AMBITIONS TA

Ambitions Tamed

Urban Expansion in Pre-revolutionary Lyon

PIERRE CLAUDE REYNARD

McGill-Queen's University Press
Montreal & Kingston • London • Ithaca

ISBN 978-0-7735-3492-6

Legal deposit second quarter 2009
Bibliothèque nationale du Québec

Printed in Canada on acid-free paper that is 100% ancient forest
free (100% post-consumer recycled), processed chlorine free

This book has been published with the help of a grant from the
Canadian Federation for the Humanities and Social Sciences,
through the Aid to Scholarly Publications Programme, using funds
provided by the Social Sciences and Humanities Research Council of
Canada.

McGill-Queen's University Press acknowledges the support of the
Canada Council for the Arts for our publishing program. We also
acknowledge the financial support of the Government of Canada
through the Book Publishing Industry Development Program
(BPIDP) for our publishing activities.

Library and Archives Canada Cataloguing in Publication

Reynard, Pierre Claude, 1951–
    Ambitions tamed : urban expansion in pre-revolutionary Lyon /
Pierre Claude Reynard

Includes bibliographical references and index.
ISBN 978-0-7735-3492-6

    1. Urbanization – France – Lyon – History – 18th century.
2. Cities and towns – France – Lyon – Growth – History – 18th
century. 3. Morand, Jean Antoine, 1727 – 1794.
4. Entrepreneurship – France – Lyon – History – 18th century.
5. Lyon (France) – Politics and government – 18th century. 6. Lyon
(France) – Social conditions – 18th century. 7. Lyon (France) –
History – 18th century. 8. Architects – France – Lyon – Biography.
I. Title.

HT169.F72L96 2009   944'.5823034   C2009–901115–8

Typeset by Jay Tee Graphics Ltd. in 10.5/13 Sabon

Discovering a city is an adventure.
Rediscovering it is more introspective. Les deux, un privilège.
À PMCD.
À mes parents, merci.

Contents

Tables

Chronological Landmarks

1727   Birth of Jean-Antoine Morand in Briançon, Dauphiné.

1735   The City of Lyon buys the large islands located at the confluence of the Rhône and the Saône, with the intention of eventually expanding the crowded city southward.

1741   Soufflot receives a commission for the reconstruction of Lyon's Hôtel-Dieu hospital.

1743   The Hôtel-Dieu is granted a royal monopoly over ferry crossings of the Rhône within Lyon.

1744   A silkworkers' revolt shakes the city; Jean-Antoine Morand undertakes his first professional activity in Lyon on behalf of Soufflot.

1748   Morand opens his first professional account book; Soufflot designs a new stock exchange building.

1750   Soufflot and several associates initiate the development of the new Saint-Clair quarter.

1753   Morand returns to Paris for training.

1755   Soufflot brings Morand in on the completion of the new theatre.

1757   Morand buys a lot in the rising Saint-Clair neighbourhood and builds his first apartment building, to be sold upon completion; he later designs other buildings in the same project. Construction begins on the dome of Soufflot's Hôtel-Dieu.

1757   Morand is named inspector of the new Lyon theatre.

1759   Morand marries Antoinette Levet.

1760   Morand works in Parma and travels through Italy; birth of Antoine, Morand and Antoinette Levet's first child.

1762   Morand receives his Lyon residency status; birth of
       Eléonore, Morand and Levet's second and last child.

1763   Morand's name appears on the list of Lyon architects
       compiled by the *Almanach de Lyon*.

1764   Morand builds a second house at Saint-Clair; the Laverdy
       reform recast the city's municipal powers.

1765   Morand buys a large field in the open lands across the
       Rhône, to the east of the city.

1766   Morand presents his "Plan circulaire" promoting an
       expansion of Lyon across the Rhône; he builds a third
       house at Saint-Clair.

1768   Morand and his associates propose construction of a
       second bridge across the Rhône; he becomes architect to
       the archbishop of Lyon.

1770   Antoine-Michel Perrache receives royal letters patent for
       his project to expand the city by pushing the confluence of
       the Rhône and Saône southward to join several islands to
       the Presqu'île.

1771   Morand and his company receive a royal monopoly for a
       second bridge across the Rhône; a Conseil Supérieur is
       established in Lyon.

1772   Construction of the bridge starts; Morand is named a
       bourgeois de Lyon.

1775   The new Saint-Clair bridge opens.

1776   Major political battle around the city's *octrois* (excise)
       tax; Morand briefly moves his family to a new house in
       the Brotteaux.

1777   Morand becomes architect to the Saint-Jean chapter; he
       revives plans for an expansion of Lyon to the Brotteaux,
       across the Rhône; he also initiates efforts to acquire a title
       of nobility.

1778   Morand buys a country estate at Machy in the Beaujolais,
       in his son's name.

1779   Morand's son, Antoine, is called to the bar of the Lyon
       Sénéchaussée.

1780   Morand is named voyer (surveyor) of the Lyon chapter.

1781   The rectors of the Hôtel-Dieu agree on a plan to develop
       the Brotteaux.

1784   First flight of a Montgolfière balloon in Lyon, from the
       Brotteaux.

1785   Marriage of Antoine Morand, who becomes procureur du roi (king's attorney) at the Bureau des Finances of Lyon.

1786   Marriage of Eléonore Morand.

1788   Morand is associated with the real estate project that has grown around the lands made available by the closing of the Célestins religious order.

1787   Opening of the new provincial assembly of the Lyonnais, under the presidency of the Lyon archbishop, Monsignor Montazet.

1793   Siege of Lyon by the armies of the revolutionary government.

1794   Execution of Jean-Antoine Morand, for participating in the defence of the counterrevolutionary city of Lyon.

1810   Judge Antoine Morand receives the Légion d'honneur and the title of Imperial Knight.

1819   Death of Antoinette Levet.

Key Institutions in
Eighteenth-Century Lyon

The following sketch of some of the key institutions based in Lyon is intended to give an idea of the large number of individuals and groups involved in public affairs in Morand's time, and of the influence they wielded. For contemporary listings, see the *Almanach astronomique et historique de la ville de Lyon* (available from 1711, and known simply as the *Almanach de la ville de Lyon* after 1760), or the *Indicateur alphabétique des curiosités, établissements réguliers et séculiers; des personnes de qualité; officiers de judicature, police et finances; Notables, bourgeois, négociants, gens d'affaires et principaux artistes de la ville de Lyon, avec les noms des rues et des maisons de leurs demeures. Pour l'année 1788* (Faucheux, Lyon).

ROYAL POWERS

Government of Lyon and the provinces of Lyonnais, Forez, and Beaujolais:
  Gouverneur (military governor; generally in Paris; Louis François Anne de Neuville de Villeroy until 1763; his nephew, Gabriel Louis François de Neuville de Villeroy, to 1790).
  Lieutenant général to the King (generally in Paris).
  Commandant (chief officer) to the King, based in the Pierre-Scize fortress.
Généralité de Lyon – administrative district similar to the intendancy; minimal differences between the two jurisdictions, which served close to 700,000 inhabitants at the end of the Old Regime.

Intendant
The indendant was assisted by a subdelegate (subdélégué)
general, a subdelegate for the city of Lyon, and some twenty
other subdelegates posted in as many districts throughout the
généralité. Six or seven secretaries oversaw specific fields,
including public works.
    The intendants during the period under study were Rossignol
(1751–55), H.-L. Bertin (1755–57), de la Michodière (1757–62),
Baillon (1762–67), de Flesselles (1768–84) and A. Terray
(1784–89).
Sénéchaussée de Lyon
This tribunal, effectively the lowest level of royal justice, was
headed by the Sénéchal de Lyon et de la province du Lyonnais
(who, however, often resided in Paris).
Présidial de Lyon (appeal court for the three provinces)
Lieutenant général of the Sénéchaussée et Siège Présidial.
Cour des Monnaies (sovereign court responsible for the large
southern third of the kingdom)
Premier président, four présidents, etc. (some thirty magistrates).
    The Sénéchaussée, Présidial, and Cour des Monnaies merged in
1705 but retained their specific attributions; they were seated in the
Palais de Roanne, on the right bank of the Saône. Sénéchaussée et
Siège Présidial denotes a few selected jurisdictions that together
formed an expanded bailliage, or bailiwick.
Bureau des Finances, including the Chambre du Domaine et de
voirie, which was responsible for matters related to the royal
demesne and the streets of Lyon.
Trésoriers de France (officials of the Bureau des Finances),
procureur du roi (King's attorney), etc.
Election de Lyon
Juridictions des Traites, des gabelles, des aides et droits réunis:
The body arbitrating disputes related to customs duties, the salt
tax, wine and alcohol levies, and a range of other indirect taxes.
Maîtrise des Eaux et Forêts: the regional authority for forests and
rivers, regulating uses such as hunting, fishing, and others.

CHURCH OF LYON

Archdiocese of Lyon (seven dioceses, the Lyon diocese including
some 850 parishes spread over three provinces). The archbishop

of Lyon is also primat (primate) des Gaules. The following held this position in the period under study: Pierre Guérin de Tencin, 1740–1758, cardinal and minister of state; Antoine de Malvin de Montazet, 1758–1788; Yves Alexandre de Marbeuf, 1788–1799.

Comtes de Lyon – canons of Saint-Jean (thirty-two)

Chapter of Saint-Nizier (seventeen canons)

Abbey and Chapter of Ainay

Saint-Just Chapter

Saint-Irénée Chapter

MUNICIPAL AUTHORITIES (AFTER THE 1764 REFORM)

Assemblée des notables:
   seventeen notables, two officers from the Cour des Monnaies, Sénéchaussée and Présidial, plus the members from the Corps de ville and Consulat; the notables were elected by representatives of trade corporations, the conseillers de ville (town councillors), several officers, etc.; in turn, they elected the town councillors.

Corps de ville: an intermediary administrative level between the Consulat and the Assembly of Notables.
   Twelve town councillors, as well as a King's attorney, a secretary, a treasurer, and members of the Consulat

Consulat (city council, the highest municipal authority)
   Prévôt des marchands (head of the Consulat, chosen by Versailles): P. Dugas, 1751–1753; J.-B. Flachat, 1753–1764; de la Verpillière, 1764–1772; Regnault de Bellescize, 1772–1776; Rivérieulx de Chambost, 1776–1779; Fay de Sathonay, 1779–1785; Tolozan de Montfort; 1785–1790
   Four échevins (aldermen); two elected annually, on paper, by the Assembly of Notables – in practice, they were coopted by their predecessors
      Procureur général (attorney general) de la ville
      Trésorier et receveur (treasurer and receiver) de la ville
   Tribunal de la Conservation des privilèges royaux des foires de Lyon
   Hôpital Général de Notre-Dame de Pitié du Pont du Rhône, et grand Hôtel-Dieu de Lyon (fourteen recteurs)
   Hôpital de la Charité (eighteen recteurs)

Bureau de l'Abondance: established in the seventeenth century, the bureau was responsible for maintaining the price of staples within affordable limits through the purchase, stocking, and regulated sale of grain in particular, as needed.

Bureau de Santé: overseeing public health.

OTHER INSTITUTIONS

Chamber of Commerce (created 1701)

Collège des médecins

Ecole royale vétérinaire (created 1761)

Académie des Sciences, Belles-lettres et Arts de Lyon (founded 1700)

Académie des Beaux-arts (founded 1736)
  The two academies merged in 1758.

Société royale d'agriculture (established 1761)

Société philosophique des Sciences et Arts utiles de Lyon (founded 1785)

Collège de la Trinité, run by the Jesuits until 1762, and eventually by the Oratorians.

Freemason lodges: La Bienfaisance, La Sagesse, La Sincère Amitié, etc.

INNOVATIONS

Conseil Supérieur (1771–74)

Assemblée Provinciale (created 1787; forty-four members, twenty-two chosen by Versailles, who in turn selected the remaining twenty-two)

Grand Baillage (Bailiwick; 1788)

Units of Measurements

The following data concern only measures that are relevant to this study. The key reference is the thorough, and thoroughly didactic, *Instructions sur les nouvelles mesures* (Lyon: Balloncle et Barret, Year 10). Eugène Vial used it for his slightly more accessible "Les anciennes mesures du Lyonnais" (*Lyon et sa région* [May-June 1920]: 71–4, and [December 1920]: 179–85).

Aune de Lyon : 1,188 metres
Lieue du Lyonnais = 2,450 toises de Lyon = 4,775.05 metres
Toise de France (or de roi) = 6 feet = 1,949 metres
Pied de France (or de roi) = 12 pouces = 0.324 metre
Toise de Lyon (or de Ville) = 7.5 pieds = 2.568 metres
Pied de Lyon (or de Ville) = 12 pouces = 0.342 metre
Bichérée de Lyon = 11.025 square feet = 12.93 ares (or: 1 hectare = 7.33 bichérée)
Toise carrée de France = 3.798 square metres
Pied carré de France = 0.105 square metre
Toise carrée de Lyon = 6,598 square metres
Pied carré de Lyon = 0.117 square metre
Livre de marc = 244.75 grams
Livre de Lyon = 418.75 grams

In an undated note, Jean-Antoine Morand made the following remarks on the differences between *mesures de ville* (town measures) and *mesures de roy* (royal measures) relevant to his work:

"The pied de ville counts 7.5 lignes more than the pied de roy. The toise courante de ville exceeds the toise de roi by 1 pied 10 pouces 8 lignes 1/4. The toise carrée de ville exceeds the toise carrée de roy by 20 pied [carré] de roy 3 pouces."[1]

Monetary Units and Prices

1 sol (st) = 12 deniers (dt)
1 livre tournois (lt) = 20 sous
1 écu = 3 livres
1 pistole = 10 livres
1 louis d'or = 24 livres

Morand's personal papers yield a great numbers of prices that help to place the many figures that are mentioned (most notably in 14 II 007) in context. Early in his career, he recorded the following yearly household expenses:

1752: 1,368 lt total expenses (including 126 lt for bread, 245 lt for wine, and 216 lt for meat)
1753: 1,206 lt total expenses (including 232 lt for bread, 300 lt for wine, and 136 lt for meat)
1755: 1,949 lt total expenses (including 421 lt for bread, 246 lt for wine, and 552 lt for meat)

In 1771 the hotel Platrière in Lyon offered rooms ranging from 25 st to 12 lt per day, and board at 40 st per day wine included; *Affiches de Lyon*, no. 1, 3 January 1771. Twenty years later, Morand spent 42 lt for the services of his barber, plus 18 lt for a new wig.

Broader comparisons may be made with the following average prices and average wages in France, quoted by Arthur Young early in the revolutionary decade:

Beef: 7 st/lb; Mutton: 7 st/lb; Veal: 7.5 st/lb; Pork: 9 st/lb
Butter: 16.75 st/lb; Cheese: 9 st/lb; Eggs: 9 st/lb
Bread: 3st/lb; Wine (bottle): 4.5 st
Male labourer, per day: 19 st; mason and carpenter, per day: 30 st
Silkworkers (working on what Young estimated to be some twelve
thousand looms in Lyon, each loom employing five people on aver-
age): 25 to 50 st per day, depending on the quality of the fabric.

In 1756 Morand himself hired a painter for 700 lt per year, while
another employee whose duties were less precisely defined received
480 lt per year (this same sum was given to another worker of
whom it was specified that he was not fed and that each month
counted twenty-four work days). At the same moment, labourers
working on the reconstruction of the Hôtel-Dieu received seventeen
sols per day (at best, for a full year of employment, less than 250 lt),
while stone-cutters earned twice as much.[1]

In 1790 Arthur Young recorded the cost of the sixty relays from
Lyon to Paris, i.e., three hundred miles, including the inns and three
louis for the post-chaise, an old cabriolet of two wheels: fourteen
pounds sterling, i.e., 1 sol per English mile for two persons. A decade
earlier, after a brief stay in Lyon, the young architect Delannoy had
contracted for passage to Rome for himself and his friend, 300 lt
per person, food and lodging included.[2] Finally, we may note the
monies paid to a provincial engineer with Ponts et chaussées
(Bridges and Roadways): Emile Gauthey received 1,200 lt, upon his
nomination in Burgundy (1758); by 1776 his yearly salary was
1,700 lt, and three years later, 2,500 lt. To these figures must be
added some modest bonuses: 500 lt almost every year and, rarely,
3,000 lt for his preliminary study of the future Charolais canal.[3]

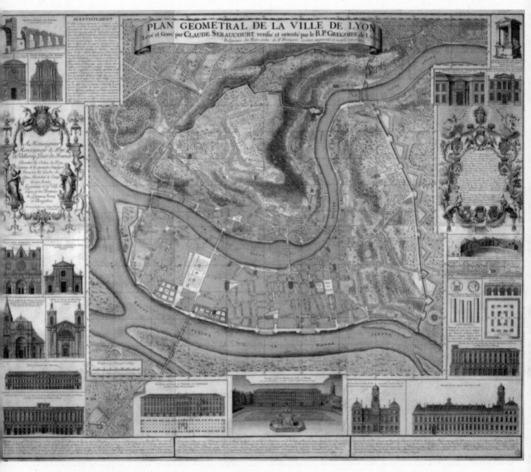

Lyon in 1735–40 – "Plan Séraucourt"
Map of Lyon drawn and engraved by Claude Séraucourt and the
Reverend Grégoire in 1735, revised 1740, with illustrations of important
buildings; dimensions: 1.36 m x 1.19 m; approximate scale: 1/3000.
Nineteenth-century reproduction. (Archives municipales de Lyon, 1s10a)

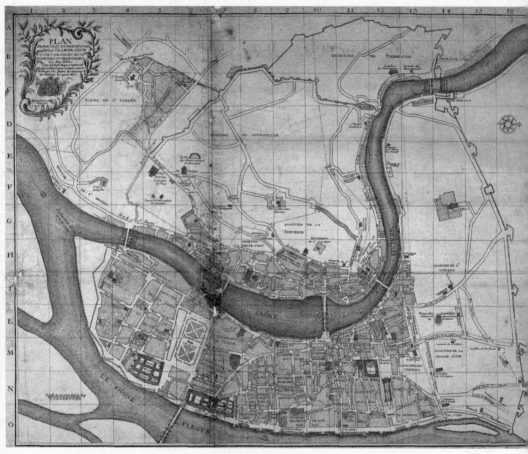

Lyon in 1747 – "Plan Jacquemin."
Map of Lyon showing the twenty-eight districts, engraved by Clair
Jacquemin, 1747; dimensions: 0.56m x 0.43m; scale: 1/6200.
(Archives municipales de Lyon, 3S693)

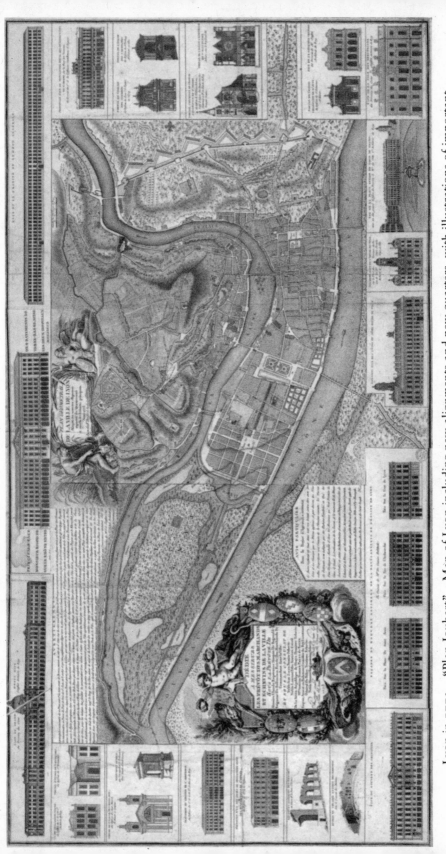

Lyon in 1773 – "Plan Joubert"   Map of Lyon including new alignments and new quarters, with illustrations of important buildings, drawn and engraved by Louis Joubert, 1773; dimensions: 1.03m x 0.54m; scale: 1/6900. (Archives municipales de Lyon, 1590)

"Plan circulaire" – J.-A. Morand (1775)
Map illustrating J.-A. Morand's project to expand the city of Lyon across
the Rhône, drawn 1764 and reproduced 1766, 1768, and 1775;
dimensions: 0.44m x 0.60m; scale: 1/9000. (Archives municipales de
Lyon, 3SM0208-1)

PROJET

D'UN PLAN GENERAL

DE LA VILLE DE LYON,

PRÉSENTÉ A MM. LES PRÉVOT DES MARCHANDS,
ET ECHEVINS.

Par leur très-humble & très-obéïssant serviteur, Morand, Architecte. 1766.

PRINCIPAUX AVANTAGES DU NOUVEAU PLAN.

1°. L'Avantage de renfermer le Rhône, ainsi que la Saône, dans le sein de la Ville.

2°. De donner à la Ville une forme circulaire, la seule capable de faire une ville d'une vaste étendue, en même temps qu'elle rapproche tous les Citoyens les uns des autres, & qu'elle rend leurs besoins onéreux.

3°. De pourvoir aux moyens de démolir, par succession de temps, sans frais & sans blesser l'intérêt des particuliers, toutes les maisons bâties sur le pont de pierre, tendant de la place du change à Saint Nizier, & dont l'élargissement fait l'objet de votre attention présente.

4°. De parvenir de même à la démolition, si désirée depuis long-temps, de toutes les maisons bâties à la pêcherie, qui interrompent le quai, qui régneroit dès-lors depuis la barrière d'Alincourt, jusqu'à la place de Louis-le-Grand.

5°. De restituer à la rive droite de la Saône, tous les quais, les ports & les tirages, dont le commerce du plus ancien quartier de la ville est privé par la chaîne de maisons bâties le pied dans l'eau, depuis la porte Saint George, jusqu'à Pierre-Scize.

6°. D'assurer par cette translation la grande route de Paris, qui peut être interrompue, & d'éviter les embarras, sans nombre, des voitures qui abordent à la place de la douane, depuis la rue de Flandres, jusqu'à la porte du faux-bourg.

7°. D'assurer l'approvisionnement des bois à brûler, soit de moule, soit de fagot, par des chantiers immenses, en face du bastion Saint-Clair, & d'en fixer par ce moyen le prix, qui rejaillira même sur les bois qui viennent par la Saône.

8°. De former des chantiers de bois à bâtir, qui, descendus à Ainai, augmentent considérablement de prix, & courent de fréquents dangers aux plus légeres inondations.

9°. De l'approvisionnement des pierres de taille, des marbres, des atteliers pour les travailler; de l'approvisionnement des tuiles, carreaux, briques, plâtre & moëllons.

10°. Des constructions d'écuries, remises & fenils, pour suppléer à celles dont on a fait un autre emploi, & à celles que demande la multiplication des voitures.

11°. De procurer des terreins nécessaires à de grandes manufactures, dont nous avons été forcés de nous priver jusqu'à présent.

12°. De l'enlévement des boues & des décombres.

13°. De parer, par la construction d'un pont de bois, de la largeur de 40 pieds en face de la rue Puits-gaillot, aux inconvéniens des trailles, qui naissent des grandes & basses eaux, de la trop grande affluence des vents, & de l'impossibilité d'y passer des chars, charrettes, carrosses, bêtes de charge, &c.

14°. De la liberté du tirage du Rhône & de la Saône.

15°. Du débarras du pont de la Guillotiere & de l'économie dans ses réparations.

16°. L'avantage de la salubrité de l'air (bien si précieux) procuré par l'étendue des promenades; celui d'un canal, qui diminuant la hauteur des inondations, assure par son enceinte les droits du Roi & les vôtres, & celui enfin de la splendeur & des embellissements inséparables de l'heureuse position de la ville, à la tête de laquelle vous êtes placés.

Project to expand the city of Lyon – J.-A. Morand (1764)
Prospectus printed in 1764 to publicize J.-A. Morand's project to expand the city of Lyon across the Rhône, detailing sixteen principal advantages of the project and meant to accompany his "Plan circulaire," on the previous page; dimensions: 0.35m x 0.17m. (Archives municipales de Lyon, 3S115-3)

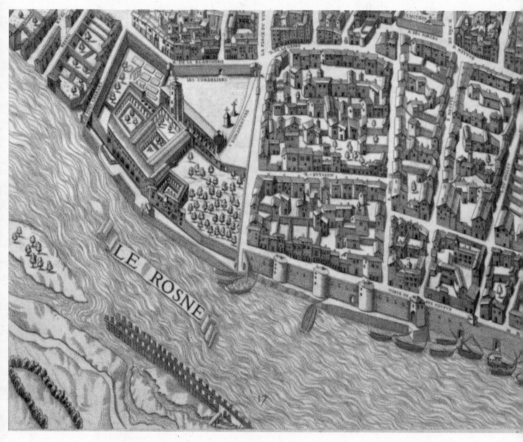

Right bank of the Rhône, mid-sixteenth century.
Detail of map of Lyon, ca. 1550, known as "Plan scénograhique";
dimensions of complete map: 1.70 m x 2.20 m; approximate scale:
1/1200 to 1/1400. Reproduction dated 1872–76. (Archives municipales
de Lyon, 2SAT6-Planche7)

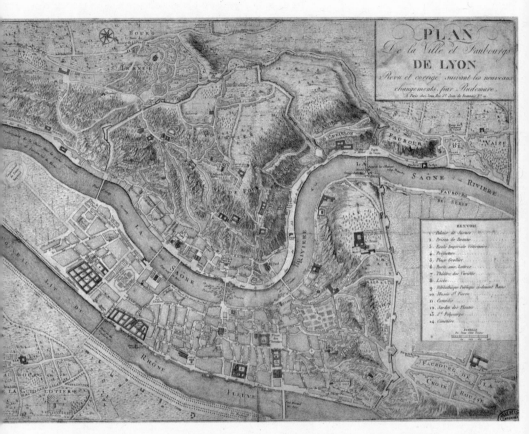

Lyon in 1805 – "Plan Rudemare" Map of Lyon drawn by Rudemare,
ca. 1805, engraved by C. Inselin, including a list of fourteen important
buildings and sites; dimensions: 0.48m x 0.36m; scale between 1/7000
and 1/8500. (Archives municipales de Lyon, 3S121)

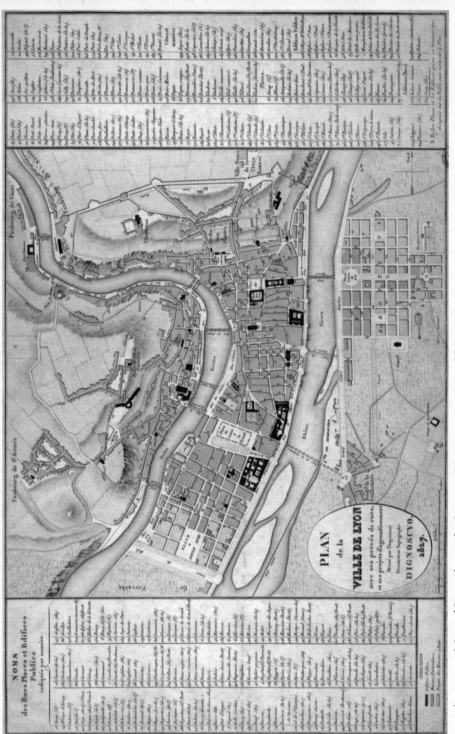

Lyon in 1827   Map of Lyon drawn by Laurent Dignoscyo, engraved by A. Tardieu, 1827, showing planned expansions and including a list of streets and public buildings; dimensions: 0.47m x 0.30m; scale: 1/10000. (Archives municipales de Lyon, 3S122)

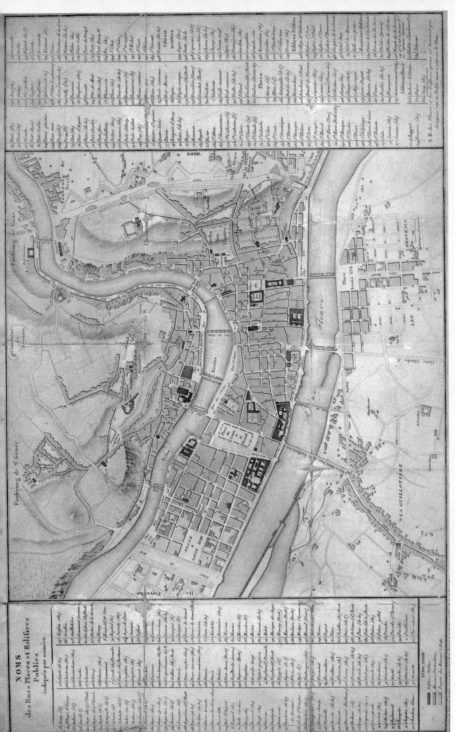

Lyon in 1840 Revision of a map by Laurent Dignoscyo, engraved by A. Tardieu, 1840; dimensions: 0.48m x 0,30m; scale: 1/10000. (Archives municipales de Lyon, 3S124)

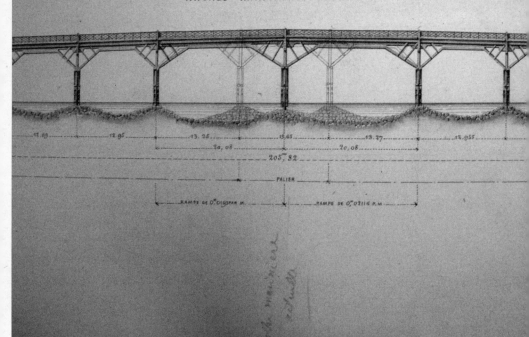

ÉLÉVATION

Echelle de 0.ᵐ0025 pour mètre (1/400)

ARCHES MARINIÈRES PROJETÉES

Pont Morand, Elevation (1867)
Photography by the author of an elevation drawing by the office of the
Service Spécial du Rhône, 1867, on the occasion of the modification of
J.-A. Morand's bridge to open a wider central arch to facilitate naviga-
tion. (Archives départementales du Rhône, s 1376)

AMBITIONS TAMED

Entrepreneurship in a Premodern Context

Upon reaching Lyon, the traveller discovers small, narrow, winding streets, poorly paved. Only a sample of the sky is visible, a narrow strip between overhanging roofs. Earlier residents must have feared the benign influences of air and light ... I could barely breath in these tiny streets.[1]

The river embankments are the greatest asset of the city. That along the Rhône is particularly beautiful, almost a league long and eighty feet wide, with a broad sidewalk for pedestrians.[2]

The foreigner [who sped through Lyon] missed the unattractive side of the city, its narrow, muddy streets, ill paved and ill maintained; however, his imagination will never forget the grandiose spectacle of this city with its great buildings, where nature mixes its gifts with the labour of men ...[3]

Upon entering Lyon in 1788, Mr C*** de T***, secretary to the king, decried the city's narrow, ill-paved, and winding streets. In doing so he was intoning a well-known refrain. A bluish strip, a pale "sample of the sky," suggested to him that the busy citizens feared air and light. Luckily, he was soon able to escape to the new Saint-Clair quarter, where he discovered a magnificent row of tall houses facing a superb promenade with a grand panorama looking eastward across the Rhône. Earlier in the decade, François de la Rochefoucauld, who, despite his elevated origins, was not blind to material realities, had also wondered how so many people could live and work in such tight confines. He too praised the new embankment along the great alpine river, one league in length and more than eighty feet wide. Two generations later, the speed of train travel only enhanced the enduring contrast between Lyon's old dank neighbourhoods born of medieval and Renaissance wealth, and its new boulevards and neoclassical facades that matched an Enlightened desire for air and light, order and grandeur.[4] Gothic clutter and modern alignments coexisted in many other European cities, often late into the nineteenth century. In Lyon, however, geography and power focused the transition around the Rhône, the great river that had hitherto marked the eastern limit of the city and offered the only space for expansion and renewal in that hilly setting. This book probes the dreams and battles of a newcomer to Lyon, a talented and versatile architect who opened the city to its potential but could only, in the end, advance the dynamic yet unpolished mix that arrested travellers for decades to come.

Jean-Antoine Morand settled in Lyon in the 1740s, when a resurgent economy once again magnified demographic pressures in the old city hedged in by a great river and steep hills. Well served by his youthful enthusiasm and undeniable capacity to learn and work hard, he also benefited from several decisive encounters with people who mattered in this provincial capital and even beyond. In less than two decades, Morand was in a position to formulate a daring vision: France's second city would leap over the Rhône to colonize the plains to the east and make him a fortune in the process. Not only would he develop some strategically located lots but he would also build the indispensable bridge. The vision was sound, but it took generations to materialize. Morand never truly savoured the fruits of his labour. He made more enemies than friends and died on the guillotine in 1794. How can we account for his early successes and later failures? The answer takes us to the heart of the tensions between entrepreneurship, an intricate institutional context, and the great ideas of an age eager to rethink yet slow to rebuild its cities.

During the second half of the eighteenth century, enlightened visionaries, assertive policy makers, and dynamic entrepreneurs initiated many of the discussions and projects that shaped the urban spaces that we enjoy today, even if real achievements came only much later. In Lyon, their efforts fuelled surprisingly bitter disputes. Around Morand and his associates swirled rival real estate developers and ambitious architects, the formidable landowning Hôtel-Dieu hospital, and several other vital networks of power. Competing forms of profit, ranging from the careful tending of seigneurial rights to the most aggressive speculation, clashed repeatedly, while Versailles's will to reform municipal politics regularly rekindled the determination of the Consulat, Lyon's municipal council, to safe-guard its powers. Even as a self-conscious agenda of urban redevelopment resonated within the widening circle of public opinion, all parties remained sensitive to the claims of newcomers of substance or Parisian interventions.

The rough and unpredictable reception given to a project of considerable significance speaks to several topics of interest to students of prerevolutionary French and European history. The Enlightenment encouraged both economic activity and plans to rationalize and manage it, but it did so amidst wide-ranging discussions of the nature of the public good and its relation to private interest. At the same time, a changing but often ancient regulatory apparatus, limited technical means, precarious financing mechanisms, and the persistence of old social or legal structures multiplied the occasions for unexpected developments. To date, studies in urban development, economic and entrepreneurial history, intellectual history, and, to a lesser degree, environmental history have addressed many of these issues. They have generally done so, however, in a specialized manner. This book bridges the various research streams to articulate more clearly the relations among enlightened principles, established power structures, and new initiatives at the dawn of the age of urban expansion.

The history of urban development is the background, as well as the first focus, of my inquiry. Within this field, a good deal of attention has been given to the key legacies of the Enlightenment.[5] Neoclassical aesthetics, efforts to devise healthy and orderly environments, and sustained attention to communication patterns all figured in many well-known projects in France and elsewhere. The debates that surrounded Jean-Antoine Morand's initiatives confirm the extent to which such new ideas permeated even provincial circles. However, I focus less on the principles of urban reform generated by the Enlightenment as on the ways in which they were advanced or disputed. These fundamental principles formed the cogent core around which all camps articulated their arguments, but these same principles were also applied within a particular context. A range of existing forces shaped that process, including key natural features of Lyon, above all the Rhône. At the same time, Enlightened urban visions were sharp and flexible enough to circulate as common currency, lubricating alliances as well as open or hidden attacks. My analysis reads through the common language generated by the ambitions of eighteenth-century urban reformers to reveal the fundamental divergences that sustained long disputes. In so doing, I also assess the importance attached to public sentiment by all parties to the debates. Morand and those for or against him often desperately lobbied decision makers and influential personalities. Yet they never forgot that these crucial players would be influenced by their perception of the public's vision of the project at hand. The age was keen to claim the support of that sibylline authority, public opinion, at a time when more traditional influences were losing relevance.

Morand had more reason than others to reflect on what his adoptive city thought of his intentions because he was and remained, to a degree, an outsider. He had left his native Alps in his teens, and his career speaks to the importance of geographical and social mobility in the eighteenth century. Several studies have sketched migration patterns, particularly those originating in mountainous areas. Morand's career recalls the individual dimension of such a vital phenomenon. It also reminds us that the support networks indispensable to a successful career must be viewed within the context of a lifetime. The range of people involved in Morand's projects is most impressive, from the celebrated Soufflot to the head of the Church of Lyon to Henri-Léonard Bertin, a powerful voice at Versailles. Yet there was nothing static in this hierarchy of influences, and nothing predictable in its impact. Morand worked hard to gather the support he needed and he always knew how much he owed to his patrons. The record also shows, however, that he could never fully assess the many agendas that combined and recombined over decades to help or betray him. The attention that is today rightly attached to early-modern patronage networks ought not to suggest rigidities where rivalries mattered, nor security where opportunism ruled.

Still, this is not the story of a lone hero. In addition to those who most influenced his career, Morand found a formidable partner in his wife. The countless letters they exchanged when separated by the demands of business make it clear that they worked as a team. Antoinette Levet's role in this story differs from that of many of the female entrepreneurs brought to light by recent studies. She was not thrust into the business world by dire need or personal circumstances such as widowhood. She emerged simply as a willing, capable, and eventually indispensable associate of Morand's. Such marital partnerships were likely not rare but they remain generally obscure. They are certainly difficult to document, because business transactions continued to be recorded in the name of the husband, and because they were probably more common at the level of small-scale enterprises that were unlikely to generate substantial files. Here, we see that they could also blossom in an elevated professional milieu where male prerogatives were increasingly backed by specialized forms of knowledge and the exclusive connections they fostered. The technical solidity of Morand's undertakings cannot be separated from the mix of commercial and political skills that Antoinette Levet helped him to cultivate on a daily basis.

It was inevitable, during that epoch, that Morand would be the public face of the partnership that bound him to his wife. As such, he was known as an architect, but his claim to that title was tenuous. He lacked any formal training and worked at a time when the profession was asserting itself and dividing along specialized lines, honing the distinctions between engineers, developers, and enlightened thinkers who dreamed of alleviating the ills of early-modern cities. Furthermore, Lyon remained a provincial city, weary of Parisian trends or bold experiments. To overcome such hesitations, Morand pointed to his long exploration of Italian leadership in the arts and crafts and insisted on the complementarity of his artistic vision, speculative flair, engineering acuity, and managerial skills. He always consciously sought to broaden his knowledge of his chosen field. The detailed records of his professional activity also highlight the obstacles faced by eighteenth-century public works entrepreneurs. To build a large bridge was a challenging venture that stretched the limits of the material ambitions of an age that was prone to enthusiasm. Nonetheless, despite his zeal and outstanding talents, Morand remained sensitive to challenges to his professional credentials. We see here an indication of the rising importance of professional standards and specialized training, but at a time when a self-trained "artist" could still design and build one of the first bridges across France's most powerful river. Those familiar with the eighteenth century will recognize that, in this field as in others, it would be a mistake to emphasize a new trend over an old and entrenched state of affairs.

Students of the early-modern age will also quickly recognize that Morand's business strategies occupied a unique ground. They straddled the fertile border between private and public interests, an

ill-defined area where the multipolar power structure of the Old
Regime was most evident. Moreover, he worked in Lyon, a great
and wealthy but secondary city, where the dealings between royal
and provincial powers were always tense, and in an age that was
later deemed not only enlightened but also prerevolutionary. In the
tight confines of this old, dense, and volatile world, the outcome of
Morand's efforts were not predetermined by any standard of entrepreneurial exceptionalism or corporate timidity, provincial aver-
sion to royal initiatives and bold concepts, or even end-of-regime
inertia. The forces among which he operated represented opportunities as much as hurdles. They were meant to be manipulated to
suit a new project, or reconfigured to cope with an original problem. Here, as always, the ways in which structures and initiatives
combined are of interest to historians because they were neither
preordained nor illogical. Morand followed an idea that was both
sensible and radically new. His goals were only partly realized, and
the city was eventually transformed almost a century later. The
many powers at work in Lyon during the last decades of the Old
Regime reacted to his plans in ways that were shaped by their history and their interests, but also by the nature and novelty of his initiatives. Here, a lack of familiarity with the concept of urban
expansion was heightened and exposed by a unique geography. It
fuelled a collective irresolution that was amplified by the corporate
structure of the age.

The institutions of Bourbon France were vital enough to serve all
rivalries; and most often, complex yet legible relations of power
combined with the skills and stamina of entrepreneurs to decide the
fate of ventures. However, when the relevant hierarchies were challenged by a powerful new issue, ambitions met in an unpolarized
field that reveals more clearly the limits of all moves. Historians
have long seen the last decades of old regime France as riven by the
persistence of its corporate foundations and the rise of forward-
looking initiatives tied to more individualistic conceptions of social
order. More recent research has shown that entrepreneurs straddled
the divide, seeking both the freedom to pursue their initiatives and
the predictability of corporate and state-sanctioned structures. Similarly, we now believe that royal ambitions were not always central-
izing, and that regional power-brokers did not invariably oppose
royal agents but strove to shape compromises that redistributed
duties and benefits in ways that were acceptable to all parties. The

same revisionist waves, moreover, have denied the existence of a prerevolutionary storm that underwrote all that happened in the France of Louis xvi. The career of Jean-Antoine Morand certainly confirms these revised understanding of broadly structuralist perspectives that overstated the weight of institutions and trends. However, it is also clear that if Morand, like his associates and opponents, was not necessarily fighting against immovable obstacles or insuperable forces, neither was he carried forth by irresistible talents and energies. All parties to these disputes had to labouriously manipulate the alignments relevant to them. Of all the factors that shaped the battles they fought, the most important were those that loosened established configurations. These destabilizing issues best account for the mix of success and failure characteristic of Lyon's first serious steps toward urban expansion. A biographical perspective throws this most effectively into relief.

Morand's life path provides the context for a discussion of the opportunities he seized and the obstacles he encountered. In the first two chapters, I look at the various factors that cast Morand's career choices. The following three chapters are devoted to the very successful enterprise that best illustrates his abilities, the construction of a new bridge across the Rhône. This venture brought him financial security and a great deal of notoriety, giving him the opportunity to formulate an even more ambitious transformation of the city. However, it also triggered a series of conflicts that burdened the last twenty-five years of his life. Two final chapters disentangle the many forces that buffeted his plans to project the city of Lyon beyond its ancient boundaries into the age of growth and assess the balance of his career in Lyon.

A biographical approach is a familiar way to assay the respective relevance of agency and surrounding historical structures in the constitution of identity. Morand's career was too modest to stand as an exemplar of ground-breaking ambition, enlightened illusion, frustrated talent, or any other dramatic permutation. Instead, his five very active decades in Lyon expose the shifting relation between personal will and context, two poles of human existence, and highlight the disruptive nature of an idea as powerful as the projection of a city beyond its ancient boundaries. We ought not to look for any hint of predictability where he or his peers saw opportunities and risks in changing, but worthy, combinations. In a career that is without the burden of unalloyed success or complete failure, the relations between individual choice and the social, political, and cultural systems of a place and age appear at their clearest.

Today's historians, like all social scientists, wish to avoid all forms of determinism resulting from exaggerated emphasis on structural factors or, conversely, events or agents. That is perhaps best done by distinguishing between structures, not timeless but certainly slow to change, and the conjunctions of structures that are characteristic of a time and place.[6] Socio-cultural patterns may be deeply rooted but they are also arranged in shifting constellations. Unique events, particular initiatives, and original issues may challenge these specific and more vulnerable conjunctions. Entrepreneurs, or adventurers for that matter, do not face immutable structures but, rather, unique combinations of institutions and practices. Their ambition is not to change the world but to shuffle its parts to make room for their interests, even if in the process they may well initiate unprecedented transformations. For his part, Morand failed to transform Lyon radically or swiftly enough to bring him the rewards he dreamed of, yet he laid the foundations for all subsequent discussions of the old city's future. He forced upon all who had an interest in it the debate that mattered: to cross the Rhône or not, revealing the potential for a very different city. The issue was so intrinsic to Lyon's identity that no resolution was possible then, but the Rhône's left bank had definitively entered the imaginary of the city.

I

The Making of a Vocation

Sieur Morand, Painter, residing rue Tupin in the house of M. Einard, in front of the Halles, undertakes all kinds of paintings, oil tapestries, landscapes and figures, historical themes, within gold lined cartouches; tempera tapestries, monochrome or coloured, in a range of genre, screens, frescoes, varnish, everything related to the art of painting but portraits.[1]

I am carried away by the works of Palladio.[2]

Rome enchants me more everyday. I visit everything ... However, I must tell you, in confidence, that jealousy is rising ... they fear teaching me too much![3]

Leaving one's family, contacts, and daily landmarks may be painful, but it is also likely to be swift. In many cases it is difficult to explain, for the individual in question and, a fortiori, for historians. On the other hand, the process of choosing a new city, weaving the relationships that will make it home, and making the many decisions that will shape a life in a new environment generally take much longer and demand greater reflection. It is also likely to be better documented. This first chapter locates some of the key impulses behind Jean-Antoine Morand's decision to settle far from his ancestral home.

Morand was born in 1727 to a family of jurists in the small Alpine city of Briançon. His paternal great-grandfather had been a merchant in the remote village of Vallouise, as well as a tax collector and administrator in his small community. In 1640 he married the daughter of a lieutenant of the Briançon *bailliage* (bailiwick), initiating a legal vocation that still characterized the family under the Third Republic. Jean-Antoine alone escaped the vast world of the robe. Early in his teens, while still at home in Briançon, he had considered a religious life.[4] However, the early death of his debt-ridden father, and perhaps a taste for a less regulated life, led him to seek a more worldly path. In a biographical essay, his great-grand-son wrote that Morand travelled to Paris in 1742 to pursue a preco-cious artistic vocation, but there is no evidence to support this romantic interpretation of what was most likely a difficult period shaped by material constraints. We do know, from a remark made to his wife in a letter dated 1760, that Morand was familiar with the capital even before the architect Jacques-Germain Soufflot sent him there for training at the end of 1753. Yet he did not settle in Paris but rather in Lyon.[5] The reasons for this choice are not known, beyond his mention, in the winter of 1754, of the paralyz-ing effect that the plethora of talented people seeking opportunities in the capital had upon him and of the "great-enough" gap sepa-rating Lyon from Briançon.[6] More than ten years after leaving home, this young man in his mid-twenties still reflected on the cultural differences that were now his lot, reminding us of the importance, perhaps even the trauma, of such a transition in the life of a young man.

Morand was only seventeen years old and already at work in Lyon, late in 1744, when he drew the plans for a bridge over the Saône presented by Soufflot, then on his way to celebrity, to the Lyon Académie des Sciences, Belles-lettres et Arts.[7] Two important events marked that year in Lyon. In August the city's silkworkers staged a revolt and forced the merchant manufacturers to grant substantial wage increases. This paved the way for months of ten-sion and, in the long term, recurrent clashes that helped shape the events of the Revolution in this manufacturing capital.[8] We do not know how Morand reacted to the social struggles of the moment, although it is interesting to note that he never gravitated toward the world of silk fashion that employed so many artists.[9] Over the fol-lowing decades, the vagaries of the silk industry affected him as it did everyone in Lyon, but only indirectly: the silkworkers' need for housing and recreation bolstered his plans for urban expansion, and the industry's cycles dominated the financial markets he oper-ated in. The other important event of 1744 was the city's celebra-tion of Louis XV's recovery from a brush with death. At thirty-four, Louis XV was still the *bien-aimé* whose good health stood as a por-tent of the nation's stability. The king's renewed vigour had an immediate impact on Morand's future, showing him the importance and profitability of public festivities.[10] He made such occasions an early focus of his career.

PUBLIC FESTIVITIES

The impression made by Lyon's public display of affection for the king upon a young small-town man is understandable: the city had spent 42,670 lt to celebrate the 1744 royal recovery, including a wine fountain and the armed guards it called for. At a time when its finances were the object of increasing concerns, the Consulat of Lyon still regularly disbursed remarkably large sums on public festivities marking events such as the visit of a dignitary or a royal wedding. Earlier that year, more than 50,000 lt went to mark the passage of Dom Philippe, infante of Spain and grandson of the House of Bourbon (and Morand's future employer), on his way to Parma. Later visits by his wife and daughter, Louise-Elisabeth of France and Marie-Elisabeth, proved just as costly (69,330 lt in 1749 and 38,115 lt in 1753). In 1745, 31,445 lt were spent to celebrate the wedding of the dauphin, heir to the throne, and 47,976 lt were called for by the birth of the dauphin's son, the duke of Burgundy, in 1751. In 1763, 16,684 lt went to celebrations of the less-than-impressive Peace of Paris. A broad range of occasions, recurrent or exceptional, called for spending on important public festivities.

Such large sums reflect the importance attached to public representations of power, although they were also used to advance other, sometimes very mundane, priorities such as the paving of streets. In 1761 the city of Lyon was just settling the bill for almost exactly 100,000 lt it spent on preparation for a royal visit, slated for 1759, that never took place. These monies had been spent levelling ground, paving streets, renovating city hall, as well as building triumphal arches, renting ice houses, dressing scores of dignitaries and employees, and crafting the silver keys that would have been presented to the royal visitor. The architect in charge of coordinating this non-event – a well-respected role – received 1,200 lt.

Besides their specific religious or political functions, public festivities naturally also contributed to the construction of a civic identity, one suitably centred around local authorities. In Lyon, the Consulat may have been all the more eager to engage in displays of public power since in reality its own power was waning. On these occasions civic decoration often harked back to more illustrious times in the history of the city and its authorities to compensate for present weaknesses. The *Affiches de Lyon* eagerly boosted such events (see for instance number 26, 27 June 1771). Admittedly, the sums devoted to celebration pale in comparison with the cost of repression. During the August 1744 revolt of the silkworkers of Lyon, a regiment was brought in under the command of the count de Lautrec, which cost the city 248,049, in addition to the 17,417 lt paid on order from the king to compensate a manufacturer for losses incurred during the riot. Even more costly were the food subsidies called for by harvest shortages: 3,000,000 lt were spent on grain during the crises of 1750.

References. For the costs of the silkworkers' strike and food shortages, see AML, BB 311 and 312, 1745 and 1746; BB 316, 1750. Many relevant references to spending by the Lyon Consulat can be found in AML, BB 310, 311, 315, 317, 320, 329, 331. See also Gardes, *Le voyage de Lyon* and *Lyon, l'art de la ville*, especially vol. 2, "Architecture – Décor," 147–66, and the bibliography, 227–30); Gruber, *Les grandes fêtes*; Loach, "François Cuenot (1610–1686)"; Rossiaud, "Les rituels de la fête civique à Lyon"; and Saunier, *L'esprit lyonnais – XIXe–XXe siècle.*

During his first few years in Lyon, Morand also acquired a taste for independence. Late in 1748, when he was only twenty-one, he opened a first account book testifying to his new calling, that of scene painter (*peintre décorateur*). Not long after, in one of the first issues of the weekly *Affiches de Lyon*, he proclaimed himself available for all kinds of painting work except portraits. This last detail was likely intended to reassure some of his established colleagues who may have taken umbrage at his rather public announcement. We know, for instance, that the city's official painter had a monopoly on the portraits of municipal officers. He no doubt had expectations beyond this circle, and Morand was probably wise to respect his turf: his 1754 accounts show that he worked for him.[11] While willing to try new ways to become known, Morand was also aware of the need to manage the sensibilities of those among whom he intended to move. The strategy must have worked, at least to a degree; in a letter to his mother written at the close of 1751, he pointed with satisfaction to the growth of his practice while mocking his persistent obscurity. Less than two years later, he had enough business to hire an assistant, bring his mother and sister to the city, start paying down some of the family's liabilities, and travel to Paris again. By 1755 he was able to spend the considerable sum of 1,457 lt (livres tournois) on what proved to be the start of a life-long collection of drawings, paintings, engravings, and books. At the end of that year, he moved his workshop to a more spacious apartment in the dynamic Terreaux neighbourhood, at an annual cost of 650 lt.[12] The following year, more than half a dozen names appeared on his payroll as he hired people to prepare canvasses, paint, varnish, or guard a work site overnight.[13]

Most likely, Morand's successful establishment as a painter rested on his versatility, very much along the lines of his early advertisement. His painting and decorating talents, for which we have no evidence of formal apprenticeship until 1753, were applied to bourgeois interiors, church walls, art reproductions, theatre sets and machinery, and ephemeral civic festivities, a vital mix of public and private commissions. The first recorded account, spanning the months of September and October 1748, refers to wall and chimney (mantel) paintings, for a total of 342 lt, out of which 50 lt went on materials. A month later, Morand travelled a few kilometres south of the city for the modest sum of 78 lt, to paint the front of a house, a balcony, a *trompe l'oeil* window, and the owner's coat of arms. In the spring of 1751 the Jesuits gave him his largest commission to date, bringing him a profit of nearly 500 lt over some 733 lt of expenses. Later that year the birth of the duc de Bourgogne brought him a further 290 lt in orders for various representations of the happy parents, heirs to the throne. A year later, Morand was working on the new theatre building, the job that would establish him in Lyon, while completing numerous small contracts ranging in price from a few dozen to a few hundred livres tournois.

The city that Morand was starting to know had long been familiar to immigrants, and those from Alpine valleys in particular. Many newcomers had strikingly successful careers, such as the father of Louis Tolozan de Montfort, the last of Lyon's prévôt des marchands – head of the Consulat or city council – who had come to Lyon in 1717, not poor but certainly without a position.[14] But

immigration to Lyon had a broader significance. Serial data
indicate that, in the eighteenth century, only a minority of Lyonnais
were born in the city. To replenish and expand its workforce, Lyon
regularly tapped mountainous regions to the east and west whose
inhabitants had long been willing to move.[15] When business
pressed, the Fabrique, the collective name given to the silk industry,
sent recruiters to promising valleys. No doubt, cheap labour was
also brought to Lyon through other networks of varying legitimacy.
The presence in the city of a relative, or simply the knowledge of
others' experience of temporary emigration, often sufficed to give
young villagers the confidence they needed to leave home. Naturally, periodic attempts were made to regulate the flow of migrants
to the city, depending on the state of its economy. In times of crisis,
civic authorities were called upon to protect the city from the threat
that migrants posed to its charitable resources and social peace.

A surprising number of migrants came to Lyon from the remote
region of Briançon, Morand's birthplace. Now known as the
Queyras, the region had a tradition of autonomy and even "republican" self-governance. It was also facing economic contraction
since the Treaty of Utrecht (1713) had ceded its eastern valleys to
Piedmont, hampering the trade networks familiar to the pastoral
economy of the mountains.[16] The young men and women of the
Queyras and the province of Dauphiné in general (in the case of
long-distance migrations, men outnumbered women) often chose
destinations other than Lyon. Indeed, Morand often commented on
the many compatriots he met in France or Italy.[17] For his part, not
only must he have considered settling in Paris but it appears that he
had also been invited to Bordeaux by the intendant, Claude
Boucher. Had he fully appreciated the scope of the program of
urban renovation that Boucher and his successor, the marquis de
Tourny, had undertaken, he might have considered the offer more
seriously. On the other hand, Morand was perhaps aware of the
delays and difficulties that plagued their project, and of the fact that
important architects, such as Ange-Jacques Gabriel, premier architecte du roi, were already ensconced in the thriving port city, leaving little room for young and unconfirmed talent.[18] More simply, it
may be that to Morand as to many of his compatriots, Lyon seemed
the more attractive place, even if he believed that a Dauphinois
would always be subjected to the tricks of the wilier Lyonnais.[19]

Migratory statistics can never tell the whole story. Morand must
have had a pleasant personality, judging from the profitable and

lasting contacts he made among the city's elites as well as its community of artists. Most notably, he befriended Jacques-Germain Soufflot, whose career as an architect began in Lyon in the late 1730s. Fresh from the French Academy at Rome, the thirty-six-year-old Soufflot had received an extraordinary commission from the rectors of the Hôtel-Dieu hospital, the city's largest and wealthiest charitable institution, to rebuild the immense hospital that crowded the right bank of the Rhône river. In Rome, he had met several men from Lyon who were linked both to the city's key institutions and its (still small) nucleus of art connoisseurs. The abbé Lacroix, a future academician, Jean-François Genève, a future Lyon alderman (*échevin*), and Ruffier d'Attignat of the Lyon Bureau des Finances (the regional royal administration with fiscal, demesne, and financial attributions) would have known of the plans for a thorough reconstruction and expansion of the great hospital. They would also have appreciated the need for a fresh mind in a city where architecture had regularly referred to outside influences. The duc de Villeroy, *gouverneur* (military governor) of Lyon as well as the three provinces of Lyonnais, Forez, and Beaujolais, quickly came to support the young man's vision and convinced the rectors of the Hôtel-Dieu and their overseers at the Consulat. The elegant facade (and, later, the outstanding dome) that Soufflot designed immediately seduced the project's overlords, for a mix of reasons that included the contemporary taste for clear lines, noble materials, classical references, and vast perspectives, as well as its linking of form and function, in this case the social and medical purposes of the building. Significantly, Soufflot's success was sustained even though his initial admirers, and in some cases their children, never saw the hospital completed; indeed, the work continued into the 1820s. Like many of his ambitious colleagues, Soufflot had circulated many reproductions of his various plans.[20] This costly but crucial enterprise included the opening of Lyon's first quay along the Rhône, offering new perspectives of a river whose shores had, until then, presented a jumble of buildings, warehouses, and busy docks. Soufflot went on to dominate the city's transformations until his death in 1780. Long after he had settled in Paris, the position of Contrôleur général des Bâtiments et Embellissements de Lyon (controller general of buildings and improvements) was created especially for him, and he invested in all the key projects of the period: Saint-Clair, Morand's bridge, Perrache's southern expansion of the city, and the nearby Givors canal.[21]

Soufflot was a steady supporter of Morand's throughout the following decades, and of many other young artists as well. Perhaps the bold start of his own professional life kept him mindful of the importance of an early push. Souffot was not twenty when he had "borrowed" a large sum of money from his father and escaped his provincial hometown of Auxerre to go to Rome, where in a matter of months he gained admission to the prestigious Académie de France.[22] In 1744, as noted earlier, he entrusted the seventeen-year-old Morand with the job of drawing plans for a bridge over the Saône, Lyon's second great river, which he then presented to the Lyon Académie des Sciences, Belles-lettres et Arts. Late in 1753, he sent Morand to Paris for training, in anticipation of the construction of a new theatre. There, Morand seems to have worked at the office of the multitalented Jean-Nicolas Servandoni, most famous then for his stage sets and his arrangements for public spectacles and a vast range of shows combining light, music, paintings, and mime. It was during this period that Jacques-François Blondel created a school for young architects, breaking the monopoly of the royal Académie d'architecture. Although some remarkable efforts were made to facilitate access to this new institution by talented but impecunious young men, it remains unclear whether Morand was able to afford the classes in architecture, geometry, and perspective that he wished to take, there or elsewhere.[23] Two years later, having been called to Paris, Soufflot included the young Morand in the team he charged with completion of the theatre.[24]

This new Comédie, as the building became known, marked the city's commitment to the growth of the Terreaux neighbourhood, on the north-eastern edge of the Presqu'île, the name given to an elongated triangle of land between the Saône and the Rhône that constituted the early-modern core of Lyon. The decision also reveals some important aspects of the way in which public policies were shaped. In 1754 the newly arrived intendant at Lyon, Henri-Léonard Bertin, had chosen for the new venue a site behind the Hôtel de ville, which fronted on the Terreaux public square. He had done so against the wishes of the comtes (canons) of the chapter of Saint-Jean, who would have preferred that the hall be rebuilt in their fief, on the right bank of the Saône (where a fire had ravaged the old theatre in 1722). Others argued for more affordable locations. The intendant replied that the developing Terreaux, although already an expensive quarter, was more centrally located and thus better suited for such entertainment.[25] More precisely, the new site allowed for a free-standing theatre, surrounded by three streets and a small square, enhancing both visual perspective and traffic.[26] Bertin added that Soufflot's recent exchange hall (the attractive Loge des changes), a new library, and a customs office (Bureau des Fermes) had all been located in or planned for Saint-Jean. In fact, the last two projects were not built, nor was it mentioned that a new neighbourhood was being developed at Saint-Clair, immediately to the north-east of the theatre's proposed site.[27] Soufflot was, as we shall see, the key promoter of the Saint-Clair venture, which would benefit from the proximity of another prestigious public building. Public statements in favour of the project reflected two important new beliefs: that sound urban planning ought to take demographic and traffic patterns into consideration, and that the rise of a new quarter did not have to be detrimental to established areas. Meanwhile, the private concerns of those endorsing this progressive agenda remained unarticulated, though they would certainly have been known to the people who mattered. All of these issues were present in subsequent battles that Morand waged over the city's development.

On the surface, Morand's role in this theatre project seemed minor and highly specialized. Early in 1755 Soufflot left his partner in the ongoing Saint-Clair project, the architect Melchior Munet, in charge of completing the theatre but delegated to Morand the decoration of the theatre's interior, including the stage and its machinery.[28] Morand's performance was impressive enough for the city to appoint him inspector to the new theatre.[29] Morand benefited from this project in many other ways. As we shall presently see, his invitation in 1759 to the Court of Parma, for instance, very much rested on his association with this talked-about theatre. Morand also understood the enthusiasm of the age for theatre and, more precisely, for the role that a such a public venue could play in creating and supporting a new urban centre of activity. Italy had pioneered this dynamic planning around theatres, and Lyon was the first French city to act on it. For a while, theatres ranked with municipal halls (and other displays of lay power), sacred architecture, and hospitals (reflecting the Enlightenment's interest in public health and hygiene) among the key preoccupations of those in power and those seeking the kind of commissions that would display their talents and advance their careers.[30]

The more Soufflot transformed Lyon's streetscape, the likelier Morand was to appreciate the growing gap between private commissions, however generous, and public projects supported by broad social, cultural, and political trends. In an age when aristocratic patronage yielded to the pre-eminence of the state, and when even royal will had to accommodate ever more ambitious assertions of the public good, the key to fame and fortune was to combine public and private agendas. Morand's participation in the construction of the theatre opened a decisive decade during which painting and decorating gave way to the exercise of his engineering, architectural, and entrepreneurial talents. Soufflot's theatre not only focused his attention on the most dynamic part of the city but also exposed him to the kind of monies and connections associated with a monopoly, at the heart of the grey area between the public and private spheres.

This theatre was an expensive proposition. It cost the city well over a million livres tournois, and Morand's own fortunes were clearly improved by his role in its construction (see appendix 1). It was, however, a successful project that became known across Europe. It was also a very profitable enterprise. Once the theatre was completed, its yearly revenues soared from an average of 100,000 lt through the 1750s to well over 300,000 lt twenty years later.[31] This boom provoked a sharp dispute in the mid-1770s that illustrates the ties between civic life, money, and politics in Lyon at the time. The company that occupied the new Comédie, headed by Madame Lobreau, enjoyed a monopoly on all public spectacles in Lyon.[32] In 1775 the city's Assembly of Notables, the lower level of a municipal government that was always pressed for money, argued that the privilege ought to be auctioned off to the highest bidder. Until then the city's governor, the duc de Villeroy, had disposed of this exclusive contract at his discretion. Soon after, a newly formed group offered the city 30,000 lt per year for the contract. Villeroy would not let this change take place, and it eventually transpired that he had been receiving substantial, if unspecified, payments from Mme Lobreau; that she herself pocketed a yearly subsidy from the city of 5,000 lt; and that the new consortium had trespassed upon Villeroy's territory thanks to a bribe of 18,000 lt to an assistant to Turgot who, as controller general, oversaw all important municipal financial affairs from Versailles.[33] Fought at the highest level, this battle was resolved by splitting the profits from the monopoly while leaving the lease in the hands of Lobreau: the city now claimed a yearly lease on the theatre of 30,000 lt, and Villeroy still received enough to declare himself satisfied with the new arrangement. The theatre must have produced some impressive profits to permit such a generous settlement.[34] Morand was well placed to assess the fertility of this intersection between the tastes of the public, municipal, even national, politics, and private interests.

Early in 1759 Morand's new-found status in Lyon and commitment to the city were solidified when he married the only child of a Lyon notary. Everything we know of the close relationship between Morand and Antoinette Levet suggests that theirs was in no way a marriage of convenience. Still, there is little doubt that their union considerably strengthened Morand's financial situation. The bride brought a dowry of 39,000 lt, an amount that reflected her family's membership among Lyon's wealthy elite.[35] During the following decades, they received further financial support from a cousin of Antoinette's, the abbé Etienne Machério, canon of the important Saint-Nizier church, who eventually left much of his estate to Morand's two children.[36] Levet family friends no doubt provided many other helpful connections. Among the relatives and friends called to witness the official transfer of her father's estate were three silk merchants (one of whom sat on the board of the Hôtel-Dieu), two lawyers, a fur dealer, and two notaries, as many potential anchors in the turbulent commercial waters of this busy city.[37] Just as he must have felt increasingly connected to Lyon, however, Morand was offered, late in 1759, a chance to build a more creative and adventurous career at the Bourbon court at Parma. In spite of his recent marriage, he accepted the offer.

The duchy of Parma was, at mid-century, experiencing a renaissance. Following the end of the War of the Austrian Succession (1740–48), all things economic, intellectual, and artistic were buoyed by the coming to the throne of the infante Felipe, son of the king of Spain and husband of Louise-Elisabeth, daughter of Louis xv of France. While this double Bourbon ascendency may not have strengthened the family gene pool, it guaranteed the duchy plenty of goodwill at Versailles. French influence swept through its capital. French visitors put Parma on their transalpine itineraries, and French musicians and poets, administrators and soldiers, teachers and artisans of all kinds found employment at the princely court. Among those who came and stayed was Guillaume-Léon Dutillot, who had grown up and eventually found employment at the Spanish court, to which his father had long been attached. Dutillot followed Felipe to Parma. There, he quickly rose to the highest level, assuming responsibility for the prince's household and then for a vast ministry in charge of economic affairs. He quickly built himself a reputation as a "New Colbert," in a reference to the diligent minister dear to eighteenth-century administrators.[38]

Throughout his two-decade tenure at the ministry, Dutillot paid much attention to artistic matters. Even before the infante had reached Parma, Dutillot was organizing spectacles for his courts at Chambéry and Milan. Eventually, a coincidence offered him a chance to renovate the city's theatre. The coming wedding of Felipe's daughter to an Austrian archduke, the future Joseph II, called for an appropriate setting. But when Isabella's mother died suddenly, the requisite mourning put all festivities on hold for many months. Dutillot seized the occasion, suggesting that Parma's theatre could be remodelled for a grand wedding and, most importantly, that the right man for the job was due in Parma in a matter of weeks. He had already invited Morand, the new talent behind the decoration and mechanics of the successful Lyon stage.[39] This offer reminds us that Lyon was at the intersection of Franco-Italian affairs, a pre-eminent axis of European cultural exchange, perhaps another reason for Morand to have chosen this city.[40]

Eventually, the scope of French influence in Parma drew the ire of local patriots, and Dutillot fell from power in a palace coup in 1771. Long before that, however, Morand had been asked to design and supervise the building of the machinery that would provide the fantastic backgrounds needed to stage an opera in the French style then in vogue at the court. Mechanical design was precisely what Morand wanted to specialize in at that point. Most notable was his design of the mechanisms that could, in a matter of hours, bring the parterre and the stage to the same level, thus transforming the theatre into a vast ballroom surrounded by an amphitheatre.

There was more to this formative experience than working out how best to display the glittering crowds of a princely wedding. Morand quickly learned that Parma workers, no doubt like their French counterparts, were weary of innovative or complicated schemes and required close supervision. Morand was reproached by his employers for leaving his work site to go on a "grand tour" of other Italian cities, and again at the end of his time in Parma for providing too few instructions for the operation of his machines.[41] This issue dogged him throughout his career as the demands of his many affairs often pulled him away from building sites. We shall see that Antoinette Levet proved a reliable partner on such occasions. At the same time, Morand appreciated many of the skills that were common in Italy but absent in France. In Italy he studied engraving, sought out the best recipes for stucco and mastic, and admired local tiling skills. He was always interested in new products and techniques and regularly sought better ways to accomplish some of the tasks common to his trade.[42]

The journal Morand kept during his travels is filled with technical observations, revealing a keen eye for novel ideas and innovative solutions to old problems, as well as an appreciation of the importance of travel in the diffusion of techniques.[43] He had barely left Lyon when he noticed, in Chambéry, a particularly hard mortar, his interest in which eventually led him to the highly polished Venetian floor cement known as terrazo. He reflected on the potential for tile flooring to replace traditional wood parquet, going so far as to take down the name and rates of an artisan skilled in tile technique. Throughout his year in Italy, he paid attention to quarries, the tools they required and the kind of stone they produced. He also noticed a new chimney system, but his interests went well beyond construction-related themes. Already aware of the importance of river crossings to his adoptive city, he recorded details of an improved cable ferry system across the Doria, a massive twelve-boat equivalent across the Po, and the safety features of similar embarkations in Venice. He even jotted down references to a better yoke for oxen, a convenient latrine chair, and a smart grater that delivered the thinnest slices of potato.

Naturally, Morand visited all the theatres he encountered, but his artistic interests were always matched by technical curiosity. Although he proclaimed his admiration for Palladio's neoclassical buildings, and although the grandeur of Roman architecture moved him, particularly in contrast with the often overburdened appearance of more recent buildings, his journal is filled with precise assessments of the amenities of venues in Mantua, Vicenza, Padua, Venice, Verona, Reggio, Bologna, etc. And if technical observation often superseded artistic comment when dealing with man-made structures, Morand's admiration for natural beauty was expressed in a uniquely architectural language. The cliffs of the Chartreuse, the first alpine range east of Lyon, appeared to him as a gigantic wall criss-crossed with perspective lines and freshly "varnished" by the rain. Crossing the Apennines, he wondered at the parallel ridges of an angry sea cast in stone. If he clearly shared the emerging preromantic sensibilities of his age, he always reflected on the structure that lay behind natural as well as artificial splendours. Beauty, for him, was meant to be analyzed. His artistic emotions never eclipsed his will to grasp the endless play of elements and patterns that arrested his senses.

His realism is also displayed in another side of his year-long sojourn. Because Italy was a cultural centre of the first magnitude, a successful trip beyond the Alps could prove essential to any calling related to the arts in eighteenth-century Europe. Soufflot and many others had seen their careers take off upon their return from Italy. Morand was keenly aware of the formative potential of this indispensable journey. He explicitly scrutinized the opportunities it offered to forge helpful connections and gather enough prestige to overcome the jealousies that were already plaguing him in Lyon.[44] He eagerly displayed his artistic and engineering abilities to impress his hosts and encouraged his wife to spread news of his successes: someone wished to publish his road sketches, crowds gathered to admire his engineering models, the French ambassador at the court of Turin had put his compliments in writing, and residents at the French Academy in Rome guided him to the many sights of the region.[45] Conversely, he regularly tried to "manage" potentially less favourable information. For instance, he preferred his compatriots to believe that he was in Rome when he had been recalled to Parma and allowed people to exaggerate the financial rewards he had received for his services – although the 8,000 lt he got was a substantial compensation for his efforts.[46] Throughout, Morand and his wife carefully assessed the mood of potential supporters of their projects and resorted to various stratagems to advance their cause with power-brokers (such as making two copies of each letter, one for private reading and a second to be shown to others, and keeping a record of all sensitive exchanges).[47] They carefully noted comments about Morand's accomplishments that were spread in Lyon by visitors returning from Italy, but they also feared that his colleagues resented the diligence with which he had sought knowledge in Rome.

It was during this Italian sojourn that Morand and Antoinette discovered their potential as partners. Morand was no longer young and carefree. Because he came from a less-privileged background than many of his peers, he had embarked on his grand tour at an age when he was already engaged in business and married; indeed, how else could he have afforded it, since the monetary rewards from his work in Parma would inevitably be long in coming? Soufflot himself was barely twenty when he had first gone to Rome, and Victor Louis only a few years older when his turn came, but Morand was already thirty-three. Consequently, throughout those no doubt exciting months, Morand relied on his wife to manage their ongoing affairs in Lyon.

The year was not easy for Antoinette Levet. She gave birth to their son while her husband was away (he managed a brief visit to Lyon for the occasion).[48] She was left facing a stalled court case in which she and her husband sought compensation for a two-year interruption in the construction of their first house at Saint-Clair (see chapter 7). At the same time she was supervising the reopened work site. While Jean-Antoine Morand was on his way to Turin she was meeting with the prévôt des marchands to persuade him to liquidate the city's debt to them (money still owed to Morand for his work on the new theatre), seek permission for her husband to remain absent from his position at the theatre, thank him for his letters of recommendation, and, finally, broach the pending affair of Saint-Clair and other less-knotty matters related to the theatre. She quickly extended this political appeal to the two recently elected aldermen, the new forces in municipal affairs.

Because a married woman could only conduct such affairs in the name of her husband, the Morands had, just before Jean-Antoine's departure, registered a very broad power of attorney for Antoinette.[49] The two detailed pages give us at once a measure of the limits facing women in the world of business and an idea of the extent to which Antoinette Levet was expected to manage complex and often unpleasant transactions. These she carried out with ease. Over the following months, Antoinette repeatedly assembled funds to keep on top of bills generated by the construction of their house. This was a tedious matter, calling for multiple small loans, the goading of creditors, discussions of the terms of every invoice, and even the pacing of work according to what her funds permitted, at the risk of losing workers at a time when a whole new quarter was being built. She was ready to borrow officially, even if it meant

paying extra to register the loan, but she also pressured her aunt to
settle the small estate standing between them. She fought to post-
pone the due date of maturing loans, while systematically trying to
delay settlement of her own debts. All year long she struggled to
meet payments. On 7 August 1760 she was looking forward to the
thousand livres tournois that a business acquaintance, Mme Mallet,
had just agreed to advance her. Less than three weeks later the sum
was gone, and she was begging another lender to prorogue a loan
four times greater. Another two weeks elapsed before she received
an unspecified sum from Italy and could borrow another fifteen
hundred livres tournois. But mid-October only brought another
cash crunch during which she faced four creditors. The following
month, another creditor lost the Lyon carriage cab monopoly and
quickly recalled the four thousand livres tournois he had lent her.[50]

Naturally, overseeing the construction of a very large house was
not only a matter of meeting payments. Besides dealing with neighbours (see the next chapter), a great number of trades had to be
managed. That included, for instance, making sure that tradesmen
did not work when the weather could compromise the quality of
their product; ensuring that stones arrived from several quarries
before the Rhône's low-water levels interrupted deliveries; or having enough tiles on hand whenever the roofers chose to show up.
All matters of quality control rested with Antoinette, though she
often referred to friends with design questions. There was a regular
stream of problems to solve, ranging from the use of metal rein-
forcements on a load-bearing wall to recutting the roof line to allow
more light into the inner courtyard to pricing fireplaces. Throughout the year, she combined the role of a manager with that of supervisor, feeling that she was respected enough on the work site for her
presence to matter; her husband, meanwhile, worried about the
hazards lurking on the site.

As completion of the building approached, Antoinette had to
worry about finding tenants for the new apartments, a process that
often entailed modifying floor plans or finishing details. The com-
patibility of the tenants with each other had to be assessed, and
Antoinette also had to keep an eye on the ways in which her neighbours rented out their buildings. She had to manage the flow of correspondence between her husband and potential clients for his
architectural and decorating practice, and she had to obtain letters
of recommendation for him at each stage of his travels from a range

of influential people. In addition to these many demands, Antoinette Levet had to monitor the care her newborn son received at the hands of the country wet nurse to whom he had been dispatched after the one chosen in Lyon had proved inadequate. Without this release from the exigency of nursing, she, like many of the artisans observed by Maurice Garden, could not have attended to her affairs.[51] Yet like many among the city's elite at the time, she was concerned about the potential effects on her son of this necessity.[52]

Antoinette entertained a steady flow of people, many of whom were related to their business, and kept numerous social engagements. She regularly reported in her letters on her evenings at the theatre. She clearly enjoyed these outings, even if she attended for the sake of her husband's position. During the summer she paid at least four visits to the countryside, short stays at her aunt's and at the country estate of Mme de Cornabé, family friend and seigneur of the village where the wet nurse lived.

By the end of 1760 Morand was preparing to leave Italy. This meant, first, tactfully refusing the offers made by Dutillot, who had new ideas for his theatre and wished to use Morand's skills to advance his plans for a canal and to mechanize local industries. Leaving also meant trying to procure payment for his services, never an easy task at a time when even the most generous patron could be forgetful of such matters – especially, perhaps, in Italy where all financial matters were, in Morand's polite words, difficult to bring to a conclusion. Finally, after a tearful visit to Chauvelin, the French ambassador at Turin who was the key to all the contacts he had made over this busy year, Morand just managed to cross the Alps before winter closed the convenient Mont-Cenis pass.

Two significant points emerge from the numerous and detailed letters exchanged by the young couple throughout this exciting, if demanding, year. The first concerns Morand's decision to return to Lyon rather than pursue the more adventurous career that Dutillot was offering him. He could have chosen to remain at the heart of the dynamic princely court of Parma, if only in the hope of eventually reaching an even more exalted centre. Ministerial goodwill, the obvious aesthetic and creative attractions of Italy, and the lure of aristocratic patronage were the foundations of many artistic careers. Of course it was an insecure path to choose, but Morand would have known that the infante's court offered opportunities that were unlikely to be matched in Lyon. Nevertheless, he chose to decline Dutillot's offer and return to Lyon, where, he claimed in a moment of disparaging candour, "great ideas were of little use."[53] The artistic passions that fuelled the Italian voyages of so many of his peers remained tamed, in Jean-Antoine Morand, by the same rational reflexes that tempered his observations of even the most inspiring scenery or building. The grandeur of Rome and Venice touched him but never dulled his interest in the more mundane challenges awaiting him in Lyon.

The second outstanding characteristic of this period was the smooth growth of Morand's partnership with his wife. Antoinette Levet and Jean-Antoine Morand were fully aware of the demands placed on them, of the need to discuss all problems, trust each other on innumerable points, and, in the end, accept the inevitable setbacks without blaming each other. For her part, Antoinette understood the limits placed, by virtue of her gender, on her abilities to transact business. She was angry enough to note that, while she had negotiated the myriad contracts indispensable to the building and renting their new house, her interlocutors remained unwilling, in the end, to sign a final deal with a woman.[54]

The tight collaboration between Antoinette and her husband may have been circumscribed by the conventions of their age (which also skewed surviving records by attributing most decisions to her husband), but it persisted. In his short look at the place of women within the business elite of the port of Saint-Malo, André Lespagnol rightly notes that the skills they displayed could not have been improvised. They presupposed substantial education and knowledge of a given trade, as well as an ongoing familiarity with a specific business milieu. While women were seldom granted any official status in the business world – with the exception of widows who had stepped into their husband's position – they often played a substantial role.[55] For her part, Antoinette Levet, although still young, must have drawn upon all she had learned growing up within Lyon's business circles. There is no doubt that her participation was indispensable to the business path that Jean-Antoine Morand chose by returning to Lyon. By the end of 1760 he knew that his wife's skills allowed him, in effect, to be in two places at once, an enormous asset in an age when personal contacts mattered so much while communications remained slow and difficult. Little of what happened during the following three decades can be understood outside the context of this partnership, even if the sources remain do not always reveal its true extent.

After his Italian travels, Morand rooted himself firmly in Lyon. In 1762 he received his residency certificate, the first step toward becoming a bourgeois de Lyon with all the fiscal benefits it carried.[56] Their second child, a daughter, was also born that same year. Morand's career acquired its final shape when he was given a chance to participate in and profit greatly from the construction of the Saint-Clair quarter, one of the most successful real estate operations of the period.

2

Decisive Years: The Saint-Clair Experience

I am eager to see your house, and the second one you are mentioning ... but will you own both?[1]

For rent, apartment, 14 rooms on one floor, view over the quai along the Rhône, the rue Royale, and the rue Dauphine, with cellar and attic, in the house of M. Pitiot, to rent as a whole or in parts: to inquire, see M. Morand, architect, rue Royale.[2]

For rent, very nice apartment, furnished, six rooms plus rooms for servants, kitchen, second story of M. Morand's house, with cellar and attic.[3]

A private individual seeks house in this city, 70 to 80,000 livres ...[4]

The construction of a new quarter in Lyon was the making of Jean-Antoine Morand and Antoinette Levet. The Saint-Clair development, on the northeastern edge of the Presqu'île, brought them wealth. It also familiarized them with the social and cultural trends behind large-scale real estate ventures, the networks of forces indispensable to such projects, and the range of obstacles likely to stand in the way of success. By the mid-1760s, Morand was in a position to formulate the grand plan that stood at the centre of his career. In the following pages, we will explore the key parameters of this project – the real estate context in which it took place and its remarkable profitability; the private and public interests it attracted; and the roles played by various key institutions and the inevitable conflicts that arose.

A CHANGING REAL ESTATE CONTEXT

The city of Lyon had originally grown on a steep hill on the right bank of the Saône, before spreading down to the riverside. Its late medieval and Renaissance prosperity had led to the settlement of the Presqu'île, the peninsula formed by the confluence of the placid but busy Saône with the less-predictable alpine Rhône. This low-lying triangle was enclosed, to the north, by the slopes of the Croix-Rousse. Across the Rhône to the east spread a vast plain, reached only by a medieval stone bridge leading to the main road to Grenoble and, beyond the Alps, Italy. The land at the confluence of the two rivers and the left bank of the Rhône remained unstable, characterized by shifting islands of gravel and the threat of inundation. Not only was the Rhône a greater geographical barrier than the Saône but it had long played a defensive role in the history of Lyon, which sat so close to the borders of the kingdom. This vocation remained visible in the administrative map of the kingdom, which showed the Rhône as a provincial border and a major customs line.[5] The result was a very congested city. On the eve of the Revolution, a population of perhaps as many as 150,000 lived on 150 hectares: a substantial part of the area enclosed by the city's walls was given over to gardens and other undeveloped land, much of which belonged to religious institutions.[6] Lyon's population had grown by some fifty percent since the last decades of Louis xiv's long reign, but the increase had been accommodated almost entirely by increasing the density of the city's occupied area, rather than by expanding it.[7]

Density was increased in two ways. First, and most frequently, older and smaller houses were rebuilt on a more impressive scale.[8] Lyon's houses were already high, often four to five stories, by the turn of the eighteenth century. They grew bigger and taller in the following decades; as one visitor remarked, "Nowhere can one find such economy of space as in a Lyon house" (Nulle part on ne voit dans une maison une économie de place comme à Lyon).[9] Before the Revolution many rose to five or six stories – in addition to the ground floor, an entresol immediately above, and servants' quarters under the roof. In 1791 houses of one or two stories represented less than ten percent of the city's housing stock, that is, no more than the exceptional buildings reaching six or seven stories. Almost two-thirds of existing houses reached four or five stories. Second, and less frequently, new buildings were erected on previously vacant land. In the decades before the Wars of Religion, in the wake of a long period of prosperity, wealthy landowners developed lots near, but within, the city's gates. After the middle of the seventeenth century, the erection of the new city hall on the Terreaux and, a little later, the creation of the monumental place Louis-le-Grand (later place Bellecour) and its surrounding neighbourhood marked a revival of urban development. Then, religious institutions came to the forefront of development initiatives. Traditionally attached to their large estates, they nevertheless periodically felt the need to freshen their balance sheets by selling part of their gardens. The Antonins in 1694 and the Jacobins in the 1720s did so in what is now very much at the centre of the Presqu'île. The abbey of Ainay initiated several sales further south in 1723, 1738, and 1769, while the Feuillants released part of their land on the slopes of the Croix-Rousse in the 1740s.[10] Early in the 1730s, an observer estimated that about one hundred buildings had risen on such lands.[11]

If one accounts for the indispensable (although meagre) space reserved for public use, narrow streets mostly, and for the needs of commerce (including the many trades that impinged directly upon residential and public space), it is clear that the roughly four thousand houses inhabited by close to 150,000 people and, in many cases, the tools of their trade were intensively occupied.[12] The promoters of the Saint-Clair quarter innovated both in the scale of the operation they envisioned and in reclaiming riverside land, reflecting the centrality of the Rhône to all further development. They otherwise followed their predecessors in planning for a high, dense, and profitable occupation of the ground. More importantly, they were targeting those segments of the real estate market that were well-heeled. Their logic in doing so was sound: sustained population growth and a limited expansion of the housing stock, as well as some of the urban improvements characteristic of the period, all speak to a real estate market that favoured the owners of buildings, at least until the economic difficulties of the last two decades of the Old Regime (and the demographic setbacks of the Revolution). Yet we have no solid data to support this apparently logical conclusion, since serial studies of the housing rental market are hampered by the fact that most leases remained private. Rather, surviving accounts and most subsequent studies speak of limited rent increases throughout the eighteenth century that barely matched the rising curve of prices in general, a trend that was also evident in other large French cities.[13] However, the apparent disjunction between demographic pressure and limited rent increases seems less anomalous in the light of other dimensions of the real estate market.

Most important in explaining the nature of the real estate market in Lyon is the even weaker curve of popular revenues. Since the pioneering work of E. Labrousse, and through countless monographs, we know that the income of the majority of urban dwellers rose more slowly than all or most prices.[14] The low and precarious living standards of the working masses of Lyon and many other cities strictly limited the amount that they could spend on rent, however pressing the need and however tight the market may have been. In a rigidly delimited and tightly controlled city, there was little room for the expansion of even substandard housing, however meagre the standards of the early modern age may have been. Those in the lowest income groups had to content themselves with more crowded conditions. One all-purpose room remained the basic unit of lodging for many Lyonnais well into the nineteenth century. Landlords, meanwhile, rather than simply raising rents, found themselves competing for tenants who were able to meet their obligations. In Lyon, they also sought to insulate themselves from the vagaries of rent collection by means of a practice known as *location principale*. Most house owners rented the whole of their building to a creditworthy tenant, who in turn sublet all apartments but the one he or she occupied. This "principal tenant" was responsible for uncollected rents or vacancies. Naturally, the practice cut into the returns that a landlord could expect from a building, even if a new buyer could renegotiate existing leases. The key priority of owners was steady and, as far as possible, worry-free returns on their buildings.[15]

These observations match what we know of the investment preferences of the higher social groups in early modern France, or even Europe. Real estate, be it rural or urban, had long been valued for its solidity rather than for high yields, and also because it could be readily mortgaged or liquidated should the need arise. It was the form of investment most familiar to the largest number of people, and a versatile undertaking, given the range of houses existing even in a city such as Lyon. Naturally, rental income was complemented by the prospect of increases in building prices. Finally, it is clear that the social status associated with the ownership of a house added to the numbers of those who were willing to enter what may otherwise have been a rather soft market, just as it led millions across rural Europe to court financial insolvency to buy land. In a city with as little housing as Lyon, the prestige of home ownership must have acted strongly on those who could consider it. E. Leroy Ladurie's suggestion that many investors were satisfied with a rather modest doubling of their capital over twenty-five years is certainly compatible with all recent studies of the Lyon real estate market. It is also consistent with the assessment given on the occasion of a dispute over the delay in construction of Morand's first house at Saint-Clair. This detailed report estimated the returns on the capital invested in Lyon's buildings at three percent, after all deductions including taxes.[16]

We must remember, however, that all such generalizations hide important distinctions. The housing market of a large city like Lyon was far from homogeneous and became further stratified during the eighteenth century. This meant that if, on average, only modest returns could be expected on investments in housing, more generous calculations could be made with regard to the city's better buildings. Not surprisingly, the key construction projects of the period, like Saint-Clair, were aimed at the better parts of the market. Since the second half of the seventeenth century, Bellecour, Ainay, and the Terreaux, where the principal development schemes were located, had become fashionable addresses. The success of Saint-Clair only confirmed that dynamic entrepreneurs could profit from more subtle trends than the raw balance of demand for and supply of rental accommodation resulting from demographic pressures within strict city limits.

Like many other French and European cities in the eighteenth century, Lyon was also discovering the benefits of urban improvement (*embellissement*) – a first form of what would eventually be known as urban planning. The key dimensions of this powerful movement are well known. A more rigorous alignment policy, the use of better materials, and a preference for more uniform facades and broader vistas reflected nascent modern urban aesthetic standards. In addition, there was a growing interest in a healthier urban environment, supported by fledgling statistical studies demonstrating the morbidity of existing conditions. A rising faith in the virtues of easier exchanges of all kinds strengthened calls for the opening of the dense cores inherited from earlier centuries. Not only were these factors remarkably congruent, revolving around the desire for a more orderly, more rational space that eased the flow of air, water, goods, and people, but they also reflected the new-found confidence of the age in the human ability to improve social life, notably through concrete, material initiatives.[17] At the same time, the benefits of new housing requirements, including better protection from the elements, more differentiated apartment layouts, higher standards of hygiene, and a growing rejection of disturbing trades,[18] slowly spread among the admittedly small numbers who could aspire to a greater level of comfort. Medieval heterogeneity and disorder gradually receded, or at least came to be perceived as negative elements of urban life. Those familiar with the complexity of early modern cities caution against too rigid an understanding of the processes leading toward a greater differentiation between neighbourhoods.[19] The traditional (higher, denser) rebuilding of Lyon's housing stock already tended to provide the rich with more comfort and privacy. Yet vertical segregation remained more frequent than full spatial separation, and the social composition of most neighbourhoods evolved only slowly. Thus, while distinctions between sections of Lyon sharpened during the eighteenth century, the process was less marked than during the age of industrialization.[20]

In Lyon, unique geographical and historical features combined to make these trends in urban development most visible to those interested in urban issues, whether they pursued profit or harboured loftier dreams of urban improvement. They could not fail to note that Lyon, contrary to many other cities, had no easy way to expand through a slow, quasi-organic development of its existing suburbs. Lyon's only two real suburbs were poorly connected to the city itself and remained so until much later. Traffic from Vaise had to make its way through the Pierre-Scize narrows alongside the Saône, while access from La Guillotière was confined to a long, narrow, ancient stone bridge, the city's only bridge across the Rhône. Anyone else coming into or leaving Lyon had to tackle the steep slopes of Fourvière and the Croix-Rousse, while those arriving from the south followed the left bank of the Saône for some two kilometres along the appropriately named chemin des Etroits. At midcentury the city of Lyon, traditionally centred around the Saône, was only just discovering its eastern river front. Soufflot's reconstruction of the Hôtel-Dieu made room for a wide quay and new ports on the Rhône. Once extended north to the level of the

Terreaux, this quai de Retz became Lyon's first north-south axis.[21] As we shall see, Soufflot immediately understood that the new riverfront would eventually be extended yet further north, while Antoine-Michel Perrache applied the same logic a few years later to expand the Presqu'île southward and redraw the route to the Languedoc. The last section of this long shore, at the entrance of the Guillotière bridge, was renovated in the 1770s by the Hôpital de la Charité, Lyon's second great social institution, and Rigod de Terrebasse, president of the Trésoriers de France. During this momentous "discovery" of the Rhône the last wall to be completed along the river, back in 1626, was removed.[22] A broad avenue and stately facades replaced crumbling fortifications, a water reservoir that had never proved its usefulness, dilapidated buildings, and a few ill-defined open spaces.

By 1780 the people of Lyon and their guests could stroll alongside the Rhône for about five kilometres, gaining a new perspective on the city and the vast empty plains across the river. For his part, Soufflot had very quickly grasped the potential of a small island, a sandbank in fact, nestled in an indentation of the Presqu'île, just east of the new theatre and the newly fashionable Terreaux neighbourhood. This island stood in the lee of the river's ninety-degree turn toward the south when it came up against the Croix-Rousse hill. Closing the shallow arm of the Rhône that stood between the island and the city offered a chance to extend the new quai de Retz, while providing the city with a new port and a more convenient route to Geneva than the one over the Croix-Rousse. It also provided the opportunity to build a new residential quarter. Soufflot started to buy land in this area in 1742, and he soon began building. By 1749 he and his associates received the rights to the complete project and work started in earnest.[23] Saint-Clair quickly attracted wealthy residents who were inspired by its coherent streetscapes and reassured by the high price of its new apartments. It proved particularly alluring for successful professionals. The often underestimated aristocracy of this "city without a prince" had recently settled, in style, around the new place Louis-le-Grand. At the same time, the merchant elite had discovered the Terreaux and quai de Retz, just south of Saint-Clair.[24] For their part, architects and administrators, officers and members of Lyon's various academies, an elite of talent perhaps more likely to reflect upon the city's shape and evolution than its titled or mercantile counterpart, gravitated to the new buildings of Saint-Clair in unusually large numbers.[25]

A MOST PROFITABLE SPECULATION

Morand must have quickly discovered the financial opportunities offered by the speculations that supported the Saint-Clair project. It is not possible to estimate the profits generated by his own successive operations since we lack information on the cost of the buildings erected on his lots, but they must have been substantial. Indeed, the returns reaped by the original promoters of the new quarter were splendid. Soufflot, Melchior Munet, also an architect, and Léopold Millanois, a prominent merchant, had spent 50,000 lt to purchase the necessary lots, to which must be added an unknown but apparently modest investment to reclaim the land, and no doubt some sizeable sums to facilitate the necessary transactions. In any case, this investment pales in comparison with the final outcome of the venture: the company eventually sold thirty lots at a price of 20,000 to 30,000 lt each.[26] Naturally, these investors also profited from the buildings they erected on the lots they kept. For his part, Morand bought his second lot for 28,680 lt in 1764 and sold the apartment building he erected on it for 250,000 lt three and a half years later. Development of the first lot may have given him more worries, because of the two-year construction delay and the twenty-year court case that followed. Nonetheless, the lot that he had bought for 38,160 lt in 1757 was sold, once built, for 207,000 lt in 1764. Two years later, Morand and Levet bought a third lot for 23,665 lt, and the building that rose on it was worth close to 200,000 lt a decade later.[27]

These speculations came in addition to Morand's activities as an architect (among his designs were two other houses at Saint-Clair). The growing scope of his operations is evident from his accounts: both his expenses and revenues doubled during the 1760s (see the detailed table in appendix 1). As early as 1765, Morand also invested across the Rhône, buying a large field, the Pré Deschamps, that played a key role in the following stage of his career. He quickly proceeded to build on it, while also selling parts of it (see chapter 3).[28] Through the contacts he established during the previous decade, and particularly through his working relationship with Soufflot, Morand had been able to participate in the development

AFFICHES DE LYON

In 1753 the Parisian owners of the *Gazette de France* and
Affiches, annonces et avis divers, sought to create a network of
publications that would link the capital with some thirty provincial cities. They placed business news at the heart of their project
and were building on precedents in Paris but also Lyon, where the
first *Affiches de Lyon, annonces et avis divers* were published in
1750. This weekly publication had been preceded by the opening
in Lyon, eight years earlier, of a "Bureau d'annonce," where
announcements were available for public consultation (the fee for
placing an advertisement was six sols, while four sols sufficed for
consultation). Eventually, some fifty similar sheets came to life
across France.

Until their transformation in 1784 into the more literary *Journal
de Lyon*, the *Affiches de Lyon* remained in great part a forum for
what would today be called classified advertisements. For six sols
an issue or nine livres tournois for a yearly subscription, readers
found offers and demands for real estate of all sorts, a great range
of services and goods, seigneurial rights and royal offices, as well as
news of spectacles, publications, trials, auction sales, scientific
experiments or drugs, etc. – all in a 95-by-240 mm format. Reports
of events of a political nature were naturally tame, but on certain
topics, such as the new practice of inoculation, fairly direct debates
sometimes played out over several weeks. Characteristic interests of
the age were also manifest, for instance in the publication, starting
in 1763, of the city's baptism, marriage, and burial statistics.

The use of this vast accumulation of weekly data is clearly
fraught with difficulties, because of the complex role played by
such a medium. The *Affiches* nevertheless sketch the range of
information likely to catch the attention of those who read them.
They also provide a riveting illustration of the dynamism of a
commercial and manufacturing centre such as Lyon. In the year
1766, for instance, the *Affiches* advertised the opening of two
mills devoted to the processing of tropical dyewood, some twenty
to thirty kilometres south of the city, and of a coffee house on the
edge of the Brotteaux, as well as the creation of a dairy founded
on the reputation of Swiss cows; another advertisement was taken
a year later to celebrate the success of this last venture. Also in

1766 the *Affiches* advertised the sale of one hundred portraits of Jean-Jacques Rousseau, whose *Social Contract* had appeared only four years earlier. (see nos. 1, 2, 12, and 22, 1766, as well as no. 9, 1767). In 1771 the services advertised included a "Magasin Anglais," a hotel that also provided transportation, a "pension bourgeoise," and a retirement home, as well as new products ranging from "*chaines élastiques*" to fine brass mosquito screens (nos. 1, 4, 24, 39, and 51). Only a few years earlier, M. Vincent, councillor to the King and retired treasurer of *Ponts et chaussées de la Généralité de Lyon,* had reflected on the impact of the opening of a new road from Lyon to the Languedoc: the village of Brignais, roughly twelve kilometres to the south, needed carpenters, blacksmiths, and a locksmith to accommodate a construction boom (no. 11, 15 March 1764). While even such an avalanche of offers and suggestions cannot accurately reflect the economic life of a large city, it offers a salutary reminder of the fragility of all generalizations.

References. Feyel, *L'annonce et la nouvelle,* "Négoce et presse provinciale en France au 18e siècle"; Jones, "The great chain of buying"; and Loche, *Journaux imprimés à Lyon (1633–1794).*

of a new neighbourhood at the upper end of the Lyon's real estate market. Lyon was a city of large tall houses, substantial investments intended to provide their owners with steady revenue from a range of tenants. Serial data on the value of houses in Lyon throughout the period I cover are not available, and the diversity of buildings and contexts makes any analysis difficult. However, the figures quoted in the new advertising sheet published in the city during the second half of the century are not without meaning: those who used the *Affiches de Lyon* to advertise their intention to purchase or sell a house asked for or were ready to pay between 20,000 and 150,000 lt. Data gleaned from existing studies fit well within this broad range (see appendix 4).[29] Even if they can be subjected to the usual criticisms associated with fiscal data, the rolls drawn for the new real estate tax introduced in 1791 are also consistent with these figures: almost two-thirds of all buildings fell in the range of 20,000 to 100,000 lt, but the average quote was 120,000 lt around the Terreaux and 156,000 lt for Saint-Clair.[30]

Public and Private Agendas

As a close observer and, later, an interested party, Morand was able to discover the principal alignment of forces behind the Saint-Clair venture. For at least two decades, municipal authorities had been moving away from traditional practices of urban renewal, that is, from the construction of exceptional, strategically located public monuments or buildings that projected images of wealth, respect for royal power, or civic pride.[31] More utilitarian approaches were emerging, focused on issues of health and sanitation, communication needs, and less-precise but nonetheless meaningful principles of urban civility.[32] The Lyon Consulat, however, which had considered the development of a Saint-Clair quarter as early as 1736, could not see its way to depart from its conservative fiscal practices and undertake any large project itself. It could only wish to control urban development, while entrusting the financing and construction to private initiatives. Generally, this was done through a two-tier process intended to generate and channel private investment. In Paris and in Bordeaux, for example, the authorities assembled lands (if possible undeveloped, or at least marginally developed) and opened a new area with the erection of an important public building. They then recouped their investment through the sale of surrounding lots to private interests that were keen to build housing in a future new quarter.[33] In the case of Saint-Clair, investors had to be motivated to undertake the necessary land reclamation, although in the end its cost proved modest. The Lyon Consulat chose to give all the lands to be reclaimed to Soufflot, Munet, and Millanois and added a significant exemption from seigneurial rights (see below). In return, the three developers agreed to a series of terms set by the city, including the creation of a port, a watering place for horses, several streets, and spaces for warehouses and commodities storage.[34]

This kind of compromise could only breed tensions by bringing together, yet attempting to dissociate, political power and private profit seeking. Speculation and public interest would share, more or less smoothly, for many generations to come in the restructuring of even the most essential of urban spaces. In this case, public interest would be served by a clear separation of public and private spaces, and notably the creation of a seventy-foot-wide quay. On the other hand, no warehousing space remained once the project was completed, thus precluding the development of any substantial port activity, and workshops and workers' housing never materialized. In turn, Soufflot's company and those to whom it sold lots gained a free hand with regard to the buildings they wished to erect. The welcome homogeneity of the ensemble was not the result of planned aesthetics but rather of a compromise among differing tastes and priorities that was somewhat unexpected – though it was more likely to be found in the context of a new, substantial development than in more frequent rebuilding projects.

Observers have often noted the pleasant effect of the tall facades of Saint-Clair, the regularity of hundreds of windows answering to the classic rhythm of Soufflot's Hôtel-Dieu. However, this effect did not come easily. The question surfaced soon after Morand's departure for Parma. His neighbours, Millanois and Soufflot, approached Antoinette Levet with drawings intended to provide three or perhaps four buildings with similar elevations. The Morands replied that they had agreed to match the height of the buildings but not their decoration. Evidently weary of alienating Soufflot, who had prepared some of the drawings in question, they eventually agreed to raise the cornice of their house to match those of their neighbours. A similar understanding had to be reached with regard to the shape of the roof to accommodate the wish of prospective tenants to use the attic not only to dry laundry, a common use of such spaces, but also to house domestics.[35]

Combined with a rigorous alignment, such compromises achieved a pleasant unity of style that was not dulled by an unnecessary uniformity of decoration. The limits of this process, however, are apparent. The Consulat had mandated that four twenty-four-foot-wide streets run through the new lands. Soufflot and his partners met this requirement, but using the royal unit (*pied de Roi*), which was some five or six percent shorter than the Lyon unit likely intended by the authorities.[36] The narrowness of the streets was accentuated by the height of the buildings, which was left to the discretion of the builders who evidently sought to maximize their use of the land. The problem is most evident in the case of a fifth street that clearly failed to meet the rising standards of the age for more open urban public spaces. The present rue Royale, which cuts Saint-Clair into two roughly symmetrical four-block sections, only came into existence as a service lane. Its length emphasizes the excessive height of the buildings (relative to its width) lining it tightly on both sides. It had clearly been expedient for the promoters to ignore a ratio governing these proportions that had not yet been legislated.[37] Many other technical difficulties taught Morand to balance the kind of control that he may have wished for as an architect and owner with the needs of neighbours. Shared walls and the fact that the houses were being built on a network of posts occasioned many discussions. The allocation of sometimes scarce resources, materials as well as labour, also entered into the equation of interests that shaped the new quarter. Every one of these issues risked alienating people who were at the same time partners, professional peers, and potential rivals. The need to manage these relationships remained a difficult problem for Morand, who was quick to feel himself the object of hostile machinations.[38]

ESSENTIAL SUPPORTS: FINANCIAL NETWORKS AND SEIGNEURIAL RIGHTS

The indeterminate equilibrium between private and public forces that is central to projects like Saint-Clair has been interpreted as a testimony to new-found abilities of the former to participate in large-scale urban renovations projects.[39] Yet the financing of such ventures was laborious given the absence of substantial banking institutions that were capable of draining investments in a systematic manner. The complexity of the disbursement schemes behind the new houses at Saint-Clair is remarkable. Intricate series of loans that were inherently unstable, even in a rich city such as Lyon, had to be woven together. Economic downturns regularly imperilled these financial constructions, and all parties knew the extent to which they rested on a wide network of connections.

When, on 15 September 1767, Jean-François Pitiot bought the new house built by Morand at 12 quai Saint-Clair for 250,000 lt, he paid 60,000 lt immediately. Most of the outstanding monies were settled in nineteen distinct payments over the following two years. Three payments (totalling 62,000 lt) went directly to complete Morand's earlier purchases of three lots, two in Saint-Clair and a third in the Brotteaux. Two (or perhaps three) other payments went to suppliers and tradesmen who were likely involved in the construction of the house in question (for a total of 28,000 or 33,280 lt). Finally, thirteen or fourteen payments (amounting to 74,280 or 79,480 lt) settled a series of obligations taken out by Morand to finance his various undertakings. These loans, contracted or renewed by Morand between 1760 and 1767, ranged from 1,200 to 12,000 lt, averaging 5,700 lt. Although these known payments did not even settle the transaction, they certainly expose the kind of financial juggling undertaken by Morand to finance his activities.[40] As we shall see, many other similar episodes followed.

Would-be promoters of urban development also had to contend with another set of local powers. Seigneurial rights played a key role in these matters. In Lyon, as in many other cities, they often belonged to great religious institutions, which also owned substantial lands. In the case at hand, the aristocratic female Abbaye de Saint-Pierre-les-Nonnains, whose Palais Saint-Pierre rivalled the neighbouring city hall in magnificence, made the creation of the Saint-Clair quarter possible by selling a strip of land on the banks of the Rhône. In the sale contract, the Benedictines justified their decision by arguing that they needed money to renovate their church; that the income they drew from the land was very limited (amounting, apparently, to only 1.7 percent of the price they sold it for); and that, as holders of the seigneurial rights (*directe et rente noble*), they would benefit from all further transactions.[41]

The principal of these seigneurial dues, known in the region as *lods* and *mi-lods*, was proportional to the price at which a property changed hands. In Lyon, these fees added a heavy cost to real estate transactions: for each sale, the *droit de lod* was levied at the rate of one-fifth of the sale price (*au cinquième denier*), and for each transfer of property other than a sale (such as an inheritance), the accurately named *droit de mi-lod* came into play at half the rate of the estimated value of the property.[42] Parcelling a piece of land and building houses on it would raise its value and increase the frequency of sales, thus multiplying levies of *lods* or *mi-lods*. To that end, the abbess required in the sale contract that a minimum of five houses be built, and she waived the fees on the first sale of each lot. This privileged abbey was not alone in paying close attention to the real estate market. The Consulat followed the same policy; and a few years later the other great holder of seigneurial rights in Lyon, the Chapître Saint-Jean, proved even more eager to foster the sale of lands across the Rhône by the Hôtel-Dieu hospital. As a mortmain institution, the Hôtel-Dieu was not, under normal circumstances, allowed to sell its properties. The canons of Saint-Jean knew that, by contrast, private owners would not only develop their lots but regularly put them on the market, triggering a new round of *lods* or *mi-lods* each time. If the institution of feudalism was threatened at the end of the Old Regime, or, conversely, if it was enjoying a revival (both views have found exponents), it is certainly true that urban growth offered great prospects to a minority of seigneurs.

Such prospects explain the next move of the Saint-Pierre abbey, which triggered a long legal dispute. In 1749 the Consulat had waived its seigneurial dues on the first four transactions on each reclaimed lot to be sold (an obvious sale argument for Soufflot and his associates). Seven years later, the abbey contested the city's claim to these seigneurial rights. Arguing that the lands to be reclaimed were part of its *directe* (seigneurial rent) before the Rhône had opened a new arm, the abbey extended its seigneurial claim to all the "new lands" of Soufflot and his associates. This was not an extravagant recourse to litigation but part of a long and dense jurisprudence along the Rhône and other major alluvial rivers. The Consulat, for its part, replied that "what the Rhône gave, the Rhône could take back"; that is to say, that if indeed the island had, in earlier times, been part of the mainland, it no longer was – it was fully part of the Rhône itself and thus beyond the abbey's reach.[43] This dispute offered a chance for the decisive intervention of royal power. The contested land was eventually deemed part of the royal domain, in application of the principle of *directe universelle* or *seigneurie éminente* (eminent domain or eminent lordship) on all navigable waterways, and given to the city on 31 August 1758.[44] This valuable grant was extended in part through the intervention of Henri-Léonard Bertin, who had been intendant at Lyon between 1754 and 1757 before being called to higher duties at Versailles and remained a personal friend of Soufflot's. However, the abbey's case was substantial and it was granted seigneurial rights over about one-quarter of the land in question in 1766. The matter was not fully settled until some twelve years later when this compromise was given royal assent, and then only after the abbey had conceded the same four transactions free of *lods* and *mi-lods* to Soufflot and his associates.

Morand fully understood the importance of such matters; for he found himself involved in a related dispute. He claimed to have been promised an exemption of the *lods* on the first sale of the building he erected upon the lot bought from Soufflot, Munet, and Millanois in 1757. To his mind, the promise had been made verbally to avoid creating a precedent. In 1762 he learned that a simi-

lar deal had been extended to other buyers at prices that seemed to
him better than what he had paid five years earlier. He believed that
Soufflot and his partners had taken advantage of his inexperience
and trust in their good faith. He sought some 8,000 lt in compensation. Soufflot replied that Morand had simply paid more (for less)
because he had bought earlier, and that he could have realized a
profit soon after the purchase by selling his lot. However, Morand's
claim must have had some standing, for the matter was resolved
quickly. The following February, Morand, who had argued the matter directly with Soufflot in Paris, declared himself satisfied with the
compromise and asked Antoinette Levet to go and sign it at the
notary, albeit "without showing too much enthusiasm."[45]

Morand had one further occasion to assess the importance of
rulings made in Versailles and the channels through which they
flowed. To reach its full development, the new quarter required the
demolition of a fort that blocked its northern entrance. Soufflot and
his partners had first asked for the removal of the fort in 1746.
It was done in 1772, through the support of the intendant, his supe-
riors at Versailles, and the governor of Lyon, Villeroy. This seem-
ingly small step was, in fact, an important marker in the waning
of traditional conceptions of cities as enclosed fortified spaces, a
topic to which we will return. On this particular occasion, the transition was marked in a manner reflecting both the new tastes of the
eighteenth century and its respect for tradition – with a beautiful
iron gate.[46]

FENDING OFF OPPONENTS

Though many trends and interests converged to make Saint-Clair a
reality, they could not suppress local rivalries. Besides the question
of seigneurial rights over the new lands, Morand was personally
involved in at least two other lengthy disputes that shed light upon
the competitive nature of urban development and emerging political alignments. Because the new lots stood between the steep slopes
of the Croix-Rousse and the Rhône river, the grades of the new
east-west streets joining these two limits became a sensitive issue.
When the matter was settled late in 1760 under the authority of the
city, one of the three associates behind the project, the architect
Melchior Munet, found that the ground floor of the house he was
building would be below grade, at least on one side.[47] Munet

accused Morand, his immediate neighbour, of having interfered with the decision-making process to bring forth a ruling that contradicted an earlier plan that was more compatible with Munet's interests. We do not know how the dispute was resolved (a 1764 letter from Soufflot to Morand mentions an arbitration process), but we know that Munet's case was argued by François-Pierre-Suzanne Brac, a young lawyer with a promising future in local affairs. Because he could not directly attack the Consulat or the duc de Villeroy, who had approved the change in levels, Brac focused his claims against Morand.[48] In time, he became a resolute adversary of Morand's. Perhaps because they had collaborated closely with Munet for several years, the Morands may have felt particularly betrayed by this attack. There is no evidence of further collaboration with Munet, although we know that the latter solved his problem rather elegantly by splitting the ground floor of his house.[49]

A few years earlier, Jean-Antoine Morand had been implicated in another dispute that took twenty years to resolve. This (not unusually) long court case was triggered by a powerful neighbour's claim that the southernmost new Saint-Clair buildings took away part of his river frontage. Antoine Tolozan had come to Lyon only in 1717, but he proved very successful in the silk trade and the commercial banking often associated with it. In 1735 he had purchased an office that brought him into the second order, as well as an appropriate rural seigneurie. In 1740 an aging Ferdinand Delamonce, who had been Lyon's leading architect before the arrival of Soufflot, designed for him a grand house that remains, to this day, an impressive example of classic Lyon eighteenth-century design. According to statements submitted in court, he had received assurances from the city that no building would be allowed between his house and the Rhône, guaranteeing him a vast panorama of the river, the plains to the east of the city, and, when the southern winds blew, the entire range of the Alps. After Antoine's death in 1754, ten years after the completion of his house, the new buildings going up at Saint-Clair deprived his heirs, Louis Tolozan and his siblings, as well as their many tenants, of the northern half of this view. The new grade they imposed and the ramp to Morand's bridge that was built in the early 1770s further diminished the perspective from the ground floor of the house. The family turned to the courts.[50]

Accusing the city of having broken its guarantee, they managed to obtain a stay on the construction of Morand's and Millanois's houses. The two owners won this first case fairly quickly, however, and construction resumed in January 1759. But they felt entitled to compensation for the delay and sued the city, which had sold them the land unencumbered. Soufflot, Munet, and Millanois (who evidently was involved in this case on two contradictory levels) accused the city and Tolozan of having failed to disclose the no-building clause. It could be said that Tolozan and the city had originated the problem, either through the breach of a guarantee or the rash stop-work order. Millanois, or rather his widow, settled fairly quickly, perhaps because their dual standing as developer and homeowner facilitated a compromise. The original three promoters of Saint-Clair, Millanois included, had agreed in the 1749 contract to build a port within five years. They had failed to do so by 1764, thus giving the city some leverage. Construction of a retaining wall and the creation of an open space in front of the Millanois house, as well as a small sum, settled the matter. Morand proved more intransigent, although he briefly considered dropping the suit in return for favourable treatment of his claim over the *lods* and *mi-lods*. He changed his mind, however, when he sensed that satisfaction would be his in the matter of *lods* and *mi-lods* without concession, and he doggedly pursued compensation for the degradations incurred on the idle work site as well as the loss of revenues from this rental property. He finally won a favourable settlement 1778.

Several observations may be made about these disputes, despite our limited information. First, one should note Morand's persistent feeling that he was the object of unfair attacks, and his stubborn willingness to carry on a dispute no matter how important his adversary. These are two key elements in his checkered career. Second, there is evidence here of the affirmation of the interests of the city over those of a powerful individual, in this case Tolozan – although the latter apparently won a guarantee that what was left of the free space in front of his house would remain undeveloped, as it has to date.[51] Finally, and perhaps most evident, there is the crucial role played by Versailles in settling feuds among rival factions in the kingdom's second largest city, particularly at a time when local political tensions were escalating – another key factor in later developments.

By 1760 Morand called himself an architect and, three years later, was recognized among the list of seventeen compiled by the *Almanach de Lyon*.[52] He had started his professional life as a scene painter and then acquired a reputation as a theatre engineer. Saint-Clair offered him a chance to combine his artistic, engineering, and managerial talents under the still imprecise but increasingly respected title of architect. In Lyon – that is, outside the preserve of royal or princely undertakings dominated by a few *architectes du roi* who had trained under the auspices of the royal academy of architecture (established in 1671) – it was not until the 1730s and 1740s that Delamonce, Soufflot, and a half-dozen other "artists" imposed themselves on the master masons and carpenters who had conducted most construction projects since the Middle Ages. In spite of growing official recognition, however, architecture was still a free profession, that is, without a defined course of training or formal corporate status.[53]

This lack of structure proved increasingly detrimental to the profession, as the technical competence of architects was challenged by another rising group, the engineers, backed by the very effective state institution of the Ponts et chaussées (the administration responsible for bridges and roadways, established in 1747).[54] But its relative freedom also helped architects to seize a broad range of opportunities. As the transformation of cities came to involve the creation of complete new neighbourhoods rather than the erection of monuments, architects learned to think of urban functions and urban planning, though the word *urbanisme* retained its connotation of refined manners for another half century.[55] At the same time, the complexity and fragility of the financial schemes at the heart of all important projects, as well as their inevitable political ramifications, led architects into the crucial role of "promoter," the dynamic personality behind a speculative enterprise. For many, the emerging profession proved both lucrative and honorific – one of the rising learned professions (*professions libérales*). Several of the pioneers of this calling in Lyon succeeded in marrying their offspring into the nobility of office.[56] For his part, Jean-Antoine Morand was too well positioned at the heart of the successful creation of the Saint-Clair quarter to ignore the immense potential of these trends. At the age of forty, he presented Lyon with an ambitious plan to project the city across the mighty Rhône, freeing it from its peninsular confines.

3

Conceiving the Brotteaux and Securing a Monopoly

Since 1764, [Morand] has sought only the beautification of Lyon. He conceived of its expansion within a circular plan [that minimised] all distances and brought both the Rhône and the Saône within ... the city ... He sacrificed six precious acres [... and] opened tree-lined promenades.[1]

A Company has been created to pursue M. Perrache's project, that has received support from the Consulat, the [Assembly of] Notables, and the King ... This Company intends to sell shares ...[2]

Perrache is turning into an architect!"[3]

As early as 1761, that is, soon after his return to Lyon from Parma and before the full potential of the Saint-Clair venture had become clear, Morand was already scouting lands directly across the Rhône from the new quarter. Although he was there on behalf of a client, we know that he was also, at the time, seeking opportunities beyond private architectural commissions.[4] In 1763, for instance, he drew plans for a canal to ship building stones to Lyon and discussed a project of "private public garden" west of Paris.[5] When the sale of his first Saint-Clair house allowed him to act, he turned back to the left bank of the Rhône. Early in July 1765 he bought fifty *bicherées*, or about 6.5 hectares, for 30,000 lt.[6] He already had plans for the area, since he immediately sold two lots while making provisions for a network of public alleyways to be managed by future owners of these lands.[7] The following summer, Morand drew a sketch of the Rhône's eastern shore and listed the owners of its islands.[8] At the time, Lyon was renewing its efforts to control the river, which regularly threatened the low-lying lands to the east as well as the medieval stone bridge that was known simply as *pont du Rhône*, since it was the sole bridge for hundreds of miles. Most worrisome, to many, was the idea of a new channel further east that would deprive the city of its riverfront, a potential calamity for its commerce, salubrity, and new quay. In 1764 the city built another series of dikes in an attempt to eliminate an arm of the river on its left shore, north of the old bridge.[9] Morand likely believed that the lands to be reclaimed could be put to some profitable use.

Early in 1767 Jean-Antoine Morand published his *Projet d'un plan général de la ville de Lyon et de son agrandissement en forme circulaire dans les terrains des Brotteaux*. These four printed pages summarized the benefits of a radical expansion of the city eastward across the river Rhône, and the means of achieving it. In the previous months, Morand had presented his new project in some detail to the city's Consulat, using a thirty-nine-page memorandum and several indispensable maps.[10] He had presented a first formulation of his vision in 1764 to the rectors of the Hôtel-Dieu, who, as the principal landowners of the Rhône's left bank, would play a central role in any such initiative. The interview had been cool, and Morand decided to raise the discussion to the highest level in the city and the broader public. Eventually, a map of the projected "circular city" was engraved and printed. It retailed at the cost of three lt in 1775 and has remained one of the best-known illustrations of the innovations sought by eighteenth-century urban thinkers.[11] In these various documents, Morand proposed to give the city a circular shape some three kilometres in diameter, centred on the Saint-Nizier church in the heart of the Presqu'île. In effect, this meant respecting the natural limits imposed by hills and rivers on the northern, western, and southern sides of the existing city (thus excluding the southern expansion planned by his rival, Perrache; see below), while settling a substantial population across the Rhône. The two rivers and their new quays, linked by several broad east-west streets, would bisect this recentered city in a pleasant symmetry. The new eastern neighbourhood would be bounded by a wall and a canal that would help control the Rhône. Residential, institutional, and commercial buildings would line an orthogonal grid of streets, boulevards, and open squares. A new bridge would join this planned community to the Terreaux and Saint-Clair.

This new section of the city, across the Rhône from the northern part of the Presqu'île, was eventually named Brotteaux, a word that referred to the gravel banks and islands deposited and regularly reshaped by the great Alpine river. These banks and islands remained uninhabited, although not unused, since some form of vegetation established itself rapidly and since it proved convenient to locate various polluting activities at a safe distance from the city. Beyond stretched a vast alluvial plain crossed by earthen levies and ditches recalling old arms of the river.[12] To the south, the faubourg de la Guillotière had grown along the road to Italy, at the end of the pont du Rhône. This settlement was dominated by artisans seeking cheap rents, inns, and other trades related to a major transportation axis. Until the seventeenth century, the pastures and fields east of the Rhône (administratively within the Dauphiné province) had generally been owned by wealthy Lyonnais. Then, in a little more than a century, the Hôtel-Dieu had built, through donations and purchases, a remarkable empire that left only a few isolated lots to a half-dozen other owners (see chapter 4).

Morand's vision was not without precedents. As early as 1733, Deville, director of Ponts et chaussées for the Lyon généralité, had argued for a complete channelling of the Rhône. This would open a new "continent" to the city where artisans could settle, although he recognized that such an ambitious plan would require decades to complete. Deville's scheme had been supported by the directors of the Hôtel-Dieu, who were eager to use their holdings across the river for more profitable ventures than farming.[13] After obtaining a royal monopoly for cable-ferries across the river in 1743, they created a promenade that quickly became a favourite destination for crowded urbanites. In 1754 they wrote to the city's Consulat in favour of a new bridge across the Rhône and, at the end of the decade, again reflected on ways to enhance the revenues from lands on the eastern shores.[14] Finally, it appears that in 1763 the hospital's directors assessed a sketch by the city's engineer for a more ambitious promenade.[15] In spite of its later resistance to Morand's projects, it is clear that the Hôtel-Dieu had long been interested in developing the left bank of the Rhône.

Morand argued that Lyon needed more housing, better transportation, safer work sites, and larger marketplaces, as well as

generally healthier and more aesthetically pleasing spaces.[16] His
circular plan was also meant to minimize all distances within the
city and bring both rivers into full use.[17] New ports, stables, and
yards would secure social peace with more regular supplies, better
prices, and employment.[18] New buildings would also permit the
removal of houses that were presently crowding bridges across and
banks along the long-settled Saône, or standing in the way of
needed streets. Furthermore, a new bridge would be safer than ferries, lessen traffic on the old bridge, facilitate its maintenance, and
ease the removal of rubbish.[19] A new quay on the left bank of the
Rhône would even serve the towing of upstream navigation. Most
of these arguments were not new, but they had been used in less-
encompassing projects. The Hôtel-Dieu's 1754 proposal for a new
bridge, for instance, stands out for its remarkable embrace of
economic expansion and consumption. The directors of the Hôtel-
Dieu welcomed the transformation of the "superfluous" into necessities and praised their contemporaries' willingness to work more to
satisfy their "chimera." However, the proposal argued only for the
opening of work sites and warehouses across the Rhône. For its
part, the anonymous essay written at the end of the 1750s to discuss
means to enhance the hospital's revenues from the fledgling entertainment scene initiated more than a decade earlier focused on the
diversity of people who could be attracted to the area, provided
that their tastes were catered to with enough distinction and "reasonable" fares. More permanent forms of development were only
mentioned as an eventual possibility.[20] By contrast, Morand's plan
is notable for its breadth and coherence. Settling large numbers of
people away from the city core made sense if communications were
improved and distances minimized by the new circular plan. At the
same time, demographic growth was to be supported by new work
sites and ports to better tap the vast region that served Lyon's needs.
More broadly, Morand's plan renewed the relation between the city
and its environment. What had long been perceived as a natural
limit to the city was crossed but replaced by a harmonious tripartite
division between hills, Presqu'île, and Brotteaux, neatly carved by
the "v" of the two rivers. The wide Rhône and the spacious grid of
the future Brotteaux promised a regenerative mingling of urban and
natural environments; at the same time, the wall and canal, as well
as the very circularity of the new city, recreated the contained urban
space familiar to the early modern age. Morand also addressed the

taste of the age for historical perspectives by fitting his proposal to cross the Rhône within the city's long, if slow, eastward advance.

The completeness and balanced nature of Morand's circular plan stands out when contrasted with the competing vision of Antoine-Michel Perrache. Perrache was known as a sculptor until he proposed, also in the 1760s, to expand Lyon by pushing the junction of the Saône and the Rhône southward. Only three years older than Morand, he had been born in Lyon to a family already connected to the arts. His father was a sculptor, successful enough to have received several commissions from the city.[21] Antoine-Michel also regularly appeared on the city's accounts and joined the Lyon Academy in 1753, an accolade that always eluded Morand. He had worked alongside Morand on the new theatre hall and had been among the first to buy a section of the Deschamps field from him, in 1765.[22] Soon after, however, their rival plans soured their relations. Perrache planned to expand the city southward by incorporating the île Moignat, a vast sandy island at the end of the Presqu'île. Once again, this was not a new idea. As early as 1677, the celebrated Hardouin-Mansard had proposed to expand the city southward on a grandiose scale.[23] In 1735 the city had bought the island and, three years later, the "jardins d'Ainay" immediately south of the city's southern wall. A second plan had then been formulated by Guillaume Delorme, albeit in rather lyrical terms. However, the Consulat acknowledged its inability to act a few years later and modestly decided on a tree-planting program to consolidate the island.[24] For his part, Perrache planned to link the island to the peninsula through two levies, one along each river. Where the old confluence had been, a canal from the Rhône to the Saône was to power several mills and provide access to a large port on the Saône side. Finally, a bridge across the Saône would link the new southern tip of the peninsula with the road to the Languedoc at la Mulatière. In the reclaimed lands, Perrache envisioned a mix of industrial and residential buildings, as well as recreational spaces and the indispensable celebratory squares.

Neither Perrache nor his successors at the head of the company he created could make the venture profitable. In spite of substantial public subsidies, the dike alongside the right bank of the Rhône stood as his only achievement for decades. The bridge to the Languedoc road did not finally open until 1792 – the first version crashed barely six weeks after its opening, early in 1783. Perrache's assessment of the lay of the land had been flawed; the mills never turned, and the lands to their south remained too low for building until a mountain of earth had been carted across the Saône.[25] The southern edge of the peninsula remained an unhealthy swamp for decades and never developed as a mature residential part of the city. From an entrepreneurial point of view as well as from that of urban development, Perrache's project was an unmitigated failure, while Morand's proved a promising, if modest and incomplete, success. Both initiatives were designed to transcend the natural and historical limits of the city to address issues characteristic of the age and make a fortune at the same time. Yet some very fundamental differences stand out.

Perrache hoped to create a new environment, not *ex nihilo* but nevertheless new enough for him to claim, under royal privilege, its ownership, just as Soufflot and his associates had done at Saint-Clair. His project could not become profitable in stages, or at least not until it was advanced enough for the mills to be operating. The real estate phase could not proceed until this low-lying area had been substantially raised, which called for large public and private investments.[26] For his part, Morand targeted existing lands, and his plans were carefully layered. The bridge to the Brotteaux would generate revenues and offer access to cheap entertainment venues that in turn would provide a second level of income.[27] Further development of the Brotteaux could proceed on an incremental basis, as lots were sold. It did not even require a controlling ownership of land. Initially, Morand argued that the company that built the bridge, the semicircular canal, and the fortifications should be granted ownership of the land thus delimited. Yet he had already put himself in a position to share in the profits of development, and he was magnanimous enough to suggest that the leading role in the venture could be played by the city itself, the Hôtel-Dieu, a company of private interests, or a combination of the three. Finally, Perrache's plan accentuated the city's north-south orientation, rather than rebalancing it in the way Morand proposed to do.[28] While Perrache's reclaimed lands appeared better connected to the existing city than the Brotteaux, they would also by definition remain ensconced between two rivers – a physical reality that partly explains the city's continuing failure, more than two centuries later, to integrate this area into its core. By contrast, the left bank of the

AN ILL-FATED CONFLUENT

In what may seem at first a curious coincidence, two major urban planning mistakes compromised the place of Perrache's new lands in the city of Lyon, the first one century and the second two centuries after the difficult initial reclamation effort. In the 1850s, when it came time to choose a location for the first railroad station, the city balked at the obvious location, on the eastern edge of the Brotteaux. This would have meant that trains arriving from Paris and then continuing south would bypass the Presqu'île, which was still the heart of Lyon. Thanks to local political pressures, the new station was built in 1856 at the northern edge of the lands reclaimed by Perrache. The massive east-west structure (naturally prolonged on both sides by tracks) irremediably separated the core of the city from the area beyond the *voutes*, the tenebrous vaults under the train tracks that gave access to the tip of the peninsula. Eventually, that is, late in the twentieth century, the advent of fast trains called for the construction of a new central station – exactly where the first should have risen, on what was by then a military site.

Not long before that, however, the fate of the Presqu'île's southern tip had been further sealed by construction of a massive freeway interchange. Sometime in the 1960s, it was decided that the great new autoroute linking Paris with the Mediterranean should come right into the city. This choice called for the creation of a tunnel under the southern edge of the Fourvière hill and the upshot was a gigantic complex entirely devoted to speedy transit just north of the railroad station. The roots of this decision remain unclear; it has been suggested that it was the result of a combination of two distinct wishes: Lyon urban planners wanted to facilitate communication between the Presqu'île and the western suburbs, a reasonable plan that was appropriated by Parisian decision makers who saw an opportunity to connect the freeways to the north and south of the city. In any case, the area was shaped by several politically charged mistakes, the later ones facilitated, perhaps, by the earlier in what may be seen as a case of "path dependency" – a major transport infrastructure paving the way for a second one. Yet it may be that the tip of the Presqu'île created by Perrache was bound to remain peripheral. What is, on one hand, a simple extension of the Presqu'île is also, on the other hand, a narrowing strip of land bounded by two great rivers, and thus physically separated from other neighbourhoods (neither the Rhône nor the Saône have been bridged between the station itself and la Mulatière). While the city eventually spread far across the Rhône, the lands reclaimed by Perrache attracted large-scale industrial and transportation infrastructures rather than residential or even commercial buildings.

Most interesting, in this regard, may be the future of this area: to date, the city is once again intent on reviving what it now terms the "Confluent." To be properly connected to the rest of the city and to take full advantage of a potentially impressive geographical setting, the area will have to be freed from its communication burden, expressways in particular – a daunting challenge by all standards.

References. Aynard, *Histoire des deux Antoine*; Cottin, "Trois propositions pour le confluent au xviiie siècle"; Delfante and Dally-Martin. *Cent ans d'urbanisme à Lyon*; Fontanon, "L'échec du projet industriel sur les terrains de Perrache"; Labasse, "Réflexions d'un géographe"; and Rivet, *Le quartier Perrache (1766–1946)*.

Rhône eventually became Lyon's most dynamic sector, and its northern reaches, the Brotteaux, its fashionable bourgeois quarter.

Morand's circular plan was sound and well crafted. It combined a seductive vision fitting the history and geography of the city with a step-by-step approach that placed him at the centre of the activity it intended to generate. Lyon's civic authorities did not fail to see the opportunities presented by his proposal but, not surprisingly, they judged it too ambitious (*trop immense*). They agreed, however, that a new bridge across the Rhône would satisfy immediate recreational and warehousing needs. Perrache's venture, examined at the same time, received a more categorical rejection, based on the need for further technical assessment and, more ominously for both projects, on a lack of consensus on the city's need for new residential and commercial land.[29] While both projects frightened Lyon's timid councillors, Morand's offered them a chance to act with a minimum of risk. Civic leaders of all ages could appreciate such an opportunity. As it turned out, events unfolded in a manner quite different from that envisioned by these prudent decision makers. Perrache revised his project slightly under the guidance of Soufflot. He obtained royal letters patent in 1770 and the support of the Consulat soon after, although this reversal of its earlier stance is not explained by the records that we have.[30] Construction got off to a good start but dragged on for several decades, leaving the city with a controversial and unprofitable work site. For his part, Jean-Antoine Morand was not able to develop a new neighbourhood in the Brotteaux, but his new bridge across the Rhône proved a mighty money maker. Before he could start construction, however, he had to overcome a potent coalition of opponents to secure an indispensable royal privilege, losing the Consulat's support in the process.

Late in 1767 Morand had started to assemble the business partners he needed for the bridge. He had at least two meetings with the Flachon brothers and Messieurs Guyot, Roux, and Guillard. Early the following year, they were joined by de Myons, Monlong, Guillin du Montet, Barety, and Mievre. By then, some members of the group were meeting almost daily, usually around dinner and more often than not at Morand's table.[31] We will meet most of these names again, but a brief sketch of their position in Lyon society will give a measure of the forces that Morand was able to gather at the start of the most original part of his career. Ferdinand, Maurice, and Etienne Flachon were respectively King's engineer, Trésorier de France (a regional official of the Bureau des Finances), and banker. Notary Guyot would be the legal counsel of the new company as well as its treasurer. He was well connected with religious authorities, notably as head of the diocesan accounting services. Léonard Roux was a colleague of Morand's, an architect who had invested in the successful Saint-Clair venture. Pupil de Myons was embarked on a brilliant and, as we shall see, controversial political career. Jean Monlong was a silk manufacturer and merchant, brother-in-law of J.-F. Genève, a former alderman and one of Morand's earliest friends in the city. Monlong was also among the new dwellers in Saint-Clair. Marie-Aimé Guillin du Montet was a lawyer, seigneur of the nearby town of Poleymieux, rector of the Hôtel-Dieu, and future alderman. Evidently, Morand was now able to draw the attention of people who mattered in Lyon.

Morand presented his project to the board of the Hôtel-Dieu on 3 February 1768 and the Consulat soon after. A first estimate of the cost of the projected bridge, reaching just over 300,000 lt, accompanied his sketch of the partnership he was seeking. He offered the hospital a twenty-five percent stake in the operations of the bridge (revenues and expenses, taxes included), in exchange for abandoning its ferry monopoly and the lands necessary to the bridge. Morand also asked the comtes de Lyon, seigneurs of the left bank, to lower the rights attached to the expected transfers of property, a concession that would be amply repaid by the new life brought to the seigneurial rent due to the comtes (*directe*). Recognizing the Saint-Jean chapter's broad interest in civic affairs, Morand added to the list of benefits that his bridge promised to the city. Not only would private owners defend their properties against the Rhône, in effect voluntarily funding what had been until then a costly battle for the city, but the bridge would increase the toll fees (*octrois*) levied at the gates and eliminate the dissipation associated with the ferries. The comtes agreed to share the first four *lods* or *mi-lods*, under several conditions.[32] On 25 May 1768 the Hôtel-Dieu declared itself willing to pursue the project, but on terms that could only be rejected by Morand and his partners. Thus began a four-year battle. At stake was a monopoly for a second bridge on the Rhône, with the concomitant cancellation of the ferry privilege that had been granted to the Hôtel-Dieu a quarter-century earlier, and a controlling voice in any future development of the left bank. This fight can be seen as representative of many other similar struggles. Yet its details remain difficult to follow, if only because much of what transpired during these years was meant to remain hidden. To make sense of it all, we shall turn first to the manoeuvres that stretched from 1768 to 1772 and assess the various forces behind these campaigns in the following chapter.

1768

Naturally enough, the rectors wished to make the venture more profitable and less risky for their institution. They insisted on retaining control of the cable ferries, or *trailles*, as long as possible, limited the company's ownership of the bridge to sixty-three years, and asked for one-quarter of its revenues on top of a yearly payment of 15,000 lt. They also wanted the company to pay all maintenance expenses and taxes and to lease the necessary lands from them. Finally, they asked to be formally included in the letters patent that would make the bridge possible.[33] On 18 June 1768 Morand took the matter beyond the municipal level, sending his plans to Bertin, the minister responsible for Lyon, who received the hospital's objections a week later.[34] The minister quickly turned back to the city to try to engineer a rapprochement. However, the tone of the discussions had already changed. In his submission to Bertin, Morand pointedly referred to the hospital's failure to meet its engagements with regard to the capacity of the ferries to transport anyone or anything except pedestrians, the frequent service interruptions it tolerated, and the excesses of the brothers operating the boats. He had also started to recruit allies for his project, and letters of support were reaching officials in the capital.[35] The hospital's counterattack opened on a suitably humble note, acknowledging the king's right to take back the crossing monopoly given in 1743. The rectors argued that their demands were simply meant to protect the interests of the poor in their care. They estimated revenue losses from the cessation of the ferry service at 20,000 to 25,000 lt and saw the profits that could be expected from future development of the left bank as speculative, ill-matched to the immediate and constant needs of their mission. They also offered the minister a way out of the dilemma, suggesting that the city's first administrative level, the Assembly of Notables, be consulted.[36] By then, Morand was in Paris to advance his case.

Morand and Antoinette Levet left Lyon on 20 May 1768 for a three-month sojourn in the capital. They chose a hotel on the rue Saint-Honoré, leased a carriage to facilitate their errands, and proceeded to meet all those who could advance the project; we know of at least sixteen trips to various ministerial residences outside the city. The day after their arrival, Morand met Lyon's prévôt des marchands, M. de la Verpillière. Soon after, he submitted his plans for the bridge to Soufflot and to Gabriel, premier king's architect. Then, Bouchet and Gendrier, inspectors of the Ponts et chaussées, introduced him to Trudaine, head of that rising institution. Although ill, the latter received him at his country estate and ordered his staff to draw plans to their own specifications and to submit a report on the project, a necessary step before Morand could see Bertin. Morand also sought and received support from the archbishop of Lyon, M. de Montazet, and M. de Montmorillon, canon of Saint-Jean, count of Lyon. Finally, he met another aristocrat with

Lyonnais roots, the count Duzelle, who could provide more support
– as soon as he received a letter from M. Prost de Royer.[37]
Antoine-François Prost de Royer was a lawyer who became alderman, lieutenant general of police, rector of both the Charité and
Hôtel-Dieu hospitals, and president of the Tribunal de la Conservation. At the time, however, he was surveyor (voyer) to the comtes
of Lyon, overseeing all matters related to streets and buildings
within their jurisdiction, a reflection of their claim to some authority in the most concrete of urban affairs. In this position, he could
relay the support that Morand expected from the thirty-two canons
of Saint-Jean.

Morand had carefully prepared for his meeting with Bertin at
Versailles. When it finally came, on 18 June 1768, the minister
was well informed of the project and willing to ask the rectors to
further explain their opposition. It must have been a long day,
since it included dinner with Jean-Rodolphe Perronet, who agreed
to provide another positive report from the Ponts et chaussées. By
the end of the month, Morand believed that it was time to inform
the board of the hospital indirectly of the favourable dispositions
within these high-level circles. This was a sign of his inexperience:
nothing moved fast at Versailles. Morand discovered the limits of
his advances in Paris on 22 July, after a long wait among the
crowd besieging the offices of Bertin. His secretary, de la Barbérie,
assured him of the minister's goodwill but confirmed that he
would ask the prévôt des marchands to broker an agreement
between the bridge company and the Hôtel-Dieu. This raised a
new alarm in Morand's mind, since Lyon's first magistrate would
know of a new objection raised by two powerful neighbours of the
future bridge: Messieurs Auriol and Pulligneu feared that its access
ramp would raise the ground level in front of their properties to an
unacceptable level. The matter was serious, since the requirements of navigation imposed a minimum height on the bridge, and
because the Auriol family was a leading merchant dynasty and
Pulligneu a rising political figure.[38]

Throughout these exchanges, Morand appears to have been
impatient, no doubt because he was still unfamiliar with the work-
ings of high administrative and political circles but also because it
was his nature. Guyot worked to reassure and calm him, but
another associate, Flachon de la Jomarière, expressed the worries
of those left in Lyon more directly. After Morand had repeatedly

suggested that he wished to move decisively to *"couper la tête au poulet"* (decapitate the opposition), Flachon reminded him that they had agreed to use their "ultimate weapon" only in the last resort.[39] This weapon of last resort was a very political, hence risky, move: it referred to the fact that the board of the Hôtel-Dieu could not, in the end, resist royal will. A substantial claim of independence on the part of the rectors could bring down the wrath of the minister. Yet this was not something that could be easily piloted through the meanderings of court politics. Instead, Flachon proposed an indirect approach. He suggested that they focus on the completion of a new road to the Bresse province alongside the Rhône. Such a road would enhance the value of Saint-Clair properties, something of importance to several partners, and bring traffic closer to the proposed bridge. It also offered a chance to cultivate the friendship of several important people in Lyon and Paris. The company continued to strengthen its plans, notably by seeking investors for venues that were likely to produce revenues quickly, such as warehouses and a tennis hall.[40] Morand left Paris disappointed, without a favourable decision.

1769

On 21 February 1769, the company revisited its offer to the Hôtel-Dieu. It offered an annuity (*rente foncière*) of 5,000 lt for the lands that it would need for the construction and service of the bridge. The loss of the ferries would now be compensated by a yearly payment of 10,000 lt, altogether providing the hospital with 15,000 lt per year once the bridge became operational. The company also agreed to run the ferry service for the benefit of the hospital until it was no longer needed, and to hand back the bridge to the hospital after sixty-three years.[41] Unconvinced, the rectors replied with a lengthy and alarmist memorandum highlighting the dangers created by the planned bridge. Not only would navigation become more difficult but the suburb of La Guillotière, the new neighbourhood of Saint-Clair, and the entire left bank would suffer from the constraints put on the river by the bridge. The hospital itself risked losing a great deal of the more than 50,000 lt of revenues it claimed to draw from the threatened areas. To support this fearsome scenario, reference was made to several great floods going back to the year AD 592. Still, the hospital declared itself willing to accommo-

date the project, if only the company met its demands: 19,000 lt per
year as compensation for ferries and land, the land being simply
leased and not sold as Morand's offer of an annuity implied; free
crossing for all of the hospital's business; and no commitment
to maintain the bridge after the sixty-three-year concession. This
virulent memorandum marked the emergence of François-Pierre-
Suzanne Brac on the front line of Morand's opponents. The politically ambitious lawyer who had argued against Morand in his dispute with Melchior Munet five years earlier was now on the board
of the Hôtel-Dieu and engaged in several tight political contests,
notably against Pupil de Myons, one of Morand's early and important partners.[42]

In a draft reply to an unnamed Crown minister that was probably
never sent, Morand forcefully argued that in the end, even the interests of the poor – the hospital's strongest rhetorical claim – should
yield to the greater public good. He also suggested that if the three
toll bridges on the Saône generated 24,000 lt of yearly profit, 6,000
lt should be fair compensation for the ferries and lands needed from
the hospital (he added that the Hôtel-Dieu exaggerated the income
from the ferries by failing to account for its investments and selecting its most profitable years). At the same time, he received an
unsigned letter from Paris, likely from Soufflot, telling him that Bertin was urging him to refrain from using his "secret weapon," to
keep sending documentation, and not to rush to the capital.[43] Nevertheless, two months later Morand again took the road to Paris,
where he stayed just over a month. He met Bertin on three successive
days, spending six hours with him on 29 November at his country
estate. A complete file was assembled, with the help of Ponts et
chaussées. As he returned home, Morand believed, once again, that
he could have obtained a ruling from the minister, although he had
now learned that it was better to give the hospital another chance to
reply positively to the Crown's support of the project.[44]

1770

Morand's optimism was again premature. Few people believed that
the minister would dare to go against the will of the hospital's directors.[45] Nevertheless, on 15 January 1770 Bertin asked the intendant
at Lyon to attempt once again to reconcile the company and the
hospital but for the first time indicated a willingness to overrule the

rectors. In turn, the province's chief engineer, de Lallié, recommended a meeting of both parties in the presence of the intendant. Not surprisingly, the hospital ignored a request that made light of its elevated status.[46] Instead, in late May 1770 the rectors' issued another draft of their demands, with the added suggestions that the left bank of the Rhône would need full protection and, most ominously, that Morand and his associates were trying to "surprise" (that is, deceive) the authorities. Morand replied that all parties had been kept fully informed and that a levee along the left bank of the Rhône would cost at least ten million livres tournois. He then spelled out his understanding of the profits that might be expected from the venture, suggesting that an investment of 350,000 lt would produce a return of only 16,000 lt (or 4.57 percent); any profit would come from lands left in the company's hands on the newly accessible left bank.[47]

The intendant proved sensitive to this last argument. In the belief that such ventures required a ten percent return on the capital invested, he set the compensation to the hospital at 6,000 lt, plus the value of the ferries. On the other hand, he favoured letting the company simply lease land from the Hôtel-Dieu, which he thought, should retain one ferry boat. De Flesselles also called for further studies and a tight schedule of inspections (to be performed at the expense of the company by the provincial chief engineer, none other than de Lallié, who was advising him on the matter). Morand was quick to reply that leaving a ferry crossing to the hospital, burdening the project with more inspections, or depriving the company of the right to own – and thus, more importantly, to sell – lands across the river compromised the financial viability of the project. He added that the Ponts et chaussées had already given a positive report on the project, and that it would be in the company's interest to maintain the bridge to high standards.[48]

In the following months Morand tried to revive his connections in Paris, notably by proposing secretely to raise his offer of 6,000 lt to the Hôtel-Dieu by thirty percent, only to be told by his "man on the scene," M. Martin, to back off. Early in November Morand clashed with de Lallié in the waiting room of the intendant, perhaps because Perrache's project had just received royal assent.[49] Yet because the support of the Lyon intendancy was crucial to his project, Morand steadied his nerves enough to agree, a couple of weeks later, to allow regular inspections by the Province's engineer, provide a further 1,000 lt of yearly compensation to the hospital in exchange for the third ferry, and lease land from the hospital, as long as the company was reimbursed for its investment on those lands at the end of what he still wished to be a ninety-nine-year lease.[50] In light of later disputes among the associates, it is interesting that this last concession (which meant that the company would not be able to own or sell lands across the bridge) was less painful for Morand than for his partners. He already owned a well-positioned property across the river. His partners, by contrast, could benefit from the speculation that would follow the opening of the bridge only if the company was able to buy land from the hospital. The intendant forwarded his final conclusions to the minister a few days later, adding yet another 1,000 lt to the compensation package and staying with the sixty-three-year lease. Morand immediately agreed to the new money but insisted on a longer concession. At the same time, his correspondent in Paris reassured him that a decision was coming, and that it would likely be favourable, in spite of the fact that the king was locked in a tight struggle with the Parlement of Paris – one of the regular confrontations that have attracted so much interest from historians.[51]

1771: VICTORY OR STALEMATE?

Not convinced by this mixed message, Morand left Lyon on Christmas day, 1770, for yet another trip to Paris. First on his agenda were the modifications under consideration for the new theatre. Soufflot eventually agreed to these renovations, but the matter called for the intervention of the duc de Villeroy, because Bertin wished to charge them to the budget of the festivities planned for the forthcoming visit of the comtesse de Provence. Morand had often managed such official entertainment; this time, however, the prévôt des marchands had chosen someone else. Villeroy concluded that Morand had lost the confidence of Lyon's civic authorities. Morand protested but also had to confess that the Consulat had turned him down for the position of city surveyor which he had been actively seeking. The duke was further irritated when he learned that the Hôtel-Dieu had built a large house in the Brotteaux to block any plan for a grand avenue in line with the future bridge. It stood as very public evidence of a rift that reflected badly on Villeroy's influence on the city's public life.[52]

The decree authorizing construction of the new bridge is dated 4 January 1771, although it was not signed for another two months, since Bertin's ministry was overwhelmed with work. During that time, pressure was still being exerted to alter some of the wording of the ruling, keeping Morand and those working for him in Paris busy. The decree recognized the unresolved conflict between Morand and the Hôtel-Dieu but reaffirmed the value of the project to the public, including the hospital itself. It granted Morand's company the exclusive right to build a bridge according to specifications submitted to the Crown, and the right to levy a toll for ninety-nine years, following a schedule appended to the royal decision. It also spelled out the nature of the compensations to be paid to the hospital, but left the details to experts. The hospital was stripped of its rights over the river crossings, while Morand and his associates were allowed to operate any boats they deemed necessary north of the old stone bridge. The rectors were ordered to sell the lands that were indispensable to the construction and maintenance of the bridge to the company, at a price to be decided by experts. The tolls authorized by Versailles were the same as those granted to the operator of the ferries in 1643, except that Morand's company had agreed to reduce the basic fee (for a single pedestrian, whether carrying a load or not, or a passenger in a carriage) from nine to six deniers. Carriages and their drivers would pay four sols, horse riders one sol and six deniers, while a cart could make a return trip for three sols.[53]

In spite of this royal decision, Morand was not able to start work on the bridge for another long year, mainly because it had to be registered by the Parlement of Paris, among other bodies.[54] However, the parlements were dismissed by the famous judicial reform carried out by René Nicolas de Maupeou, chancellor of France, in May 1771. Consequently, late in October of that year, the king ordered the newly created Conseil Supérieur de Lyon to register the letters patent granted to Morand and his associates. Until then, the bridge promoters had to proceed carefully, consolidating support and soothing opponents. They had to make a start on the initial steps of their construction project, since waiting would have given too much credit to the parlement's right to challenge royal decisions.[55] They also sought to appease Auriol and Pulligneu, the residents who believed that the bridge's access ramp prejudiced their recently built houses. Luckily, both wanted to avoid pushing their opposition too far. They likely appreciated the value of the bridge to the neighbourhood, and Pulligneu's ambitions in the new Conseil Supérieur depended on the goodwill of Versailles. Still, the problem was real – precise measurements taken more than a century later show that Morand's bridge was indeed high. Not surprisingly, complaints soon surfaced regarding the draining of the area behind the raised quay giving access to the bridge. Eventually, Morand acknowledged that Auriol's house would be "somewhat more buried than anticipated."[56]

It was also time to thank supporters. After he had obtained the royal seal for Morand's letters patent, Martin reminded him that those who had worked for him in the capital were now expecting their rewards. At least 3,000 lt were made available to that end, and a "magnificent" silk habit was secured for the minister's secretary, de Barbérie. In a similar gesture intended to strengthen public support for his venture, Morand seemed ready, in April 1771, to give the Hôtel-Dieu the 6,000 lt that had been offered in compensation for its 1743 privilege, a clause not included in the royal text. He suggested that this generous move be made public in the name of M. Bertin, a tactful way to smooth feathers among the rectors and at the same time praise the minister who had made the project possible.[57] Morand also had to cultivate public support in a forthcoming *commodo-incommodo* public inquiry, a procedure designed to allow those with concerns about a project that benefited from a royal privilege to voice their opinions. While everyone understood that this mechanism could not stand up to royal will, it nevertheless provided one more official statement of the public value of the project. For a while, Morand and his correspondents believed that, taking advantage of the confusion created by the Maupeou reforms, they would have a choice of venue for such a process, perhaps turning to the Lyon Sénéchaussée. Versailles, however, was intent on promoting the new court, and the inquiry opened in front of the Conseil Supérieur de Lyon on 3 December 1771 and lasted nine days.[58] The choice of witnesses (fifteen in this case) was essential to the credibility of the process. Local administrative institutions were represented by two former aldermen and a member of the Lyon Election, the regional office responsible for the distribution of taxes. Their voices were second only to those of the Church representatives, three canons and the archbishop. Three *gens de l'art* – experts we would say – matched three legal practitioners, while a merchant and a director of the Coches du Rhône, a shipping monopoly, represented the commercial interests so important to Lyon. As in all such inquiries, giving a voice to an array of interests was more important than reaching a conclusion. Indeed, it seems that negative views of the project outnumbered the positive. However, not only was this court not bound by any such tally of opinion but corporate decision-making processes in general were not based upon an egalitarian assessment of participating voices.[59]

Supporters of Morand naturally articulated the same arguments he himself had carefully compiled. Those who spoke against the bridge went beyond a defence of the interests of the Hôtel-Dieu.[60] Several referred to the risks posed to navigation and even to the city itself by the erection of an important obstacle across the bed of an impetuous river. Others objected that the development that would inevitably follow the opening of the bridge would bleed the suburb of La Guillotière and harm the entire city's rental market. Several witnesses decried the maintenance costs of a wooden bridge, while some worried about crowds rushing back to the city at the end of a summer day. Others suggested that the city was served well enough by the existing bridge, especially since the opening of the new quai de Retz. Finally, a lawyer with an aesthetic sense suggested that Morand's company should be required to post a large bond to satisfy all potential damages inherent in such a project; he also noted that the bridge's gates and toll booths would interrupt the pleasant openness of the eastern vista.

On 19 December 1771 the Lyon Consulat openly joined the ranks of those who opposed the bridge in a submission to the Conseil Supérieur that recapitulated most of these arguments. Morand immediately replied in a four-page printed pamphlet. Sensing that his lack of experience as well as the for-profit nature of his venture were becoming issues, he upheld the quality of his design, enriched as it was by his training in Italy and approved by all the leading names of the Ponts et chaussées. He added that he was building an expensive structure and that he had been very open to sound advice.[61] Perhaps because the Consulat's objections were weakened by the installation of a new prévôt des marchands, M. de Bellecise, who was more sympathetic to Morand and his associates, the Conseil Supérieur de Lyon registered the letters patent two days before Christmas, 1771. Before the year was over, all of the texts that accompanied the royal ruling of the previous January were printed and publicly available in Lyon. Morand could breath, and acknowledge the key role played by the intendant in obtaining a favourable decision from the Conseil Supérieur.[62] He could not, however, rest. The new year brought one more furious battle.[63]

Final Confrontation: 1772

Early in February 1772, the Hôtel-Dieu sought to appeal the registration of Morand's letters patent, but there was no formal procedure for doing so. Consequently, printed petitions were sent to the Conseil Supérieur and to Versailles. At their heart was another virulent attack on Morand led by Brac. It was claimed that Morand had misled those charged with the evaluation of his plans.[64] Several anonymous letters predicted the spoliation of the hospital and the poor under its care, cast doubt upon the propriety of the land purchase that had given Morand a foothold on the left bank, and suggested that he was separated from his wife, an allegation intended to weaken his ability to raise funds.[65] Every step taken by the company sparked new attacks. On 23 January 1772, Morand attempted to initiate the transfer of the ferries by making 10,000 lt available for compensation. The rectors refused the money and claimed that the sum was so inadequate as to jeopardize the royal decision (the Conseil Supérieur agreed to a new estimate, but the hospital failed to send its own experts). Three weeks later Morand appropriated the ferry boats – giving his opponents a chance to denounce the "violent seizure of their property."[66] Just as the contract creating the new Compagnie du Pont was about to be signed (see below), rumours spread that no agreement had been reached between the eleven partners, and that the bridge enterprise would upset the regional labour market by hiring all available hands at the fantastic rate of two livres tournois per day.[67]

As Morand started to sign contracts with suppliers, opponents asked the Consulat to stop work on the bridge. A number of important users of the river and owners of nearby houses, as well as villagers on the left bank, were encouraged to seek an injunction, and a list of collapsed wooden bridges was prepared.[68] Eventually, attacks on Morand's good faith became more specific. It was suggested that the company had hidden from the city the cost of the ramps that would give access to the higher-than-expected bridge. Morand was accused of having provided false measurements of the river's depth, and, work having finally started, of not following his own plans (all of this was supported by a report from de Lallié). The Consulat ordered work to stop on 6 June 1772, a move that could not paralyze the work site but did worry subcontractors and workers at a critical time.[69]

These assaults resulted in a further spate of work on behalf of the project. On the surface, the goal of Morand and his associates was simple: to deflect criticism of their design, in the belief that a royal decision that had reached such an advanced stage could not easily be overturned. Indeed, sources around ministerial offices hinted at growing dissatisfaction with this obstinate opposition to royal will. The Consulat itself was taking risks when it used the royal injunction to oversee the project (*tenir la main* was the standard expression of such rulings) to order new investigations.[70] Yet Morand and his partners found it difficult to rest on the security of a royal decree. They had to reassure nervous investors and find replacements for those who pulled out of the venture.[71] Even if they realized that a new offer could put the minister in a delicate position by suggesting that he had been too generous with Morand, they could not help but regularly revisit their strategy. They considered offering the hospital a one-third partnership in the venture at the cost of only one-quarter of the estimated 360,000 lt and, a little later, contemplated guaranteeing it the regular income of an annuity. They also frequently discussed using the threat of withdrawal to add weight to their assertion that the profitability of the enterprise remained fragile.[72] More constructively, Morand and his partners agreed to new inspections, provided information on the state of similar structures decades after their construction, and shipped to Paris a rather cumbersome scale model of the neighbourhood of the bridge.[73] They also seized any opportunity to divide their opponents. Thus, after denying the problem, the company agreed to pay for all expenses related to access to the bridge, undermining the cohesion between the Hôtel-Dieu and the Consulat. Finally, in what was probably a delicate move, Soufflot revealed to the minister his participation in the financing of the bridge. He owned two of the thirty shares but had kept it secret to protect his credibility as an adviser. Bertin took the matter well, suggesting that Soufflot's financial stake in the project only confirmed its soundness.[74]

Throughout these crucial months, Morand and his partners also activated all the personal contacts they could muster. The comte d'Audiffret, an aristocrat with roots in the Alps, the abbé Lacroix-Laval, the vicomtesse de Noë, the abbé de Grally, and the marquis de Groslée all contributed to the campaign of support. Standing social debts were called in, for instance when Flachon contacted a relative of his, M. Minel, who regularly helped the minister's secretary, de la Barbérie, finance his own projects and could thus wield some influence.[75] Morand and his allies also urged communities on the Rhône's left bank to reject the petitions circulated against the bridge and tried to expose some of the connections between the project's opponents.[76]

Throughout this tense spring, Morand's mood fluctuated widely, perhaps hitting a low point in June 1772 when he confessed to Etienne Flachon that he was almost too angry to show the respect due to a minister when writing to Versailles.[77] He was evidently not the only participant to this affair whose nerves were frayed. When the matter was finally resolved in favour of the bridge following a discussion in royal council in mid-June, the ministry fired off extremely strong letters to the Consulat, the hospital board, and Brac, condemning the manoeuvres of the bridge's opponents. Brac, who had gone to Paris to pursue the matter, had to leave the capital in a hurry and labouriously explain that he had made the trip only because the letter confirming the royal decision had not reached him in time. Meanwhile, the board of the Hotel-Dieu apologized to the controller general, admitting that its zeal had led it too far in defence of the poor.[78]

This was a very political decision, an assertion of royal authority. Yet there was no need to expose the real nature of this exercise of power. As far as Versailles was concerned, the royal decree of January 1771 sufficed, and all parties simply had to be reminded of their duties. The best way to do this would allow everyone to save face, confirming the hierarchy of power rather than acknowledging the challenge that had taken place. Consequently, the decision was shrouded in technicalities. M. Gendrier, inspector general of the Ponts et chaussées, reassessed the extent to which the plans for the bridge conformed with royal intentions. Morand replied in detail to his investigations, incorporating in his answers a series of new measurements.[79] Royal authority was also subtly reasserted over the Consulat. This old and ornery institution was ordered to stop opposing a project supported by a royal patent, but it was also given the opportunity to force the company to compensate the city for all expenses required to link the bridge to the existing urban landscape of the Presqu'île – something to which the bridge partners had already agreed, and quickly agreed to again.[80] Morand could now turn his full attention to the construction of the bridge. His partners simply had to remind him to "remain modest" and not appear too triumphant. We must, however, stop to consider the nature of the formidable opposition they had faced for over four years.

4

Opposition in Context

"This Monday, Eleven of March, at nine in the morning, all the Magistrates nominated to the Conseil Supérieur created for the city of Lyon by the Edict of last February, having gathered at the offices of the intendant, also first president of this new institution, started at 9:30 for the Justice Hall. The streets, bridges, and places were lined on both sides by the Militia ... intent on expressing its satisfaction for all the benefits the city of Lyon will receive from this institution ... All went off with great dignity, without any other display than that of public rejoicing."[1]

The development of the Rhône's left bank had many implications for Lyon's elite, which perhaps justified much of the resistance encountered by Morand. All house owners legitimately feared the impact of a large residential and commercial venture on existing real estate prices. Economic and demographic conditions were not only volatile but also hardly known and certainly poorly understood. This meant that few people would have had solid reasons to believe that further economic and demographic growth would likely justify the planned expansion of the city. They also knew that many religious institutions could be led to sell part of their large holdings of undeveloped land within Lyon's traditional limits. A handful of such institutions had done so over the first part of the century, and there were reasons to question the vitality of many religious orders.[2] On an even broader level, while most taxpayers would have wished to see the Hôtel-Dieu balance its accounts with the profit from its lands, those with capital shared an interest in sustaining the hospital's debt, which helped strengthen local interest rates. Many people and institutions also had a vested interest in preserving existing boundaries along the Rhône. Municipal finances depended largely on the *octrois*, a customs levy that was routinely sidestepped by the expedient of locating businesses just beyond city limits; a new gate and a new neighbourhood would multiply opportunities to avoid the levy. The rise of new suburban entertainment sites also threatened the financial interests of the bourgeois who enjoyed the privilege of selling wine from their country estates free of tax in the city.[3] These worries were no doubt shared by the massive institution of the Ferme générale, which managed the collection of a substantial share of royal revenues drawn from a complex system of customs using the Rhône as a key border. An inland customs line would be more porous than a large river. Finally, should the city gain control of lands across the river, it would be expected to buy judicial rights for the area, if only to provide its business community with a coherent legal context.[4]

The economic difficulties that regularly plagued Lyon compounded these various concerns. Rising food prices, disruptions to international commerce, rumours of financial shortages at the four great fairs and cascading bankruptcies were all familiar threats. The prosperity of the city was fickle, susceptible to royal mourning as well as the safe arrival of the Spanish bullion fleet – early in 1767 it took two public announcements in the *Affiches de Lyon* to quell rumours that the Spanish gold fleet from Vera Cruz had been lost.[5] Economic difficulties quickly translated into substantial outmigrations of unemployed workers that in turn weakened rental revenues. On the heels of the Saint-Clair venture, and while Rigod de Terrebasse started to rebuild several blocks in front of the Charité hospital, concerned investors also feared the rivalry between Morand and Perrache. Perrache was said to have raised two million livres tournois between 1765 and 1771, a substantial drain on local capital despite an infusion of Parisian funds. More would be needed over the following years. Significantly, these projects came of age in less than favourable conditions, at the end of a dynamic cycle after a period of heavy fiscal pressures exerted by the Seven Years War.[6] Under the circumstances a degree of resistance to Morand's plans for expansion was predictable. All of these concerns found an outlet in the reservations stridently expressed by Morand's key adversary, the Hôtel-Dieu.

Evidently, the great charitable institution stood to lose the steady source of income provided by its monopoly on crossings of the Rhône. However, because it was also the largest landowner on the left bank, it could expect windfall profits from development of the area. Ostensibly, the choice facing the hospital was one between an assured income and potentially large but speculative gains. Yet the forcefulness and bitterness of the stance taken against Morand and his associates suggest that more was at stake. A brief look at the history of the hospital will show the significance of the left bank in the context of the Hôtel-Dieu's fiscal strategies. Like all such foundations, it relied on its endowment to provide revenues that were more stable than the unpredictable liberalities of wealthy Lyonnais and subsidies from the city. Its property portfolio was built through donations, careful transactions, and attentive management. Starting in 1637 the Hôtel-Dieu had taken control of most of the large estates immediately across the river. Its rectors eventually recognized their unique value, close to a great market and easy to supervise. They started selling distant properties and strove to round out their holdings across the Rhône. If the hospital's lands reached a maximum acreage late in the 1720s of almost a thousand hectares, the following decades saw their value increase even as they shrank in size: from some 600,000 lt around 1720–30 to more than a million livres tournois in the 1760s.[7]

As late as 1731 the Hôtel-Dieu generated sizeable surpluses. Inevitably, this led to increased demands not only from its constituency, the city's sick and dying poor, but also from Lyon's elite, who came to expect the hospital to participate in the renovation of the city's waterfront on the Rhône. The hospital rose to the occasion and commissioned Soufflot's grand plans. This was, however, an expensive undertaking. From 1736 to 1766, the hospital spent some 2.5 million lt on capital projects with little help from the city, which was by then the most heavily indebted municipality in the realm. The construction of the dome (1757–61) definitively pushed the hospital's accounts into negative territory.[8] Through the 1760s and 1770s, its debt grew to over 3,000,000 lt. Eventually, royal letters patent allowed the hospital to borrow two million from Genoese bankers, collect one-twentieth of the city's octrois, and sell properties. Yet the Consulat had to advance the same sum to the hospital soon after.[9]

In spite of such difficulties, the Hôtel-Dieu did not fail to exploit its properties across the Rhône. It contributed a third of the sums needed to protect the left bank from the river and continued to rationalize the management of its lands and capitalize on the city's need for recreational space and storage facilities, installing a third cable ferry in 1763.[10] Accustomed to dealing with these matters in an autonomous if ponderous manner, the Rectors were justifiably wary of Morand's proposal for further developments, since their financial woes curtailed their ability to participate actively enough to give them the control they expected to wield east of the Rhône. When Morand bought the Pré Deschamps on the left bank soon after they had rejected his first proposal, the rectors of the Hôtel-Dieu must have been convinced of his intention to have a say in (and profit from) the future development of the area. When he offered to sell the land back to the Hôtel-Dieu, he was accused of having artificially inflated its price, perhaps in accord with the previous owner, to deprive the city's poor of "their inheritance." The accusation was credible, as the pasture in question stood at the end of the promenade that was the hospital's most recent investment in the area. To make things worse, Morand had bought from the comtes de Lyon an exemption from the *lods* on the first sales of any portion of this land, barring a sale to a mortmain institution such as the Hôtel-Dieu – an understandable condition since such a sale would have deprived the comtes of any further *lods* or *mi-lods*. Should Morand sell to the hospital, he not only would have to forego the profits that he stood to make by parcelling out the land to investors but he would also be bound to repay the Saint-Jean chapter 4,000 lt for something for which he had already paid 2,000 lt. This meant that Morand had to ask for more money from the board than he had paid to the owner of the field. It was suggested that he was willing to "despoil the poor," and he was branded as a shady speculator at a time when, to assemble financing for his project, he had to convince everyone of his good faith. To expose the opposition of a private interest to the public good was a sensitive matter in an early modern context where the two were never clearly separated. Morand's next move did nothing to smooth tempers: he quickly tried to seal his controversial deal by selling two small lots, instantly recouping more than a third of his purchase price. The hospital responded by building a large house at the end of its walkway and further cutting access to Morand's lot with deep ditches. The vengeful nature of this gesture was apparent, so much so that the popular name for the house was "Hôtel de la vengeance."[11]

The grounds for the board's opposition to Morand's plans were plainly formulated at a meeting of the rectors on the last day of 1766. A report on the hospital's financial trials acknowledged the heavy capital expenses of the previous twenty years and denounced the excessive "brilliance" of some of those investments (this was likely a reference to Soufflot's designs) and, above all, the speculative nature of many others. The board resolved that it would never again "sacrifice to luxury" and to the "laws of probability." Eighteen articles drawn in the report were henceforth to be read three times a year to the assembled rectors. The first renounced the use of *pensions viagères*, loans settled on the life expectancy of one or more persons that were much in favour at the time. It called for an end to all construction work in the Brotteaux, be it new buildings, improvements to standing ones, or any other venture on land or shore (again, the dreaded word *spéculation* was used here). Maintenance work on existing structures would now require approval by a plurality of the rectors.[12] It must be remembered that this move so detrimental to Morand's project, came just a few months after Morand's initial presentation of his project to the city.

Naturally, the board and Morand found other opportunities to clash, for instance in the matter of compensation for the ferries. It is simply not possible for us to know what a fair compromise might have been, but available figures suggest that the loss of income was real for a financially shaken Hôtel-Dieu, while it is also clear that no one could reliably assess the profits that the hospital might expect from land development in compensation for ceasing its ferry operations.[13] The rectors must have known, however, that such profits could only come from the sale of property, since the hospital could not undertake any large-scale building of its own. Revenues generated in this manner would have to go towards reducing the hospital's debt load.[14] This would ultimately leave a sounder but also smaller institution. The loss of the prestige associated with these holdings could only compound the pain of financial trimming. Agricultural land may not have been the most profitable investment available to Lyon's elite, but its visibility, so close to the city, certainly contributed to an image of solidity that was obviously important to an institution like the Hôtel-Dieu.

One final dimension of this complex situation remains. One of the thicker files to have survived among the hospital's archives concerns a lengthy dispute between the board and Barthélémy-Léonard Pupil de Myons. He had succeeded his father as lieutenant general of the Sénéchaussée and, in 1764, as premier président of the Cour des Monnaies. The Sénéchaussée was Lyon's only important judicial body (it had long ago merged with the Siège Présidial), and the Cour des Monnaies had the prestigious rank of a sovereign court. Since these two courts were nominally associated (although functionally independent), the long history of the former compounded the prestige of the latter.[15] Both were keen to assert their claim to oversee municipal accounts, a claim strengthened by a ruling of the Parlement of Paris in 1763. De Myons, a rector of the Hôtel-Dieu (his 1766 mandate was renewed in 1768), was also a member of the Assembly of Notables, to which the 1764 municipal reform wished to entrust the selection process of the members of the Consulat (more on this below).[16] Conscious of the possibilities of the moment, or simply eager to match his father's success, Pupil de Myons claimed an ex officio seat on, and the right to preside over, these assemblies. He never was able to assert his claims fully, for they generated much opposition, and he fell early in the 1770s. Before that, however, he had mounted a bitter campaign against the management of the Hôtel-Dieu. Early in 1768 the assembled rectors asked him whether it was true that he had publicly declared that the hospital finances were in dire straights, that its management was "vicious," and that he was a rector "in perpetuity". De Myons replied tersely that there was no denying the gravity of the situation. His colleagues countered that hospital finances had always "fluctuated" but never collapsed, and that the measures put in place in December 1766 were starting to bear fruit. The struggle intensified over the following months.[17]

At the same time, we know that Pupil de Myons had been among the earliest backers of Morand's project. He does not appear to have owned shares in the bridge, but he had been among those who gathered at Morand's table to plan for it early in 1768. Almost three years later, Morand visited him in Paris. When the time came for the *commodo-incommodo* public inquest, we know that Morand wanted it held in front of the Sénéchaussée, on de Myons's ground. No clearer sign of the association between Morand and de Myons has surfaced, although the latter may have been behind the attempt to have the Assembly of Notables, rather than the Consulat, select the commissaries charged with examining Perrache's, and most likely Morand's plans, two years later, to give the assembly the final say in the dispute between the Hôtel-Dieu and the bridge company.[18] In both cases, de Myons had reason to believe that he could wield more clout in a broader assembly. Soon after, the Sénéchaussée and the Cour des Monnaies were suppressed and replaced

with the Conseil Supérieur. When, in 1774, the Sénéchaussée (but
not the Cour des Monnaies) recovered some of its former powers,
de Myons had been pushed off the local political scene.

Pupil de Myons was interested in Morand's project, and he was
intent on gaining some control over the board of the Hôtel-Dieu.
Had he succeeded in this latter goal, would his understanding of the
calamitous state of the hospital's finances have led him to guide the
board toward an accommodating settlement with Morand? Would
he, for instance, have argued that the hospital ought to divest itself
of lands across the Rhône to lower its debt load – land that the
investors around Morand would have been eager to buy? Did the
rectors react so virulently to Morand's every move for so many
years because of Pupil de Myons's attack on their institution? Were
Morand's plans hurt by the fracas caused by de Myons, who has
been described as ambitious, irascible, and quarrelsome – "un
esprit inquiet, enflé des prérogatives de sa charge ... avide de domi-
nation, ennemi des corps" (an obsessive mind, with an inflated
understanding of his office, domineering, and enemy of established
institutions)?[19] It is not possible to answer these questions; nor do
we need to add to the rectors' perfectly sound reasons for refusing
Morand's projects.

What we know of the factions on the Lyon political stage suggests
that alliances and interests combined in a complex and changing
pattern – a topic to which we will turn presently. If Pupil de Myons
represented, to any degree, the claims of royal officers in the city
wishing for a greater role in municipal affairs, he would have been
on friendly terms with those who favoured intervention by Versailles, whence much of Morand's support came. At the same time,
if he was among those who wished to reform municipal practices,
he would likely have been a political opponent of some of Morand's
key supporters, such as the prévôt des marchands, Regnaud de
Bellecise. These conflicts occurred, however, within what was after
all the small milieu of the city's elite, among people who might well
be friends, allies, and rivals at the same time: de Myons and
Bellecise were among the notables who stood side by side, a few
years earlier, to sign the marriage contract of a noted reformer,
Prost de Royer.[20] At the very least, this illustrates the complex context in which the clash between Morand and the Hôtel-Dieu ought
to be located – a clash that, incidentally, remained puzzling two
generations later. In 1821 the board of what had become the

Hospices Civils de Lyon called for an investigation into what was still called the *spoliation du privilège en 1771*. The ensuing report concluded that royal will ought indeed to have prevailed, but that legal mistakes made by Morand accounted for the lengthy fight.[21] The belated investigation still did not satisfactorily explain the board's resistance to Morand's development project, but it reminds us that Morand's initiative had been traumatic for the custodians of the great hospital.

POLITICAL CURRENTS

It is only logical that the Consulat worried about the political challenges posed by development of the Rhône's northern left bank. The Brotteaux could threaten la Guillotière, distort the city's real estate market, undermine its fiscal base (as well as that of the Ferme générale), challenge the status of bourgeois de Lyon, and defy provincial boundaries. Four decades ago, Richard Cobb argued that "in Lyon, perhaps more than anywhere, the borders between private life and political militancy were less apparent, running into one another in a city in which people lived on top of one another."[22] While he may have overstated the city's uniqueness, he was reflecting an enduring opinion. Since then, the narrow but tense world of Lyon politics has been studied in enough detail to suggest that its shifting factions may be divided into the two broad camps of conservatives and progressives but only with the greatest circumspection.[23] There were many other important fracture lines, for example between those who strove to emancipate local power and those who favoured royal intervention. Deliberately deprived of key institutions such as a parlement or even a university, where those inclined to question royal edicts traditionally gathered, Lyon tended to find its voice through the Consulat. By the eighteenth century, much of the Consulat's power had slipped into the Crown's hands, yet it retained effective management of local affairs and municipal finances after satisfying the Crown's onerous fiscal claims. A good deal of the royal supervision that limited the Consulat's power was in the hands of the intendant. The role of governor, a position consistently held by the Villeroy family, was more ambiguous and less prominent during the second half of the eighteenth century than it had been earlier. Yet because the governor could support the city at Versailles, the Consulat still deferred to his will and patronage. The

Consulat was also frequently at odds with the many officers of the
Sénéchaussée et Présidial, Cour des Monnaies, Bureau des Finances,
Election, and Maîtrise des Eaux et Forêts.[24] Taken together, these
bodies did not amount to a sovereign parlement, although the
ambitious creation of the Conseil Supérieur came close to providing
such a voice and drew the ire of the Consulat throughout its short
existence. Nevertheless, they provided power bases from which
could be claimed a share of power on the regional scene, most
directly through criticism of the Consulat's spending habits. The
most bitter fights revolved around claims to the right to inspect
municipal finances. Pupil de Myons explained his belief in the right
of royal officers to tame the Consulat in the sharpest of terms:
"Royal Justice has always rightly claimed its superiority; a claim
always denounced by the Consulat, a kind of administration more
republican than municipal; and, in fact, more despotic than republican, left over from centuries of barbary and chaos that myriad
wise regulations have been unable to master; hence the endless disputes."[25]

A second fracture reflected the Enlightenment interest in forms of
power. While some favoured an authoritarian approach to municipal affairs, others fought for accountability and a degree of participation. Periodically, the latter found support at Versailles, where
attempts were made to remedy administrative malfunctions and to
build consultative structures that would enhance the legitimacy of
royal power.[26] At other times, they drew the ire of ministers who
were intent on upholding respect for established authorities. Such
anomalies remind us that the line between reformers and conservatives is often blurred. Reformers might seek a decisive royal
intervention or call for the reassertion of older forms of local representation, but conservatives, depending on the circumstances, might
wish for the same. Indeed, in the political climate of the last decades
of the Old Regime, ministerial rulings raised cries of despotism,
while the representativeness of assemblies remained questionable –
and not only in Lyon. In his recent study of prerevolutionary Paris,
David Garrioch suggests that the many initiatives taken by the monarchy to advance a broad and much-needed agenda of urban reform
raised fears of tyranny.[27]

There were other spheres of influence that had to be considered in
a large city such as Lyon. Anyone interested in a large real estate
operation had to take into account the interests of the city's many

religious institutions, which were at the same time important landowners, holders of seigneurial rights, and guardians of certain
highly symbolic landmarks in the city. Prominent figures of the
clergy continued to be sought as intermediaries in many issues since
they had access to elevated circles of power as well as forms of
address, both public and private, that could reach the majority of
the population. The archbishop, the comtes de Lyon, and several
other notable chapters had certainly not accepted the *devoir de
réserve* – the expectation that religious figures would not intervene
beyond their own sphere – that was increasingly thought to be their
due. When, in 1787, Archbishop Montazet was chosen to preside
over the new provincial assembly, he proved to be no neutral
observer but was fully engaged in the sharp debates that had arisen
before the Revolution.[28] Morand could generally count on support
from religious quarters.

These were among the forces at play in myriad conflicts, some of
historical importance, others apparently trivial. I have suggested,
without going beyond the available evidence, that the Hôtel-Dieu's
opposition to Morand's project, amply justified by the state of its
finances, may also have been related to initiatives originating with
the president of the Cour des Monnaies, Pupil de Myons. Another
dispute that interfered in matters of urban development concerned
the Bureau des Finances. Because the fiscal attributions of the bureau
had steadily eroded, its officers fought to maintain or increase their
influence in all fields within their reach. In particular, the Trésoriers
de France steadfastly pursued a long-standing claim to all matters
related to roads and streets, including the right to decide *aligne-
ments* (the crucial process of drawing the limits beyond which no
building could encroach), a key tool of urban planning. This claim
naturally conflicted with the attributions of the city's own surveyor
(and even those of the surveyor of the chapter of Saint-Jean – as of
1780, Morand himself).[29] On 3 March 1769 the Parlement of Paris
overturned a royal order of 7 December 1763 that had given the
Trésoriers jurisdiction over the voirie, the survey office in charge of
streets and buildings in Lyon. The Crown reasserted the rights of its
Bureau des Finances on these matters at about the same speed, on 3
June 1776. Morand could not steer clear of these battles. For
instance, on 18 August 1772, the Consulat mandated the storage of
construction timber at the eastern end of the old pont du Rhône.
This was likely meant to take some of the wind out of Morand's

sails, since the Brotteaux was in part intended to provide this type of space. A royal ruling undid the measure on 8 February 1776, but the Consulat quickly sought to reassert its authority on this less than regal matter (13 March 1776). On 5 May 1776, Versailles replied again, this time threatening the city with substantial fines should it continue in this insubordinate vein.[30] Similarly, when Morand's bridge was finally ready for its official opening, both the Consulat and Bureau des Finances pressed their claim to a final inspection, even as the Ponts et chaussées involved itself in the process, following up on earlier efforts to push the city aside during the construction of the quai de Retz.[31]

These tensions reflect the deep divisions among the city's elites, and they offered many opportunities for interventions by outside powers and ambitious local forces.[32] Long before the catastrophic events of the Revolution, they reached fever pitch on at least two occasions during the time of Morand's initiatives. Royal fiscal pressures were directly responsible for a first series of clashes in the 1760s. Gail Bossenga has placed these conflicts at the centre of her "urban perspective on the origins of the French Revolution," arguing that the Crown's abuses of municipal prerogatives and "manipulation of privilege" divided elites but also alienated all factions. The situation in Lyon figures prominently in her demonstration, because of the city's importance but also because there, the persistent mercantile bent of municipal authorities sheds light on the ensuing battles.[33] Faced with an unsustainable debt load caused in large part by royal claims made on the city during the Seven Years War, the Consulat wished to extend its tax base to include some traditionally exempt local elites, such as secrétaires du roi. It had tried to do so on earlier occasions, but then as before officers of royal courts that were most threatened by such proposals systematically counterattacked by reviving their claims to examine municipal accounts. Such clashes occured in many other cities, and to ensure the viability of the municipal fiscal vein, Laverdy, controller general of finances, chose to broaden the political base of municipal administrations, starting in 1764. Little came of his initiative. In Lyon, the Consulat managed to dash the hopes placed in a revamped Assembly of Notables that gave a substantial voice to royal officeholders. Here as elsewhere, however, the process rekindled local political struggles.[34] Without pushing the analysis further, we may note that these battles could only be prejudicial to a project such as that advanced by Morand.

Early in the following decade, the extraordinary reform initiated by Chancellor Maupeou abolished the parlements and created five Conseils Supérieurs, including one in Lyon. At stake was the monarchy's ability to push through several reforms that were deemed essential by the aging king, although in Lyon the matter of control over municipal finances again quickly emerged as a key object of dispute. The Lyon Conseil Supérieur was established rather smoothly, but the Consulat could not accept this consolidation of the local power base of royal officers. Late that year (1771), Regnauld de Bellecise became prévôt des marchands, and Nicolau de Montribloud treasurer of the city. This represented a victory for what has been termed, with all the reservations mentioned earlier, a "conservative" party that included many of the people enriched by, among other ventures, the Saint-Clair project, and a group with which Morand had become closely associated.[35] Although the new Consulat opposed the establishment of a Conseil Supérieur in Lyon, its "authoritarian" program, which focused on moral order as well as tax increases, could be denounced as being linked to the despotic moves taking place at Versailles. Before this complex new situation unfolded, the political winds turned again with the accession to the throne of Louis XVI in 1774. Maupeou was dismissed, the parlements recalled, Bellecise forced to resign, and Montribloud's financial dealings attacked in court. A new reform-minded minister, Turgot, was called to power as controller general of finance, only to lose the confidence of the king in 1776. His successor, Necker, once again tried to put Lyon politics on a sound footing. Before that, however, and for several painfully long years, Morand found himself in a most awkward position. The Consulat was firmly opposed to his project, although the new prévôt des marchands had a more positive view. All parties were bent, however, on undermining the newly created Conseil Supérieur, which, although staffed with many officeholders who were unsympathetic to Morand, in the end followed Versailles's lead, if only thanks to the work of the intendant, who was president of the new institution. At the same time, the Conseil Supérieur, although fairly well accepted in a city that had long wished for a high court, remained tainted by the despotic nature of the Maupeou edicts that had created it. No important initiative, let alone one that could

potentially change the city and enrich so many, could navigate such
turbulent waters unscathed.

Several other bitter contests were caught up in this political
whirlpool. Factions clashed over the system of subsidies known as
l'Abondance. Going back to the 1640s, it was designed to maintain
the grain stocks essential to social peace. Here again, national political preoccupations, such as Turgot's desire to liberalize the grain
trade, combined with chronic local deficits, opaque managment,
and the unforeseable, in this case a bad winter and attendant shortages.[36] At the same time, as we saw in chapter 2, the theatre monopoly fuelled clashes that, in the end, stained even Turgot's reputation.
Finally, there was the infamous skirmish concerning the handling of
Lyon's main tax revenues, the *octrois*. From 1772 to 1776 the city
had managed this sensitive enterprise directly to overcome recurrent cries of malversation. Versailles ordered a return to earlier
contracting-out practices, forcing the city to auction off the new
contract for the collection of these taxes. The city resisted, however,
choosing a group of bidders that would leave effective control in
its hands. Versailles reacted harshly to this act of municipal resistance and imposed a group of its own choosing known by the name
of Stunz.[37]

Throughout these eventful years, those who wished to inquire
into the financial practices of the municipality and who called for
greater municipal autonomy (and a revival of the parlements) had
found in the Hôtel-Dieu's willingness to resist Morand's enterprise
a great opportunity. The financial health of the hospital and its
counterpart, the Charité, bore directly upon that of the city, but
both institutions also played a crucial role in assuaging its social
tensions.[38] The boards of the two establishments provided the perfect platform from which to launch bids for greater influence in
municipal affairs. François-Pierre-Suzanne Brac did just that when
he became a rector of the Hôtel-Dieu at the end of 1768. Fond of
publicity, the lawyer who became an alderman in 1774 pushed for
investigations into the Consulat's spending habits, sought a reform
of the city's fiscal affairs, demanded more transparency in contract
negotiations, tried to wrestle away from the governor some of the
profits generated by the theatre monopoly, courted public support
by demanding a more interventionist food supply policy – and,
as we have seen, fought Morand. The royal reprimand that he
received in the summer 1772 for continuing to oppose the bridge

was no accident. In 1777 his refusal to sign the Stunz lease almost earned him a short exile.[39] Another ministerial injunction silenced him again a few years later, following his strident involvement in another complex real estate project (see below). How many public figures in any city could boast of three sharp royal reprimands in a decade?[40]

The many compromises that facilitated relations between central and regional powers are now central to our understanding of the Old Regime, when a fundamental concentration of power was balanced by an equally cardinal respect for corporate identities.[41] It took Morand and his ministerial backers half a decade to secure a modest royal privilege for a fraction of a project that raised stubborn local opposition. This detailed analysis of a small-scale but characteristic battle highlights the multipolarity and fluidity of the forces at play in Lyon, where all parties were bound in countless ways. When circumstances did not require or permit the application of overwhelming force, conflicting interests combined and recombined in ways that were not always politically coherent and were easily disturbed. Because these alignments were rarely decisive, Morand and his rivals rushed back and forth between Lyon and Paris to advance their cases and cope with inevitable set-backs, often managing to reopen even apparently settled issues. Indeed, few issues appear to have been definitively solved during the last decades of the Old Regime, although the age was almost unanimous in its recognition of the need for forceful initiatives. For his part, Morand was now in a position to build a new bridge across the Rhône, but the fate of the lands to which it would give access remained uncertain. Nevertheless, he made the most of the opportunity.

5

The Saint-Clair Bridge:
A Well-managed Enterprise and
Successful Monopoly

[The Saint-Clair bridge] is among the most beautiful ... [It] is a miniature, one could say, although full scale, very clean, a tight and most solid work of carpentry. It is painted bright red, none of the construction details visible. The roadway is divided in three parts. The centre, convex and lined with shiny benches and gutters, is clean and paved with small stones; on both sides, the sidewalks, between the benches and the bannisters, are neatly tiled. Pedestrians, riders, and carriages thus share the bridge. At each end of the bride stands an arched gate, in cut stones, finely detailed, etc. as well as an office for the toll keeper.[1]

The successful bridging of a large and powerful river such as the Rhône, that *"monstre indomptable,"* was a remarkable achievement.[2] Perhaps even more impressive is the fact that Morand managed this feat on schedule, within budget, and to standards that proved remarkably sound. Before the industrial age, such efficacy was rare enough to deserve attention. Although the group of investors assembled by Morand late in 1767 had greater plans, the company formally constituted in March 1772 was concerned exclusively with the construction and exploitation of a bridge across the Rhône. The company consisted of Morand and ten associates, who were to provide thirty shares of 12,000 lt each and to divide ownership and profits accordingly. A distinction was made between three classes of investors, as Table 5.1 shows.

After an immediate credit of 60,000 lt, biannual advances of 30,000 lt were to be made until 1 January 1776, when a final installment of 90,000 lt came due. The initial group of investors

Table 5.1
Société du pont Saint-Clair (30 shares, 1772)

First Class	Jean-Antoine MORAND	10 shares
Second Class	Ferdinand BALLET, banker (Paris)	12 shares held in
	Maurice FLACHON, Trésorier de France	common
	Etienne FLACHON de Barrey, banker	
	Ferdinand FLACHON de la Jomarière, *ingénieur du roi*	
	de BOUSSIEU, knight (Grenoble) – sold to Flachon before 20-2-1775.	
Third Class	René DAFFAUX, seigneur de Glatta, *commissaire aux revues des troupes* – 1 share sold to GUYOT (27-3-1772)	3 shares
	Jacques-Germain SOUFFLOT, *contrôleur des batiments du roi* (Paris)	2 shares
	Jean-Baptiste MAURO, agent for the Court of Parma (Paris)	1 share
	Gilles GAUDIN, merchant – sold to M. TERRASSE (25-3-1772)	1 share
	Marguerite de Tarnezieu, wife of Count d'AUDIFFRET – sold to MINEL (20-5-1772)	1 share

The society's founding charter was registered with Charles-Odile Guyot, notary, who was to act as its treasurer and soon join the group of investors (14 II 22, Acte de société du Pont Saint-Clair, 21 March 1772). Claude Mermet sketched the evolution of this company in Dureau et al., *Hommage à Morand*, 101–3. See references to the early sales of shares in chapter 3, note 71. Unless otherwise specified, investors were based in Lyon; Ballet was an uncle of the Flachon brothers.

remained unchanged until the mid-1780s, when they were joined by Morand's son and nine other individuals. When the Revolution temporarily deprived the company of its assets, it still counted only twenty associates, among whom the founding members retained a controlling interest. Initially, much of the executive power was delegated to Morand along with Ballet, who represented the second group of associates, and a delegate from the third class of investors who were elected yearly. All transactions conducted by the company, from the signing of purchase contracts and their eventual settlement to the hiring of personnel, required their three signatures (but a majority of two voices carried a decision). Management of the construction project, on the other hand, was in the hands of Morand. He was also charged with all necessary travel, and he had to provide someone to replace him on site when he was away. His pay was fixed at 8,000 lt for each of the project's three years. Flachon de Barey oversaw the operation of the ferries until their demise and supervised all bookkeeping (for which he received 3,000 lt as well as 300 lt per year to hire help). For his part, the notary Guyot acted as treasurer of the company as well as its legal agent (also for 3,000 lt).

This contract bound the associates personally, although they could sell or dispose of their share at will. A five percent charge was to be levied on late contributions, while anyone who delayed beyond six months risked forfeiting investment and status. A general assembly was held on the first Tuesday of every month at Morand's house, at which all "important or major" affairs were reported. The first scheduled disbursements were to compensate the Hôtel-Dieu for its ferries, and Morand and the Flachons for early purchases and securing the necessary authorizations. A brief last sentence referred all "difficulties" to the arbitration of experts. What we know of the construction of the bridge and its subsequent management suggests that these measures proved adequate, though as we shall see, they had to be revised in 1783.

TECHNICAL CHOICES

Morand's design was original to a degree and certainly very sound but also rather plain and uninspiring. The first choice all eighteenth-century bridge builders faced was that between stone and wood. In an age of great transportation needs, many wooden bridges were still built. Yet as an alterable material, wood was generally denounced as a poor choice, especially given the Enlightenment attachment to solidity and purity of form. Nevertheless, stonework and carpentry had long shared a common history and continued to be used until iron revolutionized the field.[3]

Although clearly preferable to boat bridges, wooden bridges were deemed vulnerable to major stresses. The Saint-Vincent and Bellecour bridges on the Saône had fallen in ice break-ups in 1697 and 1709.[4] A wooden bridge was often seen as a stopgap until such time as it could be replaced with a stone structure; when the Serin bridge was destroyed by another brutal ice break-up in 1789, the city argued that it should be rebuilt in stone at royal expense since it opened onto the road to Paris.[5] Similarly, stone piers and wooden arches could be combined until the stone spans became affordable. More rarely, a portion of the original wood construction might be retained, as with the first bridge over the Rhône, which remained wooden into the seventeenth century at its eastern, Guillotière end where aesthetics were less crucial.[6] The relative merits of each solution were often unclear since the science of materials could not yet provide solid data and comparisons between existing structures were largely empirical. Not surprisingly, technical arguments were soon overtaken by financial, aesthetic, and political considerations. In an age most interested in the movement of fluids and aesthetics, the traditional reliance of bridge builders on the weight of massive structures was yielding to a new goal of determining what sort of structure offered the least resistance to water. Morand tried to lighten his bridge as much as possible. He limited the piers to a single row of heavy timber, topped by thin flat spans. The "Y" braces connecting spans to piers, which Morand claimed to be inspired by Italian precedents, only reached to a quarter of the length of each span.[7] This structure was thoroughly reviewed by Perronet, Soufflot, and other experts from plans and scale models. Perronet's opinion must be seen as particularly meaningful, for he was fully involved in such technical questions himself. He was working on his celebrated design for the "stretched arch" that completed the revolution initiated by the introduction, earlier in the century, of the "basket handle arch." A few years later he again challenged his fellow engineers by using single rows of columns for the piers of his Sainte-Maxence bridge over the river Oise.[8] Morand also reinforced his piers with cribs and ice-breakers but, most originally, he made each span independent from its neighbours. The spans were assembled on land, allowing for greater precision and tightness, which made for a light yet resilient structure. It also facilitated repairs, an important point since one of the arguments advanced against wooden bridges was their high maintenance costs.[9]

Morand's design proved sound for over a century, but its first serious test came in January 1789 during one of the most brutal ice break-ups in memory. After several anxious days, it appeared that only a few posts had been destroyed. Morand expressed his relief and pride in the *Journal de Lyon*.[10] An arch was ruined by a heavy raft in 1823, and four more were carried away by a flood two years later. Their replacement proved fairly easy. In 1867, almost a century after it was built, it became necessary to provide a broader shipping channel under the bridge. The engineers found it best to stay with Morand's original design and simply strengthened some timbers to replace three arches with two longer ones.[11] While more daring bridge builders sought new designs in stone and, soon, metal, Morand never considered building anything other than a wooden bridge. In his mind, this was very clearly a commercial, for-profit venture.[12] That understanding may well have grated on the nerves of those who believed that public design ought not to be in thrall to private financial interest. Morand also stood aloof from another great debate of the age. Much of the discussion on the relative merits of various materials in the design of bridges and other innovative structures revolved around an emerging gap between architects and engineers. At a time when the latter sought to affirm their professional supremacy through the use of increasingly sophisticated calculations, the former remained attached to a more empirical approach.[13] Morand refused to be seen solely as an artist, a technician, or an entrepreneur but rather wished to combine all three in his work. At the height of the battle for the bridge, he feared that his enemies were trying to reduce (*avilir*) him to the function of entrepreneur, although we know that he was proud of his business sense. Eight years later, he still counted himself among the many multitalented artists who had to suffer the narrow-mindedness of lawyers.[14] Again, some of his peers may have felt some discomfort at his independence of mind on these matters. Soon after the collapse of the Mulatière bridge only a few weeks after it was built (see below), a local wit derided the lack of specialization that allowed a carpenter to build a road; a painter, a bridge; a sculptor, the new Perrache quarter; and a watchmaker, the trouble-prone Givors canal.[15] Here we see some of the roots of the opposition Morand encountered, which among other consequences denied him an invitation to join the Lyon Académie.

"ON BUDGET"

To those familiar with important early-modern construction projects, one of Morand's most remarkable achievements is that he completed his bridge largely within the terms of the budget approved by the partners early in the venture.[16] Sometime in 1768 Morand had compiled a short estimate that reached just over 300,000 lt (see Table 5.2). This estimate was obviously incomplete; it made no provision for a covered work site, pile-driving machines, scaffolding, ladders, ropes, boats, carts, hand tools, administrative fees, nor the cost of interest on capital. It is likely that other esti-

Table 5.2
Estimated cost of a wooden bridge across the Rhône (1768)

Nature of expense	Cost	Nature of expense	Cost
Oak timber	169,518 lt	8 offices, wooden	3,584 lt
Labour	56,506 lt	Roofs	3,072 lt
Iron	27,700 lt	Gates	882 lt
"*Gueuse*"	2,736 lt	Paint	8,000 lt
Abutment, Brotteaux	11,378 lt	Paving	2,014 lt
Abutment, Presqu'île	7,900 lt		
4 guard-houses, masonry	10,329 lt	Total	303,618 lt +

Drawn from 14 II 020, doc. 24 (also appended to the company book of deliberations, after 21 March 1772, p. 35, 14 II 023).

mates were made, but in their absence we must assume that final calculations approached the 360,000 lt called for in the March 1772 charter.[17] This figure must have seemed reasonable. A few decades earlier, the Charité hospital had paid a combined total of nearly 300,000 lt for two wooden bridges across the Saône, but they were smaller structures across a tamer river. In 1772, early in his own project, Perrache estimated that a wooden bridge over the same river at the tip of the reconfigured Presqu'île would cost 200,000 lt, but he was not very good at such assessments.[18] For his part, Perronet estimated 300,000 lt as the cost of a projected bridge across the Seine that would be somewhat smaller than Morand's but with an expensive lead covering for its wooden structure built over masonry piles.[19]

The final cost of Morand's bridge became a contentious issue between the associates soon after its completion. It is nevertheless possible to arrive at a coherent set of figures. Late in 1775, Morand repeatedly suggested that he could agree to a total cost of between 450,000 and 455,000 lt. He had more precise numbers at his disposal. In a note appended to the company's account book in May 1776, he noted that Me. Guyot had received 436,716 lt to pay for the construction of the bridge; his own calculations drawn from the payment orders (*mandats*) spent on construction, tallied at 431,914 lt. My own computation of these same 563 payments comes to 437,621 lt.[20] This total included over 32,000 lt spent to secure the letters patent, as well as 30,000 lt paid to Morand, Flachon, and Guyot for their respective duties and 3,000 lt for renting a covered work site. The best evidence of the integrity of these figures is that Morand's associates tried to force him to set the final cost of the bridge at 600,000 lt, a much higher total. Regardless of their reasons (see below), it suggests that 600,000 lt was a reasonable figure for such a structure. Morand himself was not above some manipulation of numbers. In a plea for a concession on the *vingtième* tax that applied to the revenues of all industrial and commercial ventures, he reported their investment as 550,000 lt (see below). However, when it came to the final cost of his bridge, Morand understood that a lower sum would serve his reputation best.[21]

A WELL-MANAGED ENTERPRISE

In just over three years, Morand built a substantial bridge consisting of seventeen arches that rested on sixteen piers and two abutments. Twelve metres wide and 208 metres long, it boasted four equal and separated lanes, two for pedestrians and two for riders and wheeled traffic. By late 1771 Morand had already begun selecting and purchasing timber, and posts were being driven into the riverbed a month before the bridge company partnership was formalized. In February 1772 the details of the foundations of the first abutment were being worked out,[22] as was the final design of the arches amid much discussion of the respective merits of metal and wooden parts. Bolts were certainly costly (four to five livres tournois per unit, more than three times the daily wage of a labourer), but wooden joints, besides taking a few more inches out of the crucial space below the arches, were less adjustable and required more labour.[23] After several exchanges (which included finding out how a similar wooden key had weathered the previous twenty years in Agde), Morand found a compromise that allowed for a finish that was flush with the undersurface of the structure. In so doing, he overruled two of the Flachon brothers, including the engineer. We shall see how this contributed to the later clash between partners.[24]

Not surprisingly, the first few months of work were busy. In May 1772 Flachon de la Jomarière was responsible for preparing sketches and plans, overseeing the worksite, selecting timber, paying workers, relocating and managing the ferry boats, and dealing with the incessant correspondence between all interested parties. Morand, meanwhile, was updating his plans in response to recommendations made by the inspections that had been mandated at the last minute. On Wednesday, 10 December 1772, a team started dig-

ging below the abutment, and carts had to be lined up to take away
the dirt and debris. Flamand, a supervisor, was delegated to sign a
lumber contract and arrange for shipment of the wood. The posts
of three piers were cut down to level and a row of old posts was
taken out. Construction began on a wall linking the new abutment
and the quay, using some of the old stones. The equipment used to
drive in the posts was overhauled; rafts and boats were reposi-
tioned; and a section of the quay itself was demolished and the rub-
ble removed.[25]

Early in 1773 Morand had the satisfaction of seeing the first pier
in place. Eight more followed before high water levels slowed the
pace in November. After several months, Morand decided to use a
leather boat of his invention to resume the driving of posts.[26] The
process proved arduous and risky, but it helped preserve momen-
tum. It was important to keep the work going as far as possible; for
the enterprise was still the object of attacks. Versailles, however,
maintained a resolute silence that amounted to support for a project
that was quickly becoming a reality.[27] By July 1774 Morand was
discussing paving alternatives.[28] When the partners met on 15 January 1775, the bridge must have been nearly finished, for their agenda
was almost entirely devoted to last-minute preparations for paying
customers: opening a new book for the bridge's operations, settling
matters such as the number, wages, and quarters of toll collectors
and controllers, and planning for the guards and custom officers.
The company and the Consulat also had to settle on a formal process for opening and closing the new city gate.[29] Some time in
March 1775 a celebratory dinner was held for the work crews. The
bridge opened on 7 April 1775 to pedestrian traffic and the company collected 642 lt in tolls; a week later the bridge had garnered
1,989 lt and the second week 4,879 lt. At the end of the first month,
revenues reached 8,819 lt. A quick calculation based on the receipts
for the first three days (Friday to Sunday) and the fee schedule suggests that there were an astounding sixty thousand crossings, that
is, a return visit across the bridge by some thirty thousand people –
a fifth of the city's population. The bridge made money continually
until the Revolution. Morand had good reason, late in May
1775, to commission an engraving of his bridge from a noted artist,
J.-B. Lallemand.[30]

The steady pace of construction is borne out by the account book
in which all payments were recorded. Up to the end of 1772, some

Table 5.3
Construction of Saint-Clair Bridge: Expenses, by category

Nature of expense	Cost	Nature of expense	Cost
Metal (inc. some labour)	32,000 lt +	Rental (accommod.)	3,575 lt
Wood (inc. some labour)	129,281 lt	Legal and administrative	32,833 lt
Other materials (inc. lab.)	34,428 lt +	exp.	
Others: spent by Morand	20,363 lt	Labour expenses	108,000 lt
but not specified, used		Honoraria	30,000 lt
equipment, and for		Total identified expenses	390,480 lt +
ferries		Unidentified expenses	47,000 lt +
Total expenses recorded	437,621 lt		
"Somme des mandats"			

Drawn from "Livre des mandats," 1772–76, in 14 II 023.

136,000 lt were spent to secure the necessary authorizations and to start work on the bridge. In the following year, the company spent more than 147,000 lt on the project and 93,000 lt the year after. A further 60,000 lt left the company's accounts during the first three trimesters of 1775, although some final bills were settled the following winter, as allowed for in the original charter. Monthly outlays were also quite regular. The months of January, April, July, and October stand out, however, since many payments were traditionally settled at the time of the city's great fairs. The expenses recorded in the book of accounts covering the whole construction project (some 563 payment orders) can be divided into eight rough categories, as shown in Table 5.3. A comparison, where possible, between the 1768 estimate and the actual recorded expenses shows that Morand's early figures were based on sound information (Table 5.4).

We know enough of Morand's role during these busy years to say that he had very effectively managed a complex and large-scale construction project. By early modern standards, this was a rare achievement. To illustrate the point, the 1766 reconstruction of a bridge over the Loire at Blois, considered a successful project, delivered a classic stone monument spanning 302 metres in eight years at a cost of some two million livres tournois, just over twice the cost and the time its planners had calculated.[31] The two-decade saga of Perrache's Mulatière bridge at the southern tip of the Presqu'île throws Morand's mastery into starker relief. Perrache's plans included a bridge over the Saône immediately before its confluence with the Rhône, opening onto the new road to the Languedoc.

Table 5.4
Construction expenses compared to 1768 estimates

Figures drawn from 1768 estimates	Figures drawn from book of paid mandates
Expenses related to the use of lumber (lumber, labour, and "wooden offices"): 229,608 lt	Expenses related to lumber and all labour as spent by Morand: 237,281 lt
Metal work ("Iron", "Gueuses", and "Gates"): 31,318 lt	Metal expenses: 32,000+ lt
Masonry (Culées, office, and pavement): 31,621 lt	All masonry related expenses, inc. pavement: 23,800 lt
Paint: 8,000 lt	Paint: 5,972 lt

For references see Table 5.2 and Table 5.3

Initially, he had proposed a wooden bridge, but after successfully damming the right bank of the Rhône, he suggested that he could build a stone bridge for 560,000 lt, with appropriate subsidies.[32] The city did not share Perrache's enthusiasm, and a compromise was reached on a wooden bridge with stone piers. Plans for the bridge were novel enough to draw serious reservations from the Ponts et chaussées, notably with regard to the use of concrete for the foundations, and financial considerations may have led to some dubious compromises during the building phase.[33] Perrache died in 1779, but his sister and associates pressed forward with what was already a beleaguered enterprise. Opened to traffic late in 1782, the bridge was promptly destroyed by the Saône on 15 January 1783. In the soul-searching that followed, much blame was laid at the feet of the late entrepreneur, not surprisingly, and his sister, who evidently shared the "weaknesses of her sex." Architects and technicians pointed to the investors' lack of support, and key investors returned the favour. De Lallié, the provincial engineer who had overseen the project, worked hard to distance himself from the disaster. The chief engineer in charge of dikes (Turcies et levées) suggested that nothing like it would have happened had he been consulted, as he should have been. Perronet used the occasion to proclaim once again that only the Ponts et chaussées was competent to oversee such projects.[34] The final word on the disaster was that the bridge, built in line with Perrache's new road, did not intersect the Saône at ninety degrees and thus unduly restricted its output at high water.

This failure, whatever its cause, stands in clear contrast with Morand's success in building a structure that withstood the far mightier Rhône for more than a century. Just as instructive, however, is the litany of complaints found in de Lallié's correspondence during the first two years of construction of the replacement bridge at La Mulatière. Naturally enough, work depended on the river's water levels, as well as regular funding and the goodwill of neighbours (notably because gravel and stone were to be procured from as close as possible to the building site). Price quotes did not always specify the unit choice, contractors failed to deliver on time, and foremen disappeared without explanation – one foreman enraged de Lallié by driving by on the way to his country retreat. Finding sound footing proved an elusive task, and removing the probe used in the search was often impossible. Ropes and tools of all kinds regularly broke, theft was an intractable problem (Morand, by contrast, had maintained regular inventories of all tools, to keep them in working order and prevent pilfering), and holidays further disrupted what cannot be called a schedule.[35] The structure was finally completed in 1793 (and carried away by a flood in 1840).

The difficulties and failures that bedevilled the Mulatière project were far from exceptional. Rather, it is tempting to view them as the norm among the great public works so eagerly undertaken during the early modern era. Thus, another Lyon investor, Zacharie, faced daunting problems while trying to build a section of a canal between Rive-de-Gier and Givors, that would have linked the Loire and the Rhône. In Lyon itself, attempts to stabilize the left bank of the Rhône met with repeated failure until the mid-nineteenth century. We might also cite the costly loss of what would have been the technologically advanced Chartons flour mills in Bordeaux, perhaps the most dynamic city in the kingdom thanks to a flourishing colonial trade (Perrache's new mills also failed, as noted earlier).[36] There were very few frank successes, that is, performing structures that were completed on time and within budget. Apart from the Saint-Clair bridge, Pierre-Paul Riquet's decade-long construction of the Canal des deux mers linking the Atlantic Ocean and the Mediterranean Sea is one of the most outstanding examples.

During the three-year construction of the Saint-Clair bridge, Morand encountered all of the problems mentioned above. He managed, however, to keep a tight rein on the various pieces that compose the puzzle of a large construction project. Many artists had grander ideas, and no doubt several engineers among his contemporaries could have provided a bolder design. And we know that most of his associates would have liked to squeeze more money out of the venture more rapidly. But Morand proved himself capable of something that, before the industrial age, was most unusual: the efficacious application of an efficient design. Yet for all of his managerial talents, Morand continued to face opposition, from outside but also from within his company.

THE REWARDS OF MONOPOLY: ENVY AND PROFITS

Throughout the period of construction, the bridge company remained structured along the lines set out in the original contract of 1772, with only a few shares changing hands:

OWNERSHIP OF THE SAINT-CLAIR BRIDGE
(NOVEMBER 1775)[37]

Morand: 9 shares instead of 10 (1 share sold to Terrasse)
Flachon brothers and Ballet: 11 shares instead of 12
Terrasse: 3 shares instead of 1 (one from Morand and one
    from Flachons?)
Soufflot: 2 shares
Daffaux: 1.5 shares instead of 3
Guyot: 1 share
Minel: 1 share
Mauro: 1 share
Tempier: 1/2 share (bought from Daffaux through Guyot,
    1 May 1775)

This stability, however, did not mean that relations between Morand and his partners were smooth. In August 1773 Morand was forced to tender to his associates two blank bills of sale transferring two more shares, to be used if he was unable to meet payments on his debts by January 1774. Just before the opening of the bridge, consultations were taking place to explore the possibility of modifying the statutes of the company. Not long after, M. Daffaux, until then one of his strongest supporters, reproached him for having complained in public about his associates who had helped him financially throughout the previous years. Morand replied that he was particularly hurt by rumours that he had "stolen the lights," the know-how of Flachon de Barey. Further accusations were made at the meeting, such as the suggestion that Morand had failed to keep the workers properly occupied, that he had not contributed his share of the investment instalments despite having sold another piece of land in the Brotteaux, that his domestics used the bridge without paying, and that he was spending too much on his new house in the Brotteaux (presumably again at the expense of his financial contribution to the bridge). His partners even complained about his choice of sweepers.[38]

Morand threatened to sell his share to the Hôtel-Dieu, a move that restored a measure of peace to the stormy meeting. Still, a month later, he was accused of standing alone against his partners when they proposed burning all account books related to the construction of the bridge and raising its official cost to 600,000 lt. Morand, who was in Paris at the time but represented by his wife's cousin, the abbé Machério, vigorously objected to a move that would rob him of what could be seen as his greatest achievement – the completion of such an important project within a most reasonable budget. The agreement apparently reached in November 1775 suggests that he yielded to his associates to a degree. The value of the shares was set at 17,400 lt, bringing the final cost of the bridge to 522,000 lt, with a supplementary statement from the partners recognizing that it had indeed cost only 450,000 lt but that a series of unforeseen legal costs had brought the final tally to this higher figure.[39] The figure of 522,000 lt that was made public represents a fictional increase of twenty percent over the actual cost of the bridge. Morand's partners' bid to raise the final cost of the bridge reflects a speculative, rather than entrepreneurial or managerial, business approach that was more interested in inflating the capital assets of the company than in demonstrating its profitability.

Throughout the summer, Morand carefully documented his financial transactions during the construction period to counter his partners' claims that he had not fully carried his weight.[40] His accounts suggest that, while in June 1773 he needed "about 100,000 lt" to keep his one-third investment share, by January 1776 he had managed to whittle down his debt to his associates to 27,237 lt and retained nine shares in the company.[41] Still, in October 1775 he turned to the intendant, M. de Flesselles, and Bertin's secretary to complain that his partners were unwilling to entrust him with the overseeing and maintenance of the bridge.[42] Once again he left Lyon for Paris. Etienne Machério, who was attending

to his business in his absence, soon informed him of a further object
of discord. The majority of partners wanted to close down the one
remaining ferry so that all traffic would have to use the bridge.
Morand, however, worried that the ferry monopoly might then be
considered to have lapsed and could be claimed by someone else, so
he concocted a plan that was unlikely to earn him new trust from
his partners: to have the ferry separated from the bridge and given
to him.[43] Before this bad idea could be shelved, a new disagreement
arose. Plans were floated to save on labour costs by streamlining
the toll collection system, a measure that, in Morand's eyes, placed
too much faith in people's honesty.[44] Morand must have garnered
enough support in Paris to fend off most of these attacks, for they
disappear from the record.[45] The bridge, however, could still arouse
negative sentiments: early in January 1780, M. Menio, a merchant
on the de Retz quay, attacked the ticket controller at the gate of the
Saint-Clair bridge. A crowd gathered to hear his loud denunciations
of the owners of the bridge for having stolen 25,000 lt from the
city's poor.[46]

Despite their frustrations, those involved in the bridge were mol-
lified by the profitability of the venture. Early in October 1775 it
was decided that revenues from the bridge's toll gates would flow
to a current account from which all operating and maintenance
expenses would be taken, and that every time the surplus in the
account reached 3,000 lt, a distribution of profits would be made to
shareholders.[47] This procedure functioned smoothly for decades.
When fair weather favoured high traffic, such profit taking sometimes occurred on an almost weekly basis. In the spring of 1787
Antoine Morand proudly reported to his mother one of the highest
receipts since the flight of the Montgolfière hot-air balloon some
three years earlier: 1,260 lt in one day.[48] As Table 5.5 shows, surviving accounts sketch a remarkably profitable enterprise.

For an effective investment of less than 450,000 lt, the bridge
yielded a yearly return of between ten and fifteen percent, squarely
around the twelve percent predicted by Morand in June 1773 (using
the higher figure of 522,000 lt, returns range between nine and thirteen percent). During the same period, Morand's share of the profits generated by the bridge apparently declined, as the number of
shares he retained fell from nine to five. However, three of the four
shares Morand had lost were intended to remain in the family: both
of his children received a share on the occasion of their marriage,

Table 5.5
Profits distributed to associates (1775–91)

Year	Shared Profits	Year	Shared Profits	Year	Shared Profits	Year	Shared Profits
1775	47,957 lt	1780	47,212 lt	1785	59,943 lt	1790	54,471 lt
1776	51,930 lt	1781	61,950 lt	1786	60,524 lt	1791	68,083 lt
1777	56,844 lt	1782	54,400 lt	1787	72,340 lt		
1778	54,906 or 43,106 lt	1783	53,154 lt	1788	64,714 lt		
1779	52,019 lt	1784	58,820 lt	1789	61,501 lt		

Figures drawn from 14 II 024 (totals available in Dureau et al., *Hommages à Morand*, 105–6). In 1777, forty-seven percent of the year's income came from the period from early May to late August (14 II 023, 5 September 1777).

and one share, transferred to Machério in recognition of his loans to Morand, was to return to the Morands upon the abbé's death.[49] Effectively, Morand was forced to sell one share before 1786, although we have no record of this transaction (he had sold one during the construction phase of the project). Ownership in the bridge appears to have broadened as of the mid-1780s, although we do not know enough about the links between many of the names that appear among shareholders to assess the meaning of this apparent trend. Family and business connections may have left much influence in the hands of original partners such as the Flachons. Still, it was felt necessary, in 1786, to require shareholders to present their original titles to thwart potential intruders, confirming a change in the nature of a company that had remained a tight club for more than a decade (see appendix 2). The bridge provided Morand with a steady income in excess of one thousand livres tournois, on average, per month (See Table 5.6).

Clearly, such an investment was well worth maintaining. Considering that high maintenance costs had been one of the arguments raised against the choice of a wooden bridge, it would be helpful to have the relevant figures for a long period of time. The information recorded in the book of deliberations attests to the company's efforts to keep the bridge in shape, provide the latest urban amenities such as lighting, and ensure the safety of its clients.[50] Nevertheless, data are not systematic enough to yield a meaningful order of magnitude of operating and maintenance costs, and, as we see in Table 5.7, only a few figures can be cited. Presumably, maintenance costs climbed as the bridge aged, raising the ratio of expenses to

Table 5.6
Morand's income from the bridge (1775–91)

Year	Received	Year	Received	Year	Received	Year	Received
1775	14,387 lt	1780	12,589 or 11,016 lt	1785	13,986 or 11,988 lt	1790	9,078 lt
1776	15,579 or 13,848 lt	1781	16,520 or 14,455 lt	1786	12,104 or 10,087 lt	1791	11,347 lt
1777	17,053 or 15,158 lt	1782	14,506 or 12,693 lt	1787	12,057 lt		
1778	16,471 or 11,495 lt	1783	14,174 or 12,402 lt	1788	10,785 lt		
1779	15,605 or 13,872 lt	1784	15,685 or 13,725 lt	1789	10,250 lt		

Figures derived from numbers cited in Table 5.5 (uncertainties related to the fact that Morand had sold a share at an unknown date before 1786).

Table 5.7
Operating and maintenance costs, Saint-Clair Bridge

	Operating costs	Maintenance costs	Expenses (distinction between operating costs and maintenance not made?)
1776 (9 months)	8,155 lt	4,941 lt	
1777	12,989 lt		
1778	11,612 or 11,876 lt	3,812 lt	
1779			12,843 lt
1780			13,471 lt
1782		1,192 lt (painting) and 1,431 lt (carpentry, etc.)	

14 II 024 (file "Etat des dépenses et recettes"); 14 II 022, 4 September 1782; 14 II 023, 23 December 1776.

revenues – but obviously never to the point of undermining profits. The bridge's profitability offers a solid illustration of the value of a royal monopoly (*privilège*).

Not surprisingly, the same state that had made this lucrative monopoly possible wished to partake of the profits. To tax revenues regardless of social order, the royal treasury relied on a levy theoretically set at one-twentieth of profits, the *vingtième* (which replaced the similar *dixième* in 1749). Not long after the bridge opened, the company petitioned for a twenty- or thirty-year exemption from the tax. To that end, it recalled the supplementary expenses incurred because of technical recommendations made by the state agency of

the Ponts et chaussées and the city. The memorandum, likely written by Morand, also expressed his willingness to use a new cement,
known by the name of its inventor, Loriot, to pave the surface of the
bridge (at a supplementary cost of 15,000 lt and potential difficulties later). Finally, the bridge owners argued that their enterprise
should be accorded the same tax exemption granted, since 1776, to
those who brought new lands under cultivation. After all, the
bridge, like cleared and cultivated land, had created new economic
value, all the more so since the ferry system opened in 1743 by the
Hôtel-Dieu was not taxed. Although the official response to this
plea is not known, it is unlikely to have been successful. The company was taxed 2,200 lt for the year 1779 (a 4.2 percent assessment
rate on some 52,000 lt in profits), at which point Flachon de Barey
acknowledged that their petition was not faring well.[51] Perhaps
because she understood how much they owed to ministerial support, Antoinette Levet was reluctant to push hard for the exemption. While Morand was in Paris, she reminded him to avoid
exposing himself too much on the matter.[52] Meanwhile, the owners
had to face another demand from the Treasury. In 1778 their company was called upon to pay an old tax on public bridges, the *droit
de pontonage*, assessed at eight deniers/lt (or 3.33 percent). They
apparently managed to fend off this levy, arguing that theirs was a
private venture already subject to taxation.[53] Other related problems emerged to do with the bridge's role both as a new city gate
and as a new crossing of one of the many internal customs lines that
divided the kingdom. The company was required to provide space
for the constables of various agencies. Could these agencies possibly
be charged rent for the space they used? No clear answer emerges
from the record, but such a request was also unlikely to have been
successful, given the sensitive nature of these matters in Lyon just
after the great political crisis of the bail Stunz.[54]

Running a profitable company naturally attracted undesirable
attention, and the company devised careful procedures for handling
the daily receipts from the toll gates. Much depended on the honesty of the two couples who acted as receivers at each end of the
bridge, as well as the extra gatekeepers brought in during rush
hours. Choosing these employees occasioned some sharp discussion
among the partners. Then came the crucial evening count of the
take, including the careful screening of dubious coins, which were
taken to the mint, where a price was negotiated for them based on

their silver content. Vigilant bookkeeping and direct supervision by the associates could not, however, prevent all cheating. In April 1777 a complex "sting operation" involving the use of marked tickets caught two employees who had sold fake tickets for more than a thousand livres tournois.[55] The bridge's owners faced a constant stream of requests from Lyonnais who sought to avoid the toll for themselves and their dependents. The matter became problematic at times since each partner felt entitled to grant such exemptions.[56] The company also tried to encourage development of the Brotteaux to generate more bridge traffic. To that end, it sold annual subscriptions, notably to people who wished to build businesses across the river, and offered discounts on certain fares. These measures were generally tested on a trial basis. On 1 January 1783 the company lowered the fee for carriages, revised it slightly upward at the end of the year, and again sharply lowered it three months later, after realizing that crossings by such *"voitures de maîtres"* accounted for only two percent of revenues but could eventually generate much traffic. Morand, however, feared that such offers might prove difficult to manage. The matter of vehicle identification was indeed delicate; for lack of registration plates, the company relied on descriptions of private carriages, of which a record was kept. Morand argued, moreover, that the congestion, dust, and risk associated with carriage traffic could potentially deter the pleasure-seeking crowds that were still the principal source of revenue for the company. Finally, and most interestingly, he feared that rates favourable to wealthy users might alienate the larger public, whose support he deemed necessary for a monopoly in an age that was coming to resent such privileges. Characteristically, all of his partners but one turned against him, brutally asking why he chose once again to stand alone in his opinion. Morand could only concede the point. Evidently, the tensions of the previous decade had not abated.[57] They may well have flared again two years later, when Morand tried to smooth his relationship with the Hôtel-Dieu (and enhance the value of his lands on the left bank) by seeking free passage for the institution's poor; we do not know how his associates reacted to this proposition.[58]

Because the new bridge stood astride a busy waterway, the company was involved in a range of conflicts with users of the river. The project had long been stigmatized as an obstacle to navigation, and Morand and his associates were quick to denounce the ineptitude of boat owners whenever accidents happened. Given the design of the bridge, however, accidents were unavoidable. The risk was minimized in 1867 when two of the original arches were replaced with one larger span.[59] More avoidable were risks posed by boats moored just above the bridge. Soon after the bridge opened, the company tried to have a floating public bath facility moved downstream, along with several boats that were used to full cloth (these boats were known in Lyon as *frises*). The matter quickly reached Versailles, where Bertin obliged with a ruling from the royal council – but to no avail. We find here an illustration of the limits of royal power in practical matters that were essential to the people who made a living from the operations in question. Two years later, in 1779, a compromise was reached and boats were surrounded with posts to secure their anchorage. In 1789 the captain of a barge remarked that these working craft, far from threatening the bridge, protected it from ice floes.[60]

In 1783 the company's statutes were modified in the hope of avoiding some of the clashes of the previous decade. Morand suggested that the partners continue meeting twice a month, which had become the norm (the initial regulations called only for monthly meetings). It was agreed that a minimum of three partners would be necessary for a quorum, but that any one partner could call an extraordinary assembly. Regular operating and maintenance affairs could be decided by a simple plurality of votes, but matters related to the toll would require unanimous consent. All negotiations with private individuals or institutions required assembly support. The hiring of key employees called for a unanimous decision (associates were still allowed to present their own candidates), and all books and titles were to be kept under triple keys, in the hands of the representatives of the three classes of shareholder. Finally, partners could no longer give direct orders to staff nor dispose of tickets. More controversial was Morand's wish to institute a voting system that limited the power of his rivals, the Flachons: he proposed that owners of seven or more shares should receive only five votes. Not surprisingly, they refused to sign the new deal; it seems, however, that some form of compromise was found a few months later.[61] Even so, institutional fine-tuning could not overcome deep-seated antagonisms. The brutal ice break-up of January 1789 generated

Table 5.8
Revenues and operating expenses, Saint-Clair Bridge (1801–06)

	Revenues	Operating Costs
1801	41,337 lt	11,081 lt
1802	32,340 lt	11,663 lt
1803	50,035 lt	11,879 lt
1804	48,229 lt	12,023 lt
1805	52,521 lt	12,608 lt
1806	67,067 lt	12,083 lt

AD 69, S 2023.

yet another contest of wills. The bridge weathered the break-up successfully but needed some repairs. Morand's associates voted to contract out the repairs rather than let him deal with the matter. Quick to overreact and evidently lost in his own private world, Morand petitioned the king for redress. Two weeks later, on 16 June 1789 – that is, exactly when the Third Estate was about to impose its will on the monarchy and the privileged orders – Morand's son reminded him that the king and his ministers had more urgent business to address.[62]

Had he been spared by the Revolution, Morand would have had the satisfaction of seeing his bridge survive the monarchy and continue to make money, after the company recovered its properties, which had been confiscated after the siege of Lyon late in 1793 (see Table 5.8). Eventually, the company came to own three other bridges over the Rhône (and one on the Saône), albeit not without new opposition from the Hôtel-Dieu, by then part of the Hospices Civils de Lyon, and other rival groups.[63] In 1860 Napoleon III helped the city to buy these properties on the condition that it offered free passage to all.[64] The bridge built by Morand was replaced with a steel structure on stone piers in 1886. Until then, for many decades, it had demonstrated that entrepreneurial good sense and royal privilege were far from contradictory. In this case a good idea, a sensible design, intelligent management, and a monopoly had combined most successfully, not only for investors but also for the crowds that rushed to the Brotteaux as soon as fair weather called. Morand, however, had greater dreams.

6

Resistance to Expansion

Imagine a row of very nice houses, five or six stories high, raised at the expense of the sky, a superb embankment along the Rhône, lined with most welcome sidewalks, a magnificent view ahead and on both sides, that is the quai Saint-Clair ... Two beautiful bridges ... give access to pleasant promenade on the other side of the Rhône, known as the Broteaux. It reminds one of the Champs-Elisées.[1]

New house, located in the Broteaux, across from Puits-Gaillot street, for rent, immediately, as a whole or in part ...[2]

In the spring of 1778 Morand took another step along the path of bourgeois respectability, buying a substantial estate in the Beaujolais, some twenty kilometres north of the city. The count de Laurencin, who would soon try to revive the Perrache project, sold him the Machy estate for the impressive sum of 120,000 lt. Significantly, this property never seems to have acquired a place in his life, though for his son, Antoine, it became central. The purchase was made just as Antoine was completing his studies, before being called to practice law in front of the Sénéchaussée. He later moved to the Bureau des Finances and, after the Revolution, made his way within the new justice system and Lyon's municipal politics. The Machy estate perfectly fit his position as a Lyon notable, and its management occupies a large part of the papers he left.[3] However, it never matched the needs or wishes of his father, who was not at all ready for retirement.

Late in June 1776 Morand had been thrilled to move into his new house in the Brotteaux. In a letter to her son, Antoinette Levet described her husband gyrating through the empty rooms of the house and watching the crowds along the promenade outside their windows. She was busy furnishing the place "as economically as possible." For his part, their son already missed this quasi-rural retreat – even as he was discovering Versailles on a school outing. Indeed, signs of genuine attachment to La Paisible, as the house was called, dotted the family correspondence for a few years.[4] Later in 1776 Morand went to Briançon to settle his father's succession, a secondary burden that had nonetheless been dragging on for years. He was particularly glad to have been well received by relatives and friends back home.[5] By 1777 he had secured the position of architect for the Lyon chapter and, three years later, that of surveyor of the chapter, supervising all construction projects for the massive institution that was the chapter of the Lyon cathedral. The position came with a substantial stipend (two thousand livres tournois per year), as well as opportunities for important commissions.[6]

Yet early in April 1777 Morand left Lyon for Paris to advance some long-standing legal disputes (see chapter 7) but also to seek support for what would be, should it take life, the most important project of his life – the development of the Brotteaux. Antoinette Levet wrote to him that the portion of his plans that had already been made public was creating a "sensation," that "people were rushing to buy property," and that even the rectors of the Hôtel-Dieu were apparently willing to talk. They were, in fact, reviving at least part of his circular plan by formally proposing to include a vast area of the left bank as part of the city. This time, the Morands believed that they could count on two allies on the board of the hospital: Philippe Choignard, lawyer and future alderman, and G.A. Gesse de Poizieux, then lieutenant general of the Sénéchaussée et Siège présidial de Lyon and eventually head of the hospital's board of directors. It is not clear why the Morands felt that they could count on de Poizieux. He has generally been seen as a vocal opponent of several of Morand's allies, most notably Bellecise and Montribloud (who, admittedly, had lost their grip on power in Lyon by then). De Poizieux was also a cousin of Tolozan, with whom Morand had clashed. All of this may explain why the couple soon found Gesse's manners ambiguous. There were, no doubt, factors justifying de Poizieux's support of Morand's plans, but when they read a memorandum in which he argued against Morand's proposal, they still did not know whether he was putting forth the arguments of the rectors or expressing his own opinions. They clung to the belief that de Poizieux was *"fin mais pas faux"* (smart but not duplicitous).[7] Once again, however, we are touching the limits of what we know of the complex manoeuvres that stirred up the political milieu of Lyon when a large project was at stake.

Perhaps more surprising, Morand encountered a cool reception from Bertin in Paris. This worrisome development was linked to a rumour suggesting that meetings of political opponents were taking place at Morand's new house in the Brotteaux. This allegation was likely related to the sharp political clashes, described earlier, between the municipal government and Versailles over collection of the city's excise tax. In any case it is not clear whether the charge was anything more than a malicious lie, but it tapped some of the fears associated with all suburbs. The matter was serious enough for Morand to call upon the services of an aristocratic protector, Madame de Nervo, to appease the minister.[8] In Lyon, Fay de Sathonay, who reached the position of prévôt des marchands in 1778, in part through the support of the archbishop, was likely favourable to Morand. So, apparently, was de Flesselles, the intendant, although his biographer suggests that he remained wary of an interventionist role for the state in large-scale urban transformations.[9]

Morand's plan was to profit from the emergence of a new neighbourhood in the Brotteaux beyond what he could reap from the sale of his own land and increased traffic on the bridge. To that end, he proposed to help finance the construction of a semicircular fortification wall, an adjacent canal, and a grid of streets and public spaces, in exchange for substantial acreage from the Hôtel-Dieu's holdings; in return the institution would see the value of its own holdings in the area increase immensely. Once again, the hospital appeared to the Morands as the key agent between them and fortune. Initially, Morand offered 800,000 lt and his participation in building the wall and laying out streets, in exchange for an unknown area of land and a concerted plan to sell building lots. Soon after, rumours of competing bids prompted him to enrich his offer, which very much revolved around the open secret of the Hôtel-Dieu's gaping deficit. He mused about offering to finance the completion of the Hôtel-Dieu's facade, an idea obviously intended to please Soufflot, but insisted at the same time that the rectors refrain from calling on royal financing for their share of the wall, a condition meant to reassure ministerial offices. As discussions continued, Morand made clear his reluctance to go beyond one million livres tournois (notably when de Poizieux hinted that a rival offer of 1.2 million was being made), and refused to consider shortening the duration of the bridge monopoly, which he understood to be his most solid source of revenue.[10]

By 1779, after two more inconclusive trips to Paris, Morand's faith in this ambitious project was flagging. Antoinette Levet had already argued that they should seek a more reasonable goal, perhaps something as simple as longer opening hours for the city gate at the bridge (although even that, as we shall see, would prove elusive).[11] They decided to work toward linking the bridge with the existing road toward Chambéry and Grenoble, a plan that would not only enhance traffic across the river but also foster development on Morand's land even if the hospital did not join him in selling lots. The company approached the intendant in the summer of 1779, a few weeks after the chapter of Saint-Paul had agreed to lease the necessary land. Several private owners followed suit (not without some resistance), and the provincial engineer responded favourably to the project. An agreement was even reached with the Hôtel-Dieu, whereby the company agreed to lower its toll to enhance the value of the hospital's properties in exchange for the right to build a road across its lands.[12] However, things moved very slowly, offering yet another illustration of the complex tangle of factors that could endlessly delay even a rather consensual project late in the Old Regime. In 1781 the bridge owners offered six thousand livres tournois to pay for the less than four kilometres of roadway needed to connect the bridge to existing roads. The engineers in charge of the file believed that to be an irresistible offer. Yet a year later, some serious objections had been raised, notably by those catering to the needs of travellers on the existing road through the Guillotière.[13] Not long after, the company's wishes ran into an issue of national importance, the suppression of the *corvée*, the labour levy widely used by the Ponts et chaussées to advance its projects. First attempted in 1776 by Turgot, the measure had been quickly rescinded, but not without creating a flurry of worried correspondence among administrators. This characteristically enlightened reform, designed to lessen the burden of peasants, proved fraught with unintended implications, notably for those charged with developing the infrastructure that was indispensable to economic development. The *corvée* was again replaced with a new tax in 1786, disrupting the construction and maintenance schedule of the Dauphiné to the point where administrators deemed it impossible even to consider opening sections of new road. Finally, in the

spring of 1789, the intendant of the Dauphiné disbursed one thousand livres tournois from a fund devoted to relief-work projects to
start connecting the bridge to the province's road network. A few
months later, however, most parties to this phase of the development were paralyzed anew.[14]

By 1780 it seemed unlikely that an official expansion of the city
would take place, but the hospital was slowly warming up to the
idea of selling lots. In that year, Morand abandoned the idea of a
semicircular wall and canal around the Brotteaux, as well as plans
for warehouses, markets, and work-related sites.[15] He worked on
a more modest vision of a new residential neighbourhood and produced a series of plans envisioning the sale of some fifty-two
blocks of land spread over forty-three hectares directly across
from the new bridge. These plans called for an orthogonal street
grid, symmetrically organized around a broad street in the axis of
the bridge. Respectful of the contemporary desire for less-dense
urban environments, Morand sketched a great public square at the
foot of the bridge and several other squares further inland. All
streets were to be a minimum of twelve or thirteen metres wide –
considerably wider than what had been built twenty years earlier
at Saint-Clair. The overall area slated for development was partly
defined by a deal struck with the comtes de Lyon, who owned the
seigneurial rights over the area and agreed to exempt all first sales
of the land in question from *lods* (eventually, an exemption was
even secured from the one percent fee owed to the royal registry of
the *centième*).[16]

Morand revised his plan more than once, but early in 1781 the
rectors of the Hôtel-Dieu settled for a slightly more modest version
drawn by another architect, Cyr Décrénice.[17] This final plan
retained the essential features of Morand's project but probably satisfied a wish, on the part of the rectors, to distance themselves from
a man with whom they had such a long history of confrontation.
Over the summer of 1781, Décrénice's plan was officially approved
by the parlement, a measure without real power but intended to
give all interested parties greater confidence in the coming transactions. More concretely, this official approval tied the projected sales
to the government's emerging plans to force hospitals to sell lands.
Only a year earlier, hospitals had been invited by royal edict to
divest themselves of real estate that provided them with a secure but
modest stream of revenues, and invest instead in the Caisse générale

du domaine (the general revenue chest of the royal domain). While the call vaunted the "solidity of the royal treasury," the measure was fundamentally intended to breathe some life into a perpetually underfunded monarchy. The hospital's new-found willingness to accompany Morand along the path of urban speculation was thus less than entirely self-motivated.[18]

The rapprochement between Morand and the hospital continued when they exchanged land to square the shape of their holdings and ease future sales, and when the bridge owners agreed to a lower toll for those who bought land across the river.[19] When sales started under the umbrella of the new plan, Morand held some 2.43 hectares of the land to be offered for sale to the public: he had bought 5.6 hectares (fifty bicherées) in 1765, set aside 1.71 hectares for streets and squares, and sold four lots amounting to 1.46 hectares.[20] If the acreage of the lands set aside for public use over the forty-three hectares is calculated in a proportion slightly inferior to the equivalent ratio set aside by Morand on his own lot (twenty-five percent instead of thirty percent), the land effectively offered for sale to the public covered thirty-two hectares, of which Morand held less than eight percent. During the following twelve years, that is, from 1781 to his death, Morand gradually sold the greater part of his remaining land in the Brotteaux (see appendix 3). He sold a lot in 1781 and another in 1783. In two transactions in 1784 and 1787, he sold his house, La Paisible, to the fashionable Freemason lodge to which he belonged (he was also commissioned to transform the house). Another lot was sold in 1785, and yet another, possibly two, in 1789. The early years of the Revolution only slightly accelerated the leisurely pace of these transactions; there was one sale in 1791, another in 1792, and two more in 1793, including the house known as La Rotonde, which had been built in 1788. These ten sales brought over 135,000 lt to the Morands (for some 160,000 square feet or 1.87 hectares; the uncertain sale accounted for 17,000 lt of that total). Altogether, Morand had managed to sell 285,000 square feet (25.85 bicherées, or 3.33 hectares) of land in the Brotteaux that, including several buildings, brought him just under 175,000 lt.

The pace of sales by the Hôtel-Dieu was comparable to that achieved by Morand, considering the size of its holdings and the fact that it offered a greater choice of locations closer to the city. Between November 1781 and July 1793, it signed twenty-two sales, covering some 6.6 hectares, for a total of 373,794 lt (a twenty-third sale concerned the Hôtel de la vengeance, sold in 1782 for 64,000 lt).[21] On average, the hospital received just over eight sols per square foot. However, this average was bumped up somewhat by the last four sales, in 1793, when inflation raged. Until the Revolution, land in the Brotteaux sold on average for less than seven sols per square foot; the price received by the hospital ranged between four and nine sols per square foot. Indeed, the rectors could realistically expect these sales prices by the middle of the 1780s when they renewed their plea to be exempt from the public auction required for the sale of lands belonging to such public institutions. The intendant agreed with their assessment and their request.[22] Morand's sales of unbuilt lands ranged from 2.5 sols per square foot to 13.45 sols per square foot, although these two figures stand somewhat outside the range of the other transactions. For an unknown reason, the first figure was much lower than what Morand had received for another sale concluded only the day before. The last figure was likely skewed by the inflationary pressures of 1792 (by comparison, the 10.7 sols per square foot attached to a sale in April 1793 speaks of a dramatic fall of real estate values, Morand's sharp needs, or the brutal political context of that year). If these two sales are put aside, Morand received between 5.2 sols per square foot (for a very large sale to Spréafico, in 1775) and 10.7 sols per square foot (for a substantial sale to Padovany, in 1785). There may have been a modest improvement in his sale prices after the 1780 agreement with the hospital. Even if investors did not greet the opening up of the Brotteaux with enthusiasm, these transactions played a large role in steadying Morand's financial accounts, although they certainly did not bring him the fortune he might have dreamed of late in the 1770s. Similarly, the less than half million livres tournois reaped by the Hôtel-Dieu could not redress its deficit-ridden balance of accounts for long. Administrators could not even agree on the best way to use this one-time relief, and Versailles kept ordering new inspections of Lyon's two hospitals.[23] At the close of the Old Regime and before the siege of Lyon stopped the whole project for several years, both parties to this vast enterprise would have had legitimate reasons to be disappointed.

Comparisons with the cost of land within the city are difficult; location evidently mattered a lot, and little land changed hands without buildings. Nevertheless, we can assess some transactions with which Morand himself would have been familiar. He had bought his own first lot at Saint-Clair, in 1757, at a cost of eight livres tournois per square foot (4,770 square feet for 38,160 lt) – some twenty times more than the average transaction in the Brotteaux a quarter-century later. Three years later, in 1760, Soufflot and his associates sold two more lots, one small and one large, the first for 5.32 lt per square foot and the second for 2.78 lt per square foot.[24] Morand also played a very minor role in the development of the more than two hectares (175,541 square feet) fronting on the Saône just north of Bellecour that had been made available by the suppression of the Célestins order in 1778 (see below). That large lot was sold for 1.5 million lt in 1785. These figures correspond to a cost of between 7.2 and 8.5 lt per square foot – again, fully twenty times more than the amount fetched by land in the Brotteaux.[25] The southern tip of the Presqu'île entrusted to Perrache fared a little better than the Brotteaux, although a remarkable drop in the price of land sold by his successors clearly reflects the public's loss of faith in the project (see appendix 3). Sales in 1777–78 averaged four livres tournois per square foot. Immediately after the death of Perrache and until the siege of Lyon, the company could not get more than one livre tournois per square foot. We also have an idea of the price of land in the Brotteaux before Morand launched his plans for urban expansion, although transactions were rare because of the Hôtel-Dieu's overwhelming ownership in the area. Morand himself had bought his land in the Brotteaux in 1765 at a price of thirteen deniers, or just over one sol per square foot. That same year, the Hôtel-Dieu had purchased the Guillotière domaine de l'Abondance, where the future veterinary school would stand, for a comparable 11.6 deniers per square foot. Five years earlier, and back in the Brotteaux, it had bought twelve *bicherées* at the price of 8.2 deniers per square foot.[26]

   In the roughest of terms, it is possible to say that the price of land in the Brotteaux had been multiplied by ten in two decades but remained ten to twenty times cheaper than in the "old" Presqu'île. By the end of the 1780s the Brotteaux were not seen as part of the city – nor would they be until much later in the nineteenth century. But they were no longer an agricultural preserve under the watch of the Hôtel-Dieu. Morand's plans for urban expansion had brought the Brotteaux within the fold of the suburban real estate market, but not within the city itself. His dream of a "machine to make money" had run up against some profound reservations.[27]

"UNE VILLE DOIT CONCENTRER SES FORCES"

While their land sales were underway, Morand and the Hôtel-Dieu intended to give prospective buyers some guaranties as to the urban nature of the new quarter. The poster that made the project public in 1781 announced that the king had allowed the Saint-Clair city gate to remain open until 23:00 hours, and that the plan drawn by Décrénice would be fully implemented and remain unchanged.[28] Yet at the end of the Old Regime, and indeed for several decades, the Brotteaux remained an unintegrated suburb, devoted mostly to entertainment facilities. When Napoleon Bonaparte visited Lyon and crossed the Rhône in 1805, he had to use his imperial vision to see the "Lyon of the future" in the fewer than two dozens buildings lining the street grid laid out a generation earlier.[29]

Few people lived in the Brotteaux, and certainly few people of note. Morand himself had moved his family back to the Presqu'île four or five years after their happy installation in the Brotteaux. In June 1779 well-intentioned friends had told him that his lonely settlement across the Rhône was detrimental to his affairs. This was not a reference to geographical distance: Morand's new house was only a thirty-minute walk from Saint-Jean, across the bridge that he owned. Rather, this was a reminder of the importance of his links with the older part of the city: Saint-Jean was the power-base of the archbishop, one of Morand's most solid connections to the city's elite – and the Brotteaux were foreign to this group.[30] Only three other people of note are known to have built houses that early in the new area: Flachon de la Jomarière, the king's engineer and an early partner in the bridge venture; M. Neyra, a former councillor; and M. Berlié, a merchant-manufacturer who bought a share of the bridge in the mid-1780s. It is unclear what use they made of their buildings along the central Grande Allée. Few would have risked losing the privileged fiscal status associated with a principal residence in the city proper. This was a widely held fear, as reported by that busy observer of the local scene the abbé Duret, who was citing M. de Monluel from the Bureau des Finances.[31] We do know that the left bank attracted associations, perhaps because it could offer larger spaces and more privacy than the crowded Presqu'île.

Morand's own house was claimed by the Sagesse Freemason lodge and by a "Company of Protestants" during the 1780s. Early in the same decade, another Freemason lodge, the Bienfaisance, opened slightly further east. In 1785 the rectors, trying to characterize this state of affairs, argued that land in the Brotteaux still had only a "value of opinion" – an ambiguous statement to our eyes that was likely meant to underline the somewhat frivolous nature of investments across the river, as opposed to a more solid basis for value, such as necessity.[32]

When, in 1780, the young architect François-Jacques Delanoy came through Lyon, the Brotteaux were still mostly a pleasant, and perhaps stylish, promenade with a handful of buildings, one of which Delaney deemed not without merit.[33] On his own or with the company, Morand rented chairs and benches along the Grande Allée, arranged for such wholesome entertainment as a puppet theatre, and added a café to his ice-retailing outlet.[34] It is likely, however, that the area became louder and more gaudy over time. Dining and drinking gardens multiplied, followed by a great range of entertainment venues. Antonio Spréafico, as noted earlier the largest investor by far in the Brotteaux, opened his famous Jardin de Flore. Two large houses sheltering several reception rooms bracketed vast lawns, flower beds, and groves of trees in a fine example of the playful nascent romanticism of the age. People could enjoy cold and hot drinks, pastries, and ices while gaming, reading, and indulging in conversation fuelled by the latest news sheets.[35] On 5 June 1784 this fanciful establishment formed the background for the first flight in Lyon of the Montgolfier brothers' hot-air balloon. Morand was in charge of building the arena and launching facilities, and he helped design the one-way traffic pattern for the event.[36] The Brotteaux were the site of several such large-scale festivities, culminating in the great Fête de la Fédération in 1790 and several demonstrations of republican enthusiasm.[37] A generation later, after the upheavals of the Revolution and First Empire, little had changed. A visitor to the Brotteaux still discovered only two houses around the great open square, then known as place Louis XVI. Proceeding along the Grande Allée, on the right hand, came a showhouse, the Petit Tivoli, followed by the Café du Grand Orient, opened in 1806 and probably named to recall the masonic past of the area. Across the broad street there were a circus (from 1818), a Chinese garden, and, further down, several beer

WHAT VISITORS SAW IN LYON

Lyon was frequently visited by French and foreign travellers, because
it was the kingdom's second largest and wealthiest city with a long
and rich history and also because it was on the way to Italy – a destination of choice for so many curious minds. A short sampling of the
many accounts that have been published leaves no doubt as to what
drew the attention of these travellers.

Most visitors were aware of the demographic and economic weight
of Lyon; many estimated its population at somewhere between
120,000 and 200,000, and several reflected on the scale of its silk
manufactures. General observations recalled the Roman foundation
of the city, the height of its houses, and its crowded, often dirty, and
ill-paved streets (the local round stones known as têtes-de-chat – cat's
skulls – were evidently uncomfortable). By contrast, the approaches
to the city drew very positive comments. From the north, the river
Saône afforded tranquil views of splendid country houses on tame
hills, followed by an appropriate narrowing guarded by the fortress
of Pierre-Scize. The new quays along the Rhône and the majestic
Hôtel-Dieu greeted those coming from the east, and if they looked
back, they might have seen Mont-Blanc. Arriving from Geneva, the
view from the Croix-Rousse must have been even more arresting, and
all visitors eventually climbed atop Fourvière for another splendid
perspective over the whole of Lyon, an impressive city to contem-
plate, with a dense and dark core.

Once in the city, visitors could follow personal taste to a certain
extent, but everyone recognized four great "must see" categories that
reveal the city's nature: churches, civic landmarks, squares and quays,
and manufactories. With regard to churches, it was an epoch in
which people rushed disparagingly past the gothic Saint-Jean cathedral but still appreciated pious paintings and rich decorations. At
least half a dozen churches were regularly mentioned in travel
accounts. Opinions about the more recent Hôtel de ville, Comédie, or
Loge des changes were more mixed. The city's two great hospitals
deserved more ink than any of these buildings. Indeed, hospitals were
of great interest in that era, and Lyon had a reputation in the field. By
the end of the Old Regime, some decried the contrast between the
magnificence of the buildings and the treatment of patients – criticism
that came from the heart or from the wallet; it was suggested that the
sums spent on such great buildings would do more to relieve pain and
poverty if they were given to individuals. Nevertheless, everyone was
impressed. The city's great squares also drew comment from visitors,

Bellecour above all. But the real originality of Lyon was evident in various lyrical descriptions of its quays. A hurried Arthur Young, eager to get to revolutionary Paris where a king and a queen were "prisoners," burst into an expressive paragraph on the relation between a city and its rivers. The range of bridges serving the needs of the busy Lyonnais was also noted, from the massive but narrow old bridge over the Rhône to the apparently ill designed boat bridge across the Saône, and back again to Morand's bright red structure. The sad state of the Perrache works, at the southern end of the penin- sula, were widely noted, of course; the potential as well as the failure were clear and spoke to the minds of a generation attuned to bold public works ventures and the controversies they fostered. Another peculiarity of a visit to Lyon was the economic foundation of the city – its silk industry. A few words sufficed to recall the ancient commer- cial vocation of Lyon, but pages could be used to describe the many stages of the manufacturing process. There were apparently several well-positioned persons who made a habit of helping visitors tour various celebrated workshops, including Philippe de la Salle himself when the young François de la Rochefoucauld came calling. And many visitors made a point of accumulating economic data that, one must suppose, proved meaningful to their correspondent.

Naturally, each new generation coming to a city will look for what- ever suits its obsessions. Yet even in an age that generally paid little attention to the environmental and economic contexts, the unique geography and manufacturing vocation of Lyon were always com- mented upon. Here, even manufacturing data mattered. See for instance the account of the visit of Henri, brother of King Frederic II of Prussia, 3–11 August 1784, as related in the *Journal de Lyon*, no. 17 (18 August 1784), or that of the marquis de La Fayette, a few months later (no. 14, 6 July 1785).

References. Delphine-Balleyguier, translator, *Journal de Mme Cradock*; Duranton and Lauvergnat-Gagnière, eds. *Journal d'un voy- age aux environs de la Loire*; Galle, "Lettres sur un voyage en France en 1788"; Marchand, ed. *Voyage en France*; Mascoli, "Sur la route de Rome"; and Young, *Voyages en France*. For the wide range of accounts they offer, see Goulemot et al., *Le voyage en France*; Lough, *France on the Eve of Revolution*; and his *France Observed in the Seventeenth Century*. For a near-exhaustive list of published accounts, see Gardes, *Le voyage de Lyon*. Finally, see Clapasson, *Description de la ville de Lyon*; and Dulaure, *Description des principaux lieux de France*.

gardens, more than one dance hall, and a row of shooting stands. At the heart of this district, the Elysée lyonnais was a vast compound in which all types of entertainment venues were concentrated. Then came the famous Montagnes, where carts roared down a steep incline, and one or more houses devoted to other racy pleasures. Often enough, fireworks refreshed the public's appetite for the area.[38]

The Brotteaux did not become the city quarter that Morand envisioned until the second half of the nineteenth century. The Revolution itself, and more particularly the republican siege of Lyon, damaged the area severely. The repression that began in 1793 with mass executions carried out in the Brotteaux, as well as memorials that were erected later and political rituals regularly enacted in honour of the victims of republican rage, further harmed the image of the area. Administratively speaking, the initial creation of the Rhône et Loire department by the new Revolutionary authorities had been favourable to the growth of the city. All suburbs had been attached to the district of Lyon-ville. But this move was reversed during the repression and the whole left bank remained under the jurisdiction of the Isère department for many decades.[39] Then the new Hospices Civils de Lyon, successors to the Hôtel-Dieu and Charité hospitals, stubbornly pursued a rather short-sighted policy. Wary of selling more of their real-estate endowment after their experiences of the 1780s, they chose to lease land on a short-term basis only, offering terms of six, nine, or twelve years (it wasn't until 1870 that they moved to longer leases of thirty years or more). This encouraged the construction of cheap temporary buildings catering to precarious and polluting trades that were unwelcome in the city proper. The trend was denounced by the rising movement of urban "hygienists," but to no avail.[40] Finally, the vagaries of the Rhône itself cooled interest in these low-lying lands. Only after the great floods of 1846 and 1856 were the necessary remedial works undertaken.[41]

The development of the Brotteaux ran up against fundamental, if often latent, resistance to the expansion of the city. The eighteenth century is often seen as the age in which cities opened up, shedding their medieval fortifications and replacing them with broad boulevards and connections to a rapidly growing road network. Nonetheless, traditional beliefs in the contained essence of urban life persisted; all the more tenaciously, perhaps, within a climate of change that challenged so many other traditional aspects of urban life. New initiatives designed to ease congestion, improve sanitation, and tackle other deleterious consequences of urban concentration inevitably disturbed many entrenched aspects of city life. The opening of wide straight streets meant the demise of many well-used buildings, and maintaining the new thoroughfares free of clutter directly threatened the livelihood of countless people. The taming of ancient marketplaces ran into protests from dynasties of vendors as well as their clients, who were often dependent on a web of marginal transactions that seemed tied to the existing tangle. The removal of cemeteries, the enforcement of minimum fire-prevention standards, more active policing, all of these changes were at the same time desirable and decried, just as the large cities in which they occurred were both admired and feared, praised and denounced. Over the century, analyses of the roles and definitions of cities multiplied.[42] The many equilibria that supported urban concentrations appeared more fragile than ever.

Some of these tensions are visible in the discussions that took place in Lyon, late in the 1780s, concerning the opening of the city gates beyond established hours. Not long after the opening of the bridge, the company considered the possibility of a night shift. The cost of such a measure was estimated at close to fifteen hundred livres tournois and the returns were uncertain, so it was decided simply to seek an extension of the city gate opening hours to 23:00. The matter was approved by Versailles, ostensibly because it would favour the sale of lands belonging to the Hôtel-Dieu, thus improving its debilitated accounts. The measure was rescinded, however, after only a few years. The objections that led to this reversal were summed up in a memorandum that began by denouncing the multiplication of inns and cabarets, which escaped the city's excise tax and encouraged all forms of smuggling.[43] Worse, in the authors' view, this concentration of dubious businesses attracted crooks from a broad region who encouraged debauchery among as many city workers as they could to build up their own clientele. Located in the Dauphiné province, the Brotteaux were beyond the reach of the Lyon police yet too far from other cities for regular patrols. Even the Lyon office of the Eaux et Forêts, a royal institution with jurisdiction over rivers, entered the fray to order the bridge's owners to provide guards to prevent attacks on late strollers. Perhaps even more worrisome to the good citizens of Lyon was the idea that restless workers used the area for their seditious plotting.[44] The belief that the strikes and uprising of 1786 could be linked to the opening of the gates beyond traditional hours gained enough currency for the city to end this dangerous experiment with evidently good results. (The tight closing of the city was also said to have helped repress the 1744 rebellion). The bridge company and those who had recently settled in the Brotteaux came back to the charge the following year, but to no avail. Pushing their analysis a little further, the authors of the memorandum drew attention to Lyon's unique geographical setting, which concentrated these unsavoury activities on the difficult-to-police left bank of the Rhône. The land reclaimed by Perrache was also attracting the wrong crowd, but at least that area was bounded by two rivers and under the jurisdiction of the city.

Beyond these fears, those who objected to a late closing of the gates feared that the very future of the city was threatened by an uncontrollable expansionist dynamic. Business and house owners as well as civic leaders feared for the revenues that made urban life possible, and they also feared the competition that unregulated suburban expansion would unleash. To them, the city's vitality depended on the concentration of energies that its boundaries fostered. The intendant echoed this concern when he came to believe, as early as 1784, that the rectors of the Hôtel-Dieu were going well beyond their mandate in transforming a recreational space across the river into a new quarter of a city that already had too many buildings losing rent revenues. The pioneer demographer Messance felt the need to address these fears when, in his famous *Nouvelles recherches*, he denounced the commonly held belief that the number of vacant houses in Lyon had grown rapidly since the late 1770s – that is, since the opening of Morand's bridge.[45]

Morand and his associates were confronted with the persistence of an organic vision of the city – "the trunk whence all the principles of life emanated," as the authors of a memorandum put it in a telling if flowery sentence.[46] Eighteenth-century reflections on the city owed much to advances in the medical sciences. Cities were increasingly understood as great bodies, complex arrangements of organs and functions, depending for their welfare and also their very existence upon the smooth circulation of not only people and goods but also air and water. Examples of urban decline and death were often mentioned.[47] This functionalist understanding of the modern city stood behind many of the arguments put forth by those who, like Morand, favoured an expansion of Lyon. They envisioned a harmonious and well-balanced city, neatly divided by its two rivers into three sections devoted to distinct but complementary uses.[48] However, this medical perspective had other implications. It also bolstered an older belief in the need for clearly defined borders around the city, for no organism could live in an indeterminate shape.

The eighteenth century is often seen as a transition period during which many cities, including many important cities, abandoned their defensive posture, dismantled their walls, and built new links with the surrounding countryside.[49] In so doing, they were shedding an old military vocation but also a fundamental distinction that had both classical and Germanic roots. The city had long been characterized by a unique legal status, a concentration of powers over but also dependency upon the countryside that called for the control of people and goods. These features were displayed in walls, gates, and restricted hours of access, as well as guard duties for its citizens.[50] In so many ways, the city was an exception to the broader social and political order of the *plat pays*, the countryside without walls. This fundamental opposition was spelled out in the daily language of those who lived in and around cities in the classic distinction between *faubourg* and *banlieue*, a differentiation that lost much of its meaning in the age of regular expansion, later in the nineteenth century.[51]

This concept of cities as series of unique equilibria of political, social, and economic ideals and realities was increasingly challenged through the early-modern age by the rise of royal power, repeated bouts of urban growth, and pressing communication needs. Enlightened thinkers eventually located the theoretical foundations of these pragmatic developments in the primacy of flow and movement. However, until the rapid transformations of the nineteenth century, even the most ambitious plans to open a city to its surroundings retained the idea of controlled access. Paris offers a telling example of this apparent contradiction. While defensive walls had all but disappeared by the later part of the seventeenth century, the government repeatedly tried to impose clear limits on the spread of new buildings. By the time it fell, the Old Regime was busy constructing a new wall for fiscal purposes – the "*mur des fermiers généraux*" – that became one of the first targets of revolutionary agitation. This will largely survived the age of revolutions. New fortifications were built around the capital and Lyon at mid-century, and now, more than a century later, municipal powers are busy designing the elusive "green belts" that will stop urban sprawl.[52] Utopian thinkers, for their part, never ceased dreaming of the perfect city as a perfect-sized city.

In Lyon, these arguments may have carried added weight because of the traditional understanding of the city as an emporium – a unique and evidently fragile concentration of energies gathered for the purpose of trade. The fairs and the "foreigners" they attracted had always been seen as essential to the city, even when the dangers they conjured compounded the dramatic religious fractures of the sixteenth century.[53] This was certainly an enduring image, portrayed again in what is likely the most famous historical representation of the city, a *plan scénographique* engraved in 1720. Its author, François Cléric, combined several distinct bird's-eye perspectives spread over some two hundred degrees to display myriad trades, activities, and movements that were intended to convey the busyness that was equated with Lyon's prosperity by residents and visitors alike.[54] More than fifty years later, this vision was still powerful enough to stall the rebuilding of the left bank of the Saône. Because Perrache's expansion of the southern end of the Presqu'île was expected to lower the level of the Saône (by pushing its confluence with the Rhône roughly two kilometres south), a group of investors under the name of Pierre Chapuis and Company proposed to narrow the riverbed and build several new blocks of houses on the extended left bank of the Saône (1777). A coalition of opponents quickly formed, led by owners of houses fronting on the river. Their arguments were at once self-interested (they stood to lose their river frontage), technical (they raised concerns about navigation requirements), and aesthetic (they saw the width of the river at the foot of the Fourvière hill as a remarkable asset). They also argued that the chaotic shores that the project was meant to bring to order were in fact the economic heart of the city.[55] Here, the jumble of so many private interests could stand for the public interest against the promoters' self-serving plans. Perhaps because this project touched at the very centre of the city, it was (surprisingly) quickly defeated. By contrast, Morand and Perrache worked in a more liminal space, making it possible for them to resist, but never fully overcome, opposition to their plans.

Bernard Lepetit has suggested that the growing importance granted to economic matters contributed to the slow retiring of earlier attachments to the walled city, the fundamental replacement of an historically as well as spatially static vision of the city with a dynamic functionalist perspective.[56] However, the case of Lyon suggests that an appreciation of economic mechanisms could accommodate a contained or fixed understanding of the city. Here, economic interests had always loomed large, but the concentration of activities seemed essential to prosperity. Expansion of the city raised fears of dilution of economic acumen, rather than the potential of growth. What was at stake in Lyon was not the discovery of the importance of economic exchange but an even more fundamental tension between an essentialist understanding of social phenomena and a more relative approach attuned to changes. This dilemma was enhanced by the contemporary taste for references to natural laws: growth could indeed be positive, inasmuch as it was natural rather than forced (by speculation, for instance).[57] Naturally, all of these factors played a role in the discussions that fostered or hampered the expansion of many other cities, in varying proportions, in France or neighbouring countries. In Lyon, however, the Rhône underscored and framed all hopes and all concerns.

The fate of Morand's vision for the Brotteaux at the turn of the nineteenth century is perhaps best described as half success and half failure, reflecting the ambivalence of the age toward urban expansion. The grandiose rebuilding of the Hôtel-Dieu and attendant opening of the first quay along the Rhône, the creation of the new and very successful Saint-Clair quarter, several other more modest neighbouring initiatives, and Perrache's southern push can all be seen as a "discovery of the Rhône." Until then, Lyon had turned its back on this alpine river and thrived on the banks of the Saône; Natalie Zemon Davis has shown how deeply embedded the city's psyche was the distinction between a "powerful, masculine ... and dangerous" Rhône and its "slow-moving feminine" tributary.[58] Eventually, economic and demographic growth combined with geography to place the Rhône at the centre of all discussions of urban transformations in Lyon. The river fostered initiatives and supplied arguments to both proponents and opponents of new plans. This process illuminates the heuristic role played by key natural features in the development of that most social phenomenon, a large city.

In Lyon, the Rhône could at the same time be an obvious and "natural" border, and a key element in planning a better city. And when the time came to consider expanding the city, it precluded the compromises, the small-scale trials that were possible in many if not most other geographical settings. Here, rivers and hills forbade an incremental, steady or hesitant but quasi-organic expansion; for many generations existing suburbs remained poorly linked to the city.[59] The left bank of the Rhône offered the only open land suited to the rational city planning so attractive to the enlightened mind, but crossing this mighty and in many ways foreign river raised serious concerns. Arguments for or against expansion beyond the Rhône reflected, on one level, a series of professional, financial, and political interests. They also articulated broadly held aesthetic, medical, and social standards of what constituted an inspiring, healthy, and orderly urban environment. Then came two distinct analyses of the nature and prosperity of this great and old city. Those favouring urbanization of the left bank of the Rhône applied a functional and rational analysis, heralding what would eventually be known as urban planning. Their opponents may, at first, appear to have adopted a more defensive perspective, doubting the abilities of engineers or the promises of a rational organization of space. However, their concerns were also founded on a positive understanding – the belief that a city, and more particularly this city, Lyon, thrived on a unique ever-renewed but fragile concentration of energies. Growth could not be forced. There is no need to read into this the premises of a liberal understanding of economic relations. Such an attachment to the (evidently vague) idea of natural growth was more likely rooted in emerging beliefs in natural law or, perhaps likelier still, in the continuing influence of mercantilist ideas.[60] In the end, both camps shared an organic perspective of the city, but the functionalist optimism of one side stood in contrast to the essentialist beliefs of the other. The Rhône easily found its place in both lines of thinking. During the following century, it became the demarcation line between the old city devoted to commerce and the new city devoured by industrialization. Until then, it simply made it clear that a different future was possible – but not everyone agreed on the meaning of this promise.

7

A Fine Balance

[The Saint-Clair bridge] is most convenient for the inhabitants of Lyon who could not otherwise enjoy the promenades on the other side of the river, the closest to the city; [it] has given a real value to the vast lands of the hospitals; [its] construction, across a broad and fast flowing river, has withstood several ice break-ups that swept mills and other boats; it was based on new principles and has been regarded as precious for the arts, yet was never a burden for the city or the state ..."

In spite of all the expenses required by this enterprise, it has proven most profitable to is owners ... It is well known that its principal shareholders have build considerable fortunes.[1]

I always strive to balance our love and the demands of work.[2]

From the completion of his bridge to his arrest late in 1793, Morand continued work on a range of projects, besides the initiatives detailed thus far. He was a busy man, successful enough to support his family in a style that only a fraction of the population of his adoptive city could aspire to, even if it required endless financial juggling. Yet a number of disappointments suggest that his career was no longer on an ascendant curve. Was he able to accept this reality in light of the comforts and satisfactions his private life afforded him, or did his evident pugnacity turn to bitterness? We cannot answer the question for lack of information about his personal feelings. Yet we can sketch the key elements that would have been on his mind whenever he found the time to weigh the positive and negative aspects of his five decades in Lyon.

Morand's professional papers are filled with drawings, but it is not easy to distinguish those corresponding to actual commissions from others that did not lead to a contract or that were simply collected

for reference. We know, for instance, that he drew plans for a botani-
cal garden in the Brotteaux that was never completed. The idea had
originated with the noted physician Jean-Emmanuel Gillibert
(1741–1814), who had bought a large lot from Morand. It was an
ambitious scheme, to include a library, laboratories, and an amphitheatre, as well as the rooms indispensable to the storage, servicing,
and display of collections; however, it could not be funded.[3] Morand
was generally luckier in his relations with the archbishop, yet even in
Saint-Jean many projects failed to materialize. He was charged with
the interior of the new choir school (1775–81) and well positioned
when the time came to rebuild the area to the south of the cathedral
and the archbishop's palace, although thanks to interference from
Paris the project was scaled down considerably. Morand oversaw the
rebuilding of the palace's *officialité* (seigneurial justice), jails, and
stables, as well as the redesign of the facade of the episcopal palace
opening on a new public space. This was a successful campaign, even
if Morand had to defend his honorarium and if the worldly prelate
found reason to worry that his new stables would not be ready in
time for the summer.[4]

Morand's association with the Church of Lyon continued even
after the proclamation of the Civil Constitution of the Clergy (July
1790), which deprived this ancient institution of its properties and
authority.[5] It is reasonable to ask whether this connection did not
add to his reputation for being on the wrong side of the political
spectrum in those revolutionary times. Indeed, Morand worked for
a great range of patrons whose positions were eventually challenged by revolutionaries, from the elevated Tonnerre of Burgundy
to the lesser Guillin brothers, who were among the first declared
opponents of the new regime.[6] Morand designed one church and
the steeples of several other and contributed to more than a dozen
châteaux and gardens. Naturally, these potentially compromising
commissions were just one part of his practice. His files also contain plans for a mill and its dam, a covered public market, many
houses, big and small, in Lyon and Paris, as well as a bridge in
Nantes, commercial and semi-industrial spaces in and around
Lyon, a fountain, and the river-port of Givors.[7] Morand also drew
plans for an ice house for the town of Villefranche – he had, it
seems, a reputation for this type of building after having built his
own in the Brotteaux and one at the Montribloud estate.

A FASHIONABLE VENTURE – THE ICE TRADE

Late in April 1763, the sieur Labonté and his Swiss partner
announced the opening of their new café, on the Brotteaux side of
the Hôtel-Dieu's ferry service across the Rhône. At the very top of
the substantial list of sweets and drinks awaiting Lyon's
promeneurs was the mention of a broad range of ices, frozen
cheeses, and chilled beverages: "Le sr Labonté associé avec un
Suisse fera Dimanche premier de Mai l'ouverture du Café qu'ils
ont établi au Broteau, au port des Trailles ; on y trouvera tous les
rafraîchissements que l'on souhaitera, glaces de toute espèce,
fromages glacés, orgeat, limonades, bière, etc. De même que le
chocolat, café, lisqueur et vins de liqueure. Ils feront leur possible
pour contenter les personnes qui leur feront l'honneur de
s'adresser à eux." (The sieur Labonté and his Swiss associate will
open next May Day his new café in the Brotteaux, besides the
ferry landing; there, one will find all the refreshments one may
wish, ices of all kinds, iced cheese, barley sirup, lemonade, beer,
etc. As well as chocolate, coffee, liqueur and wines. The owners
will do their best to satisfy his honourable clientele; *Affiches de
Lyon*, no. 17, 27 April 1763).

As Morand would a few years later, these two entrepreneurs
were capitalizing on a powerful fad. In Lyon the ice trade had
been freed from its monopoly status in 1725. Eventually, wealthy
estate-owners added an ice house to their outbuildings, and some
municipalities came to see such a building as a necessary civic
amenity.

References. De neiges en glaces ...; Ellis, *Ice and Icehouses
through the Ages*; Flandrin, *Histoire de l'alimentation*; *Glacière et
caves à neige du Rhône*; Planhol, *L'eau de neige*; and Rousselle,
La glace et ses usages.

Again, it is barely possible to know which of these projects materialized and how profitable they proved, but they generated enough
work to justify the occasional hiring of other architects.[8] In the
mid-1780s, when leaving Lyon for Paris with his wife, he left a

precise list of ongoing concerns. The man left in charge, Buisson, was to attend first to the wrought-iron gate and fence for the archbishop's palace, and then to the *salon* (or *salle de garde*) of the comte de Tonnerre. He was also to further the plans for the gardens of Madame Laroche, supervise the small but delicate work undertaken at the château de Cruzol, and regrade the slope leading to the priory of l'Argentière. Although most of these projects required trips outside the city, Buisson was also expected to collect the rents for several buildings in the city and deal with a problematic tenant whose belongings had been seized. Finally, he was to intervene in several litigious affairs, making the necessary visits, forwarding correspondence, etc.[9] Naturally, few of these ventures were trouble-free. For instance, the Morands had to move their ice-retailing storefront twice against their will, and rental records illustrate abundantly the difficulties associated with managing half a dozen large buildings.[10] Most impressive of all is the range of revenues that Morand and Levet kept flowing to meet their expenses. Through the late 1770s and 1780s, they counted on income from Morand's architectural practice and his salaried position as voyer du chapitre (2,000 lt), their shares in the bridge (in the order of 12,000 to 15,000 lt – see chapter 5), rents from several buildings (amounting perhaps to 10,000 to 15,000 lt), and the farming of undeveloped land in the Brotteaux and the Machy domain.[11] To these figures must be added a semiregular stream of property sales and an unknown number of annuities, some inherited from Antoinette Levet's father.[12] Such a long list must be seen less as evidence of financial ease than an illustration of the tenacious combining of ventures needed to support a successful entrepreneur and professional in the complex business environment of the Old Regime.

FINANCIAL PROWESSES

When gathered in a life-long summary, the family's accounts allow for some comment in spite of the inevitably incomplete nature of the data (see appendix 1). Across the decades, the higher sets of figures reflect transactions of important assets. Purchases called for new borrowing, and sales settled some outstanding debts, inflating both sides of the ledger. The Saint-Clair operations are clearly reflected in the figures available for the years 1764–67, as is Morand's participation in the construction of the new theatre in the late 1750s. Similarly, the sale, in two stages, of La Paisible is reflected in the figures stated for 1784 and 1787, as is the 1775 sale to Spréafico. The figures for the early 1770s reflect efforts to finance the bridge construction, including the sale of one share in the company. A second such sale, as well as some 12,000 lt in settlement of Morand's long legal battle over the Saint-Clair project, contributed to revenues in 1779–80. At the same time, the costly purchase of the Machy estate triggered a new bout of heavy borrowing that swelled the accounts for half a dozen years (this difficult period is detailed below). Conversely, the marriages of Antoine and then Eléonore triggered the transfer of two shares in the bridge, the Machy estate, and the Croix-Rousse house to the children. The 1792 figures, marking a sharp increase from the previous five or even seven years, included 42,000 lt received from the estate of Etienne Machério (5,000 lt of which immediately went to settle small claims on the estate). Finally, the 1793 accounts, although incomplete, included 17,500 lt received for the sale of la Rotonde, and 15,000 received for the sale of land in the Brotteaux. Without such irregular entries, Morand's accounts appear to hover around the 60,000 to 70,000 lt mark. Less than half of this figure came from regular and secure sources (salary, income from bridge, and rental returns), the rest from his architectural practice and an endless series of financial transactions. Evidently, the position that Morand had reached within the bourgeois strata of Lyon by the end of the Old Regime provided him and his family with a very comfortable way of life – but at the price of a never-ending financial strain.

Indeed, if the Morands lived well and never stopped dreaming up greater plans, they remained dependent on the goodwill of many people. All their undertakings were made possible by a stringent borrowing schedule. Their difficulties in meeting their obligations during the late 1770s are known in some detail because Antoinette Levet, often alone in Lyon, spelled out the problems she was encountering in her letters. In April 1777 Morand and his wife were considering the sale of their Saint-Clair house. They estimated their debts at 140,000 lt and believed they could get 180,000 lt for the building. Nothing came of this calculation and early in June 1777 Antoinette Levet sent her husband a detailed list of loans that were coming due on the traditional dates of payment in Lyon, the first of July, October, January, and April. She mentioned twenty-four loans from twenty-four distinct lenders, totalling 109,468 lt, for an average of just over 4,560 lt per loan (although it is likely that the 21,495 lt called in by Me. Guyot, notary, were owed to more than one lender).[13] The Morands feared that their partners would try to delay the next distribution of profits from the bridge, in order to force them to keep paying interest on the monies they owed – a further measure of the pressures bearing on them. Throughout the month of June, Antoinette Levet cajoled some lenders into postponing their claims, partly satisfied others, and simply put a third group in front of the *fait accompli* of a loan extension.[14]

The year 1779 was also difficult for the Morands, in part because of their recent purchase of the Machy estate. Morand had barely arrived in Paris when Antoinette Levet reminded him to find a modest hotel, for she could foresee serious financial clouds ahead. By the middle of March, she started to assemble the 20,000 lt needed to meet the demands of creditors. Some nineteen lenders were solicited. The rhythm of her laments matches the schedule of payments, on 1 April and 1 July, with a very slight relaxing of the pressure early in May. Week after week, she met the most urgent demands and made the rounds from lender to lender seeking extensions on other loans.[15] Her son was finally of age to help her in some of these incessant walks across the city, but the complexity of the manoeuvres must nonetheless have been problematic. Indeed, early in April, when Antoine delivered 1,200 lt in cash to a friendly lender, he was told that he was three months early. At times, Antoinette Levet went hunting for money. Late in June, she reported the death of an acquaintance but only because she wondered whether some trace had been found among his papers of a loan for 12,000 lt made by a third party – she wanted to see if that third party would now be in a position to lend her some of the money. The goodwill of a notary, the impatience of everyday suppliers, an unexpected tax levy, the 300 lt required to install their son in his first job – everything mattered and called for renewed juggling. In the end she could say, with much relief no doubt, "*J'ai tout payé*" (I have paid everything), although she had managed to do so only by using the 5,000 lt in rental income that would eventually have to find its way to its rightful owner, M. Pitiot. This had been, in fact, a difficult period for many in Lyon, triggering several noted bankruptcies. Should we need it, we can find further evidence of the tensions hidden behind these manoeuvres in the fact that several lenders relaxed their attitude upon learning of

Morand's victorious settling of one court case (see below), a positive outcome that immediately boosted their credit.

Yet this settlement could do little to ease the complexity of the
financial schemes that supported their ongoing affairs. On 1 January 1780 Morand sat down and listed all of his commitments on
two distinct records. On a first sheet he recorded 15,700 lt owed in
the form of life annuities (*rentes viagères*) due to seven lenders
claiming 1,200 lt per year, one perpetual annuity (*rente constituée*)
for 12,000 lt at five percent, and two long series of obligations, the
first (to thirteen names, including at least two notaries) totalling
160,943 lt for contracts with a few more years to run, and the second (to twenty-eight names) for contracts expiring in the coming
year, for a total of 94,406 lt. This amounted to some 285,049 lt
owing. On a second sheet, Morand counted 172,943 lt in mortgages, 99,107 lt in *obligations*, 10,000 lt in one life annuity, and
16,400 lt due to his partners in the bridge venture and two other
names that are difficult to place. This second estimate arrived at the
similar sum of 298,450 lt owing. These figures stand behind the
quasi-balanced budget shown in his accounts for the year 1779
(revenues of 112,324 lt and expenses of 109,083 lt) and the very
positive balances that followed in 1780, 1781, and 1782 (reflecting
the realization of assets).[16]

Morand drafted another summary of their outstanding obligations at an unknown later date, perhaps as late as 1792. In it, he
listed thirty-nine creditors, to whom some 258,164 lt were owed.
Some of these loans dated back to 1760, although the great majority had been contracted, or at least renewed, around 1780. Seventeen of them were for sums of less than 4,000 lt, eleven ranged
between 4,000 and 6,000 lt, six reached between 6,000 and 8,300
lt. Five much larger sums were owed to notary Fromental, M.
Barroud, and three long-time friends, the comtesse d'Audiffret,
Mme. de Cornabé, and René Daffaux, seigneur de Glatta.[17] This
treasury depended on the confidence of a great many people. The
slightest rumour of financial difficulties on the part of the borrower
or, more generally, on the financial markets (*place*), could convince
some lenders to withdraw their funds. So could any malicious slan-
der, however unfounded. This level of borrowing required tremen-
dous social effort to build and maintain goodwill on a very large
scale.[18] It is important to note that, in spite of the many battles they

fought, the Morands were fortunate to retain the trust of many
long-term lenders.

PROFESSIONAL DISAPPOINTMENTS

During the last two decades of his life, the failure to develop the
Brotteaux was not Morand's only disappointment. Early in January
1778, he sent drawings to Soufflot for a wooden structure to
replace the derelict bridge over the Saône at Saint-Jean.[19] The archbishop had also informed him that he envisioned the creation of a
new quay between Saint-Jean and Saint-George. He was reflecting
the desire to bring the kind of urban renewal operation that had
reclaimed the right bank of the Rhône to the Saône, an area that
had been urbanized, in a rather chaotic manner, for many centuries.[20] What followed is so characteristic of the manoeuvres
involved in any substantial public project that it is worth following
as far as the records permit. The city's first level of deliberation, the
Assembly of Notables, officially activated the project in the spring
of 1779. Respectful of financial constraints, the notables chose a
wooden structure, and a week later they selected two members of
the cathedral chapter to examine the matter, two positive signs for
Morand. Immediately, Guillin du Montet asked the prévôt to ask
the archbishop to recommend Morand to the examiners. However,
by the end of the month, rumour had it that someone else would
receive the commission. Morand turned again to the archbishop,
hoping that he could persuade the minister, Bertin, in his favour.
Antoinette Levet suspected that Flachon, one of Morand's earlier
associates, had worked against him.[21]

Early in May a meeting of the aldermen took advantage of the
absence of the prévôt des marchands who favoured Morand, to
bring forth yet another name, that of M. Petit, against the recommendation of the selection committee. A month later, Morand had
the further displeasure of seeing his old antagonist, Brac, argue for
a stone bridge. By 1 July 1779, after the rejection of a compromise
plan calling for a wooden structure on stone piles, the city was considering the cheapest option of all: a boat-bridge, and with a toll at
that. By then, Antoinette Levet was blaming these difficulties on
another rival, the architect L. Roux. Their hopes revived once again
when they learned that Bertin was working toward the creation of a
provincial assembly for the Lyonnais, to be headed by the arch-

bishop.[22] Meanwhile, Brac had mounted a major public campaign to radically transform Lyon's south-west entrance along the Saône, accompanied, in his polemic style, by a vigorous attack on all those standing in his way. Yet another proposal for a stone bridge surfaced early in 1782, but nothing happened, even though the old wooden structure had been demolished in 1780. The Consulat, the Saint-Jean chapter, Soufflot, the archbishop, the Ponts et chaussées, and a series of eager promoters had only managed to bring down firm condemnations from the highest level: Necker and Joly de Fleury, both at the head of royal finances, and Vergennes, secretary of foreign affairs, all intervened to stop the project.[23] The matter did not proceed until 1792, and it took another fifteen years before a new stone bridge was eventually built.

Morand and Levet may have had reason to feel frustrated by this episode and perhaps to blame certain individuals for the outcome. We know, however, that their disappointment fitted within a pattern of failure that reached well beyond their particular case. When, in the spring of 1791, the new municipality tried to convince the revolutionary authorities that the city's debt burden was largely the result of the kind of mismanagement characteristic of the fallen Old Regime, a special chapter of their submission was devoted to this latest bridge fiasco. They questioned several aspects of the project, most notably the astounding variation in plans for replacement of a bridge that had been demolished prematurely.[24] They could have reached further back. Throughout the eighteenth century, the city debated the necessity of rebuilding the old stone bridge just north of the bishop's bridge. Several centuries old, only seven metres wide, and burdened with houses, it was under constant surveillance and frequently closed. Proposals for its replacement covered the whole range of possibilities, yet nothing happened.[25]

Morand had gone through another exciting, if short-lived, "entrepreneurial bubble" in the summer of 1777. This period in his life was difficult enough for him to consider completely reorienting his career and even uprooting his family. In May he declined an offer to manage stage machinery at the Paris opera, a position he deemed too modest. In July he inquired about the possibility of purchasing the office of Trésorier général de France at Grenoble, at the (affordable) price of 48,000 lt.[26] His will to succeed revived, however, when he came up with a new design for a hydraulic pump, a classic quest of the early-modern age. He came to believe that it would suit the needs of the king, who was looking for a replacement for the old marvel at Marly. His enthusiasm proved contagious. Antoinette Levet could not help but dream of the successes that this new machine could bring them, all the while worrying about their move to Marly and mapping out the contacts they could use to reach the comte d'Angiviller, directeur général des Bâtiments du roi, who would be the true "*distributeur de grâces*" (dispenser of favours) in this case. Morand soon faced a problem common to all innovators before the age of patent: how to convince people of the value of his invention without revealing in detail how it worked?[27] Eventually, he decided to publish a detailed account of his machine in the *Gazette de France*, under the assumption that doing so would solidify his claim to the invention. The tensions associated with such a gamble were such that, in a letter to Antoinette Levet, Morand mused about its being the last project of his career. Antoinette Levet replied that she should have gone up to the capital, where Morand stayed from April to August 1777, to help him deal with these matters. The *Gazette* article brought him public recognition in Paris as he strolled through the Palais Royal or the Tuileries, as well as an appointment with Necker. However, it also brought him a sharp attack by one of the more outspoken architects of the time. In the January 1778 issue of the *Mercure de France*, Pierre Patte argued that Morand's invention was a copy of a design built a year earlier by Loriot (the inventor of the new cement used by Morand on his bridge), for the gardens of the marquis de Marigny. Shaken, Morand could only ask his supporters for help. D'Angiviller obliged and commissioned a study of Morand's design that concluded that it was indeed original. The blow was serious enough, however, to put an end to Morand's bid. The Marly pumps continued to deteriorate until the following century.[28]

These disappointments must have been all the more heartfelt because Morand was, at the time, fighting two protracted battles. The first went back to the late 1750s, when Tolozan had managed to stop the construction of Morand's first house at Saint-Clair. We saw earlier that the latter had rapidly won his case in court, and that construction proceeded while he was in Italy. However, Morand stubbornly pursued compensation for the delay, and by the late 1770s his appeal to the Paris Parlement was one of his reasons for travelling to the capital every year. He was claiming 26,500 lt for lost rental income, for damages to materials and partially completed structures, and for the cost of immobilized capital, legal procedures, and trips to Paris.[29] This complex affair resurfaced in the spring of 1777, when Morand arrived in the capital determined not to let an "unworthy" opponent frustrate him any longer. It was only settled in July 1779, after many skirmishes that mobilized a remarkable list of contacts but also risked, at times, alienating such crucial allies as Soufflot. In the end, it is difficult to know how much the Morands received of the 28,000 lt cited by the judgment in their favour.[30]

This battle was linked to another painful dispute over what Morand called his *pension*. In 1757 he had been appointed inspector to the new theatre, with a yearly stipend of 1,000 lt that was, in his mind at least, compensation for the sums still owed him for his work on the venue (see chapter 1). Ten years later, the city replaced this salary with the right to build and collect rent for thirty years from ten small boutiques alongside the back of city hall – in itself a contradiction characteristic of an age eager to open public space, particularly around great buildings, and yet prone to such ad hoc concessions. Another decade passed, and the Consulat wished to eliminate the position altogether, arguing that no contract precluded its termination. Morand claimed that he was still owed more than 15,000 lt plus interest for his work on the theatre. He took up the matter with Bertin and other influential voices in Paris in April 1777, while Antoinette Levet pressed the matter in Lyon.[31] In June the controller general ruled against Morand, although it appears that the Morands kept the Terreaux shops.[32] Once again, Morand and Levet had found themselves standing against a majority of the political elite of the city and trying to muster support in Paris. More important, however, is the fact that the outcome of these cases may well have been hollow victories. It was an age of endless legal feuds, and the stubbornly litigious were likely not viewed in an unduly negative light. Nevertheless, one cannot but suspect that Morand's actions risked eroding the goodwill he needed so much, in Paris and in Lyon, to develop the Brotteaux – or to be invited to play a significant role in what was to be the last great real estate venture in Lyon before the Revolution.

The suppression of the religious order of the Célestins by Pope Pius VI in 1778 opened a legal dispute over the ownership of their vast lands at the heart of the Presqu'île. Eventually, the duke of Savoie, king of Sardinia, managed to assert his rights. Even before that, Morand had submitted plans to locate a great new building for the Douane de Lyon on this site.[33] The move was wise not only because the tax farm was a wealthy institution and thus a potentially generous patron but also because Perrache had been trying to lure it to his new quarter. Nothing came of Morand's proposal, and the property was sold to a Parisian investor at the head of a group of associates with roots in Lyon.[34] This group included a Parisian architect, Jean-François Colson. Morand was chosen to be the project's second architect. This secondary role was not what he had hoped for. In an undated record of his discussions with Madinier, a key partner in the venture, going back to April 1788, Morand noted that he would have liked at least to be officially associated with the project as "free architect," or consultant. When he had suggested that the public would respond favourably to his name on their brochure, the promoters had replied that, on the contrary, raising his profile would be seen as a problematic.[35]

The project was explicitly inspired by the residential complex built earlier in the decade by Victor Louis in Paris on the grounds of the Palais Royal. A large administrative or commercial building (covering some 17,000 square feet of ground and expected to cost well over 300,000 lt), a theatre, and rows of five-storey houses were to surround a vast garden. The whole was meant to form a "controlled public space," separate from but open to the surrounding streets. Morand drew plans for two types of house and regularly revised his drawings to meet the promoters' calculations. By the summer of 1789 he appeared to be involved in demolition work and some early stone-cutting contracts, and as late as 1791 he was submitting plans for passageways between two streets.[36] Colson's theatre was ready by 1792, just in time to profit from the end of the monopoly on public spectacles and other new-found freedoms. However, the houses were built only over the first part of the nineteenth century, and the privacy of the development envisioned by its promoters never materialized; in fact, little remained of the original design. More relevant to our study is the fact that Morand's participation in the project had been strictly circumscribed and was far more limited than he had wished. A disillusioned tone crept into his notes, and he wondered, after a new set of plans had been returned to him, who would pay for the expenses he incurred on this venture. In the fall of 1792, there must have been rumours of his intention to retire; for he received a letter from a young architect who had briefly worked for him, asking whether his practice was for sale.[37] We do not know how Morand responded. It is clear, however, that he was no longer in a position to influence the transformation of the city.

A last illustration of the mix of stress and disappointment that characterized these difficult years for the Morands is found in his failed quest for a title of nobility that would bring him not only fiscal exemptions but also official recognition. His claim was double in nature. First, he presented evidence related to the judicial services of his family in the Briançonnais, as well as to services to the crown of Savoie on his maternal side. Second, he maintained that his own achievements entitled him to the distinction accorded to artists for exceptional services, the cordon de Saint-Michel.[38] When he first mentioned the matter in May 1777, Antoinette Levet feared it was one goal too many, when so many pressing issues were already bearing on them. She agreed that it could be important to the future of their children but never believed that it would materialize. Bertin also tried hard to convince Morand that Louis XVI had refused to consider such requests even in more meritorious cases, and he insisted on paying for the marble vases that had been given to him to avoid being indebted to Morand.[39] A year later, they approached Vergennes through the comte de Tonnerre; in 1779 they were trying to reach Maurepas; and by 1781 de Flesselles, the archbishop, and the princesse de Lamballe had intervened on his behalf. However, it proved impossible to move the matter any further.[40]

LIFE'S COMFORTS

Enough evidence has survived to suggest that the Morands lived very comfortably in a city where the vast majority of the population counted their yearly revenues and expenses in a very few hundreds of livres tournois, not tens of thousands. During his early years in Lyon, Morand kept a detailed record of his expenses, reflecting an almost compulsive nature and great respect for money. After the mid-1760s the records that have reached us are less systematic and less detailed, yet we know enough about his and his family's spending to provide a short analysis. To go beyond mere impressions we will focus on a series of perspectives that sketch the evolution of his family's way of life.

The early household daily record of expenses for the year 1752–56 speaks of a strict regimen. At the time, Morand lived with his mother and sister in a rented apartment in the heart of the Presqu'île. Bread, wine, meat, lighting and heating, as well as petty and market expenses slowly climbed from 1,200 to 2,300 lt (appendix 1). These were already comfortable figures for a small household, and when the New Year came, Morand was able to give thirty livres tournois to his brother. More telling, he had already started to build up what would become an impressive library and collection of engravings, drawings, and paintings. As early as the mid-1750s, he was able to spend some 2,500 lt on such items; his year in Italy gave him the chance to acquire another 1,000 lt's worth of books and artworks. The hundreds of engravings accumulated by Morand over the years attest to one important way to acquire the culture indispensable to his craft, in an age before photography and when travel opportunities remained limited. A recent study of this portfolio notes that it ranges from reproductions of works by old and recent masters to early efforts of contemporary artists, and reveals some clear focuses immediately related to the various projects that occupied Morand.[41] We may add that it also reflects the fact that he was self-taught and from a family that, however respectable, had not exposed him to the artifacts of the elite culture he aspired to join.

After her husband's death, Antoinette Levet kept from his library titles reflecting the broader interests of the age: thirty-six volumes of the *Encyclopédie*, as well as its thirty volumes of illustrations; treatises on mathematics and physics; Buffon's natural histories (some seventeen volumes, a much-appreciated gift to her from her husband); religious, philosophical, and historical essays and studies; old classics (Homer) and contemporary authors (thirty-three volumes of Rousseau, ten volumes of Voltaire); as well as several dictionaries.[42] Antoine Morand, for his part, inherited thirty-two sets (perhaps 150 volumes) of studies directly related to his father's professional life, as well as another hundred general volumes of mainly a historical and religious nature.[43] The professional library included several technical treatises (such as Réaumur's *L'art de convertir le fer en acier*), a range of manuals on perspective, an essay on the movement of fluids, a code of urban building regulations, guides to carpentry, stonecutting, and the drafting of estimates; illustrated descriptions of monuments and cities; studies of antique and modern architecture; countless illustrations of fountains, landscapes, chimneys, tombstones, altars, and birds, intended to support Morand's decorative talents; the immensely respected works of Vitruve and Palladio, and those of well-known artists, such as Le Brun and Blondel, as well as lesser-known artists; descriptions of memorable public events and the festivities that surrounded them; and many other texts devoted to gardening, fireworks, and astronomy. Such a collection naturally raises the question how many of these volumes did Morand actually read and use. The library can also be seen from different perspectives, however, such as those of historians of art or students of the Enlightenment. For the purpose of this study, its most striking feature is its coherence. Morand's collection on the whole is concentrated on the perfection of his talents, the pursuit of his chosen profession, and the will to belong to the cultural elite of his time. It also reflects a national and Parisian orientation rather than a regional perspective, as well as a large Italian influence. In Lyon Morand was connected to many of these cultural currents, though at times he felt that he was far from the real centres of artistic and intellectual life.

Naturally, the life of the Morands was far from purely professional. As we have seen, some of the sharpest political debates of the time proved highly relevant to many of their projects. They kept abreast of public affairs, subscribing to the *Journal de Lyon* and collecting pamphlets on the financial state of the monarchy (such as Mirabeau the Elder's essay on the state debt and Necker's analysis of the royal budget), on pressing political matters (such as the creation of provincial assemblies or the convocation of the Estates General), and on more pragmatic, yet often controversial, matters such as the deregulation of the trade in grains.[44] Morand and Antoinette Levet's letters are filled with references to local politics, not all directly related to their own affairs. They also sketch with some precision their social circles, changing over time but also steadily centred around a handful of aristocratic names, certainly not of the first magnitude but clearly out of bourgeois circles.[45] We even catch glimpses of the lighter aspects of their social life. Antoinette Levet's letters frequently mention her interest in the theatre and the musical stages of Lyon, as well as dinner parties and country outings, complete with donkey rides.

Their house in the Brotteaux, like the other houses Morand envisioned for the new quarter but that were never built, also tells us something of their preferences for a sobriety that was likely as much provincial as it was neoclassical, enriched by some rather heavy decoration.[46] The facades were (to be) painted, partly in *trompe l'oeil*, reminding us of his work for various public celebrations around the city. A similar tension between austerity and display likely characterized the furnishing of La Paisible. Although Antoinette Levet reported applying great economy to the task, the mirrors, paintings, wallpapers, and furniture that were sold to the Freemason lodge La Sagesse fetched 3,000 lt.[47] The apartment on the rue Saint-Dominique, where they lived from 1779, was certainly spacious and well appointed. When the lease was renewed in 1793, we learn that 850 lt per year provided them with ten rooms on the second floor, another on the third floor, two attic rooms, a cellar, and storage space.[48] A 1797 inventory notably mentions a salon, a *cabinet* or office, a dining room, at least two bedrooms, and a long list of furniture and necessities that speak of very up-to-date and comfortable, if not ostentatious, standards. The fact that they chose to rent an apartment rather than occupy space in their Saint-Clair building reflects a set of priorities typical of house owners in Lyon or even Paris, for whom a building was more an investment than a family base.[49]

Their concerns for their children yield another glimpse into the Morands' outlook on life. Early in the 1770s, at the age of ten, their son Antoine had been sent to a college some fifty kilometres north of Lyon. Although it was a moderately priced institution, the undertaking was far from cheap – a few years earlier, an advertisement in the *Affiches de Lyon* mentioned boarding tuition costs of seventy-two livres tournos per trimester. Like many similar schools, it promised a classical education to "well-born and docile" children. The reports sent to his parents spoke of a somewhat closed, reticent nature.[50] Late in 1775 he was attending the Collège Duplessis on rue Saint-Jacques in Paris. His parents believed that he had no particular talent for the arts, but that his literary proclivities would find their most fruitful application in the field of law. For a while, they also believed they could leave him some freedom of choice, in the hope that he would find his own way.[51] However, when his father joined him in Paris in April 1777, he found him physically sturdier than they had feared but very unfocused when it came to his studies and his future. Morand reacted sternly, depriving him of his music lessons; while he recognized that music seemed to bring him out of his indolence more than anything else, he also feared it was a waste of time. His severity was only temporary. Antoine came back to the Brotteaux for the summer holidays to put on some weight, improve his mathematics (with Barbier, a noted figure in the city), and pick up the violin again.[52] After another year of school in Paris, he finally seemed more confident about his future in the law and managed to graduate by the end of the summer of 1778. He was also eager to get back to the Brotteaux, where his parents were seeking a riding instructor for him.[53] Early in 1779 he was helping his mother cope with the financial difficulties of the moment while waiting for his appointment to the bar at the Sénéchaussée. In April Antoinette Levet reminded her husband that the 300 lt "reception fee" had to be paid as soon as possible since it would determine his seniority ranking. Only then could his parents feel a little more confident that he would be able to support them in their old age.[54]

Characteristically, Antoine's marriage was directly related to his purchase of the office of King's counsellor and attorney at the Bureau des Finances in Lyon, the second step in his legal career. The contract signed on 26 April 1785 instituted him *héritier universel* (primary heir) to his parents, entitling him to their complete estate upon the death of the last surviving parent, except for the following items: 120,000 lt to settle outstanding debts, 40,000 lt that both parents wished to dispose of at their will; and his sister's *légitime*, the sum meant to settle the inheritance of a sibling who was not the principal heir (see below). Morand and Levet retained their properties until their death but immediately gave their son one share of the bridge and agreed to pay him an annuity of 6,000 lt per year, to come out of the rental income from their Saint-Clair house, which they were forbidden to sell.[55] (Not mentioned in this contract is the Machy estate, most likely because it had been bought in the son's name.) Antoine's bride, Marie-Magdelaine Guilloud, daughter of a merchant and captain of the bourgeoisie de Lyon, brought to the marriage a house estimated at 60,000 lt, and 100,000 lt. The contract stipulated that Antoine Morand could use this last sum to pay for the office that he had just purchased.[56] That transaction had taken place two weeks earlier, when Jean-Pierre François Catalan, knight, seigneur of la Sarra, conseiller du roi, lieutenant general at the Sénéchaussée et Présidial de Lyon, had sold to Antoine Morand his office in the Bureau des Finances for the price of 68,000 lt.[57] Everything we know about the Morands and about Antoine Morand's career suggests that his was a good marriage, in social terms. Yet Jean-Pierre Catalan had himself been married only a few months earlier, and the contract signed on that occasion offers a telling comparison. Catalan had married the daughter of M. de la Verpillière, a prominent figure on the Lyon political stage. Catalan had received 300,000 lt, a first account on the estate he would receive as universal heir to his parents; his bride brought a dowry of 280,000 lt and an estate in nearby Millery. The gap between this contract and the one signed for Antoine Morand's marriage is also reflected in the four pages of well-known signatures that concluded it.[58] No prominent name graced Morand's contract.

Of his sister Eléonore's education we know little, except that she had been a boarder at the Sainte-Elisabeth institution on the slopes of the Croix-Rousse and later received training in drawing. She was married at the age of twenty-four, one year after her brother, and her marriage is of interest to us for more than the transfer of capital it occasioned. Antoinette Levet apparently turned down a first suitor because of his inadequate fortune. This is all the more interesting given that she herself had married a man who offered more promise than capital and who could well have been considered less than ideally suitable for the only daughter of a notary. The marriages of their children yield another measure of the trajectory the Morands believed they had accomplished, in spite of all their setbacks. Antoinette Levet carefully noted that M. de Besson, Eléonore's husband, owned a house yielding some 2,550 lt in rents (which were due, Antoinette noted, to be raised soon), besides a worthy apartment for the new family, four estates drawing 5,200 lt a year, an office that paid him a minimum of 1,200 lt a year, and one obligation bringing another 336 lt per year. He had, however, contracted some debts to purchase his office and paid his brother's *légitime*, but he would inherit some 40,000 lt from a childless uncle. As settled in her brother's marriage contract, Eléonore brought to the wedding a dowry of 16,000 lt, one share of the bridge (evaluated by then at 22,000 lt), and a house (deemed to be worth an equivalent sum). Her great-uncle, Etienne Machério, signed on the contract to leave her 20,000 lt at his death, and her husband offered her jewels estimated at 6,000 lt. A few years later, Antoinette Levet was able to direct another 10,000 lt out of her estate to each chid.[59]

Beyond that, much of what we know about the Morands' private life concerns trips to Paris, during which detailed accounts were kept. Indeed, Morand travelled a fair amount, mostly on business.

The irascible Tobias Smollett summed up the choices facing travellers between Paris and Lyon in the 1760s – even if in the end, he spent an extravagant amount on his trip:

> There are three methods of travelling from Paris to Lyons, which, by the shortest road, is a journey of about three hundred and sixty miles. One is by the *diligence*, or stage-coach, which performs in five days; and every passenger pays one hundred *livres*, in consideration of which, he not only has a seat in the carriage, but is maintained on the road ... Another way of travelling in this country is to hire a coach and four horses [spending] ten days on the road ... [T]he third method, which is going post ... The postmaster finds nothing but horses and guides. The carriage you yourself must provide ... There are two post roads from Paris to Lyons, one of sixty-five posts, by the way of Moulins; the other fifty-nine, by the way of Dijon in Burgundy ... My journey from Paris to Lyons, including the hire of the coach and all the expenses on the road, has cost me, within a few shillings, forty *loui'dores*.
> (Smollett, *Travels through France and Italy*, 84–94; "forty loui'dores" amounted to 960 lt)

Fast and reliable exchanges between Lyon and Paris, of people as well as mail, were essential to a great range of enterprises. By the 1760s letters and small parcels left Lyon daily for the capital, except on Sunday, and arrived also daily, except on Wednesday. In 1770 the *Almanach* listed three drop-off locations, but six years later there were five. However, Morand's key concerns appear to have been not reliability or frequency, but cost and discretion. The privileged postal service ranked high on both counts. To save on postal charges, Morand and his partners often relied on acquaintances, such as the enlightened abbé Pernety. Whenever possible, the use of ministerial post – for example slipping a letter in an envelope addressed to M. Trudaine, director of the Ponts et chaussées, whose services would forward it – was a good alternative. Several close associates, including Soufflot, chose not to sign their letters, and Morand himself often advised Antoinette Levet to burn his letters.

In spite of a dense flow of mail between the two cities, Morand frequently travelled to Paris, and the pattern that emerges from his travels hints at a smooth, regular, and rather speedy process. In his *Dictionnaire géographique, historique et politique*, Expilly suggests that travellers availing themselves of the diligence service reached Paris in five days in summer and six in winter at a cost of one hundred livres tournois, food included but with a surcharge of six sols per pound for luggage. Morand rarely took more than five days, although he may have spent a little more.

Typically, having left Lyon on Wednesday, 10 April 1777, he was writing his first letter home from Paris on Sunday, 14 April, as expected by his wife (14 II 008, Antoinette Levet to her son, 7 April

1777, and Morand to Levet, 14 April 1777). A decade later, both Morand and Levet left home early on 24 May 1788 and were paying their first visit in Paris only four days later, on 28 May (14 II 007). In 1769 he had shared a coach with an acquaintance and covered the distance in four or five days: having left on 18 November 1769, he held a first meeting on 22 November at Versailles but may have arrived late the previous day. This was obviously a more expensive proposition, costing 217 lt, plus thirty livres tournois for the luggage that could not be accommodated in this private carriage (14 II 020). A year earlier, a similar sum, 263 lt, had conveyed both Morand and Antoinette Levet; the couple left on 29 May 1768 (14 II 005; much earlier, in 1758, Morand had paid 115 lt one way). Not long after, a trip by diligence, departing on Christmas day, 1770, claimed 159 lt (14 II 005).

If it was already possible for determined travellers to reach Paris in an average of four days, Morand's son was to witness some substantial improvements (14 II 028). By 1821 he travelled as fast as, or even a little faster than, the shattering news of the king's escape, late in June 1791 (Tackett, *When the King Took Flight*, 153–4). In 1789, 1795, and 1796, he covered the distance in three days, regardless of the season (in January, April, and August). In 1815 he reached the capital only on his fourth day, but in 1821 he arrived in Paris on 16 October, having left Lyon only two days earlier, at a comfortable 10:00 A.M.

References. The key links between this kind of data and larger questions, such as degrees of market integration and even the emergence of a national identity, are illustrated, albeit for an earlier period and across the English Channel, in Brayshay et al., "Knowledge, Nationhood and Governance." For an illustration of the guides at the disposal of Morand's contemporaries and, indeed, the kind of information they sought, there is the geographer Michel's long-titled *L'indicateur fidèle, ou, Guide des voyageurs: qui enseigne toutes les routes royales et particulières de la France, routes levées topographiquemt dès le commencement de ce siècle, et assujetties à une graduation géométrique, contenant toutes les villes, tous les bourgs, villages, hameaux, fermes, châteaux, abbayes, communautés, églises, chapelles, et autres maisons religieuses, les moulins, les hôtelleries, les justices, et les limites des provinces: les fleuves, les rivières, les ruisseaux, les étangs, les marais, les ponts, les gués, les montagnes, les bois, les jardins, les parcs, les avenües, et les prairies, traversés par les grandes routes &c: accompagné d'un intinéraire instructif et raisonné sur chaque route, qui donne le jour et l'heure du départ, de la dinée et de la couchée tant des coches par eau, que des carosses, diligences et messageries du royaume, avec le nombre des lieüs que ces différentes voitures font chaque jour.* See also Arbellot and Lepetit, *Atlas de la Révolution Française*, vol. 1, *Routes et communications.*

He spent a year, as we know, travelling through northern Italy and made several trips to Burgundy (mainly related to lumber purchases in the early 1770s), the Alps (Grenoble, Briançon, etc.), and Switzerland. More regular were his twelve known trips to Paris, at least three of them with Antoinette Levet.[60] In all, Morand spent more than three years in Paris – an obviously expensive proposition, as countless letters remind us. Although no precise tally is possible, the figures that we have suggest that Morand required sums ranging from 200 to 500 lt per week while in the capital. These visits reflect the stages of his professional life.

The 1768 visit that brought both of them to Paris from mid-May to late August cost more than 500 lt for the Lyon–Paris and return trips and 336 lt for the rental of a carriage, as well as 180 lt a month for food and accommodation. They also took excursions to Chantilly and Compiègne and spent some 600 lt on gifts for themselves, their son, and Morand's mother. In all, they spent close to 5,000 lt, dealing with the initial stages of the bridge project but also enjoying themselves in the wake of their successes at Saint-Clair. Morand returned to Paris the following year, a shorter and more modest trip to overcome obstacles that were starting to accumulate. He shared a carriage to Paris with a friend and only rented one by the day while in the capital. Faced with growing opposition, Morand was in Paris again a year later. This time, he chose a modest accommodation, and his spending appears more centred on unavoidable social outings than on the acquisition of personal items, although he still found it necessary to have the services of a domestic (at forty-nine livres tournois per month, including gratuities). In 1777, 1778, and 1779, three or four long stays in the capital reflect Morand's battles to get the Brotteaux project off the ground but also to advance, and eventually terminate, his pending legal battles. These were difficult times for an embattled Morand, who resented the cost of such visits, as his associates were no longer willing to support him (although development in the Brotteaux would have boosted traffic on the bridge). Letters from this period paint a moving picture of a harried yet intensely active and probing man. We see him running out in the morning for a series of appointments, suffering through endless waiting periods in ministerial antechambers, rushing out to catch decision makers in the favourable surroundings of their rural retreats, and returning to his cramped quarters. Maps and drawings occupied every available surface, and

Morand struggled to stay abreast of the thick flow of letters that were at the heart of early-modern business. Then friends came knocking on his door, calling to embark on the evening rounds of restaurants, shows, and receptions needed to reinforce the web of relationships woven by these letters. Eventually, late in the evenings, a few moments would be found to reflect on the more personal paragraphs of his wife's letters and to reassure her on the future of their son.

The demanding and in many ways disappointing visits to the capital of the late 1770s marked the end of the most active part of Morand's career. He was able to remain in Lyon for the following decades, until the Célestins venture brought him up one more time. This was not his project, however, and most of his time was spent on technical discussions. He was spared the tedious rounds of ministerial offices that seemed so crucial a decade earlier and found time, with Antoinette, to visit old friends. These many trips to Paris reflect, successively, Morand's ambitions, his determination to marshal support for his projects in the highest political circles, and his eventual inability to overcome the opposition arising from other circles in Lyon and his gradual distancing from such costly battles. In his many meetings, we see him transcending the limitations of Lyon politics. We also plainly see the toll that such battles took on him, as he retreated, abandoning one after another of the projects that had aroused his enthusiasm only a few months earlier, worn down by an endless flow of rumours, delays, and disappointments.

The enthusiasm that Morand displayed at the beginning of each project was systematically challenged in Lyon but worn down in Paris. The distance between the two cities exposed the fragility of Morand's business plans, and likely those of many others. The many hands that governed the business world of the Old Regime were perhaps not invisible and certainly far from impersonal. They were simply often beyond the reach of someone like Morand. He could participate in and even profit by some of the most important ventures that were transforming the kingdom's second city, but he was never able to reach the security and independence that was the lot of so few. It is no surprise to see Antoinette Levet briefly lose heart as she struggled to meet her July 1777 payments and suddenly proclaim her distaste for the endless round of solicitations and her dream of financial independence: *"Je fatigue de vivre en solliciteur ... vivons indépendants!"*[61]

Epilogue and Conclusions

[On 3 July 1789] The news of the union of the three Estates having been confirmed, the People gathered, and forced house-owners to display their joy by lighting their windows ... but soon this joyfulness reached an excessive level ... the People ... wishing to wrestle down the last aristocrats, moved towards the residence of M. Tolozan de Montfort, overtook its guards, and cut down the May pole ... Then, the crowd moved towards the Saint-Clair gate ... attacked the office, seized registers and papers, burned and threw all in the Rhône. [Then], the crowd descended upon the tax farming offices, at the end of the Guillotière bridge; nothing was spared ... and then a wine depot was stormed ... At that point, these over-heated heads let loose; the People seized the weapons of the guards ... several soldiers who resisted were wounded, killed, and thrown in the Rhône."[1]

Early in the afternoon of 24 January 1794, or 5 Pluviose, Year 2, Morand was guillotined in front of Lyon's hôtel de ville, on the renamed Place de la Liberté.[2] He was sixty-six. He had been arrested almost two months earlier, interrogated, and found guilty of contributing to the defence of the rebellious city besieged by the armies of the Republic. His properties were confiscated by the nation.

Morand was probably not indifferent to the political transformations that preceded the Revolution.[3] There is no evidence, however, that he involved himself deeply in the political maelstrom that brewed in Lyon in subsequent years. Most likely, he tended to his business and tried to protect his family and its assets from the new pressures mounting all around them. He continued to seek buyers for lots in the Brotteaux and was still connected in minor ways with the Célestins project. The company had to maintain the bridge and cultivate the goodwill of the new authorities. It added a night shift now that the city gates never closed and granted free passage to everyone on the occasion of various revolutionary festivities in the Brotteaux. Morand and his partners had reasons to worry. They knew all too well that their property rested on a royal privilege – two words that had lost much of their capital. In June 1791 someone tried to burn the bridge; five months later, the company hired more guards to safeguard its employees. Not long after, it asked the Garde Nationale for yet more protection, in the name of the respect due to private property. Soon, a more elusive threat materialized when a shortage of coin led the company to issue its own bills. These papers started to circulate more widely than expected, and the bridge toll booths were flooded with counterfeit issues. Other expedients had to be found, but the company was by then losing money and drawing new contributions from its owners.[4]

The deterioration of the city's economic climate, forced loans, inflation, shortages, and soon, requisitions, tense political manoeuvres and frequent violent clashes, as well as an increasingly radical redefinition of many dimensions of social relations could only make life unpleasant for those who, like Morand and his partners, were used to the comforts, influence, and respect that were the lot of the elite in more stable circumstances. Yet Morand was not in a position to leave Lyon, even if he had wanted to. His fortune was neither portable nor sufficiently secure to be left behind. The public nature of his key asset would not even let him escape into the relative safety of private life. When, early in February 1793, Joseph Chalier, the leader of the most radical republican movement in the city, called for the creation of a revolutionary tribunal to more effectively eliminate counterrevolutionaries, he wished to set the guillotine at the very centre of the pont Saint-Clair.

In all likelihood, Morand tried to avoid problems by staying abreast of the changing political landscape. We know that he contributed 1,000 lt to the 1789 *souscription patriotique*, the first of many such fiscal levies imposed by the new revolutionary authorities, and was active in the Saône section, the district where he lived. By 1793, however, everything had become even more complicated. As the Convention, the new national assembly elected in September 1792, drifted towards the Terror in Paris, and the radical leader Joseph Chalier and his allies consolidated their hold on municipal power in Lyon, moderate republicans regrouped, setting the stage for a confrontation.[5] On 29 May 1793 a short, bloody, and decisive insurrection led by about two-thirds of the sections deposed "*les*

Chaliers." Lyon's rejection of the Jacobin social revolution that was, at the same time, gaining the upper hand in Paris was soon declared counterrevolutionary by the Convention. In many ways, this development was not surprising. At least since the discovery of a monarchist conspiracy in December 1789, Lyon had been considered a potential haven for opponents to the ruling assemblies of the capital. The new municipality's affirmations of republican loyalty were rapidly eclipsed by its unwillingness to recognize the legitimacy of a truncated Convention. Early in August, republican troops surrounded the city. The two-month siege that followed allowed decidedly antirevolutionary elements to play an increasingly important role in the city, thus justifying both the proclamations of the Convention and the repression that followed when troops entered the city on 9 October. Three days later, the Convention ordered the summary punishment of counterrevolutionaries, the demolition of "all that had been inhabited by the rich," and the compensation of oppressed patriots. A column was to rise to remind citizens that "Lyon had fought Liberty – Lyon is no more." The city would henceforth be known as Commune Affranchie.[6]

During the siege, Morand's bridge was a target of revolutionary armies, albeit not without some ambivalence. On the one hand, because Lyon's defenders had set an artillery battery in the Brotteaux, cutting it would have dealt a blow to the city. On several occasions early in September, incendiary craft were floated down the Rhône. Chains across the river, quick responses, and luck saved the structure. On the other hand, as besieging forces tightened their stranglehold over the city to ensure that shortages would soon combine with artillery fire to force a surrender, the bridge became more of a potential access to the weakened city. This may explain why it survived, usable after repairs. In turn, this made Morand's participation in the defence of his bridge all the more evident, all the way to the symbolic dismantling of one arch.

Immediately after the siege, repression focused on those caught with weapons in hand. At this time, Morand was called upon to help reopen the bridge. However, late in the fall, repression intensified and expanded under the watch of the Commission temporaire, the executive body led by Fouché and Collot d'Herbois, envoys of the Convention. Early in December, all architects, masons, and firefighters who had contributed to the defence of the city were proscribed by decree. Morand was arrested, held at city hall, and inter-

rogated a first time on 23 December 1793. According to his own
account of that interview, he argued that an honest marriage and a
life of work had brought him all he had, and that he had lost everything in the siege; that he came from an ancient republican heart-
land (the Briançonnais was known for its early emancipation from
the seigneurial system); and, ultimately, that he had many reasons
to refuse to destroy his own bridge but could not ignore a military
order. His case was decided a month later, along with those of
thirty-seven other men, and he was executed the same day.[7] Several letters written to Antoinette Levet during his captivity show a
man who was at first still confident enough to mention matters of
finance and make arrangements for a minimal level of comfort in
prison. He even drafted a letter to the mayor detailing the need for
repairs to the ceiling of the great hall in which prisoners were held.
Early in the new year, his spirits were flagging. His final comfort in
life was likely knowing that his son Antoine had managed to leave
the city, and that his wife and daughter appeared to be safe.[8]

His son's early successes had offered him some consolation for
his own disappointments well before this tragic episode. Antoine
Morand had first shown his ambitions when he adopted the name
Morand de Jouffrey to recall the noble origins of his paternal
grandmother. He switched to Morand Jouffrey during the Revolution and reclaimed the *particule nobiliaire* later. He nimbly over-
came the loss of his office with the Bureau des Finances to become a
deputy judge on the new tribunal of the Lyon district in 1791.[9] He
then worked his way up to the head of the Saône section and, by
1793, to the assembly of the nearby canton of Limonest. In April of
that same year, upon returning to the city from his Machy estate, he
took care to inform the authorities of "all he had learned" during
this brief journey, to underline his desire to "serve the public
good."[10] Most impressive was his ability to leave the city before the
siege. He joined the Armée des Alpes, serving in the administration
of supplies at Briançon.[11] Eventually, Lyon reclaimed its name, and
most punitive measures were lifted in October 1794. The Morand
family recovered its properties, and by August 1795 the owners of
the bridge were allowed to reimpose the toll that had lapsed in
1793.[12] By then, Antoine Morand Jouffrey had assumed a key position on the board of what was now the pont des Victoires.[13] Over
the following decades, he became a member of the Lyon municipal
council, served on the board of the Hospices Civils de Lyon and on

the Conseil général du Rhône, was awarded the Légion d'honneur and an imperial knighthood, and worked as prosecutor and then judge under the First Empire and through the Restoration period. He carefully managed his properties, buying and selling land in the Brotteaux, expanding the company's monopoly over several bridges, and enhancing his Machy holdings.[14] Finally, he played a key role in building up a cult of remembrance for the victims of the siege and the repression that followed. A series of monuments rose in the Brotteaux, and for decades to come Lyon's good citizens treasured the memory of the city's martyrdom under the Terror.[15] Antoine Morand de Jouffrey had achieved the kind of unquestioned notability that had always eluded his father. He died in 1838. For her part, Antoinette Levet moved to Grenoble to be with her daughter; she died there in 1819.

Over the past two decades, Bruno Benoît has recast the history of the revolutionary years in Lyon and their consequences for the city. After placing the fiery clash of 1793 within the city's record of deep social tensions and recurrent revolts, he argues that profoundly shaken local elites rallied around conservative yet dynamic combinations of moderate politics and strong local authority, economic liberalism and catholic values – a pragmatic stance occasionally spiced with anti-Parisian sentiment. Throughout the nineteenth century, the memory of the 1793 trauma was cultivated to help reject the more extreme political currents that repeatedly shook the nation and the continent. At the same time, Lyon's elites slowly reconciled themselves to increasing centralization and eventually accepted a Third Republic that proved strong and conservative enough to preclude any drift toward a "social republic." Rapid industrialization inevitably bred new pressures, but economic development and the urban transformations that it financed also held the promise of a less-conflicted future. Class tensions certainly never disappeared, but they could be accommodated in a rapidly growing city under a strong administration – or at least checked when they led to brutal clashes. The Presqu'île, modernized along the lines associated with Haussmann, the celebrated prefect of Paris, remained the business and decision-making centre of the city. However, the belated urbanization of the left bank of the Rhône also made room for powerful industrial cores, while the Brotteaux finally became a fashionable quarter where the elite of the city's bourgeoisie could enjoy and display its wealth. Lyon's municipal council recovered the right to elect its mayor in 1884 and, in 1905, the rise of Edouard Herriot to that position and to national political prominence completed the reconciliation of Lyon with the Republic.[16]

Such an analysis emphasizes the management of tensions that carried the city through a potentially revolutionary century. This delicate exercise was reflected in the social geography of Lyon, the coexistence of quarters closely associated with distinct social groups, and, in an age of rising political participation, the sensitive map of demonstrations and protests that played a crucial role in building up social pressures while for the most part respecting some critical limits.[17] From this perspective, Lyon may be seen as a city where social distinctions and social tensions were neither denied nor resolved but rather managed and visibly contained. Just as Lyon's contrasting landscapes have facilitated the preservation of many historical layers, its past speaks of coexistence rather than unity, a form of political realism that is often mistaken for a bourgeois value or plain common sense.

The "terrible year" of 1793 traumatized Lyon's elites so deeply not because it had come as a surprise but because they had always feared and expected social explosions. Old Regime Lyon had been economically dynamic, but its prosperity was always fragile because of the overwhelming dominance of the silk industry. As we have seen, it was also an extraordinarily dense city, and one without a legitimate political voice. The monarchy preferred to keep it in a state of dependency, for fear of its potential power but also because any eventual recognition of Lyon's political personality entailed the creation of mechanisms for accountability and some degree of local representation that were beyond the regime's capabilities. The Consulat, caught between its prestigious past and ultimate impotence, managed its own survival and the immediate interests of the elite it represented, rather than the demands of development. The profound social tensions characteristic of this uniquely large manufacturing concentration fuelled several revolts, most notably in 1744 and 1786. When the collapse of royal power dismantled the mechanisms of repression that had contained such convulsions, a radical Jacobin movement arose that found a strident voice in Chalier and his allies. The reactions of Lyon's elites to this threat were further shaped by events in Paris, a traditional pole of resentment in Lyon, leading to the defiant stance of May 1793 and the subsequent siege and repression.

Morand was one of almost two thousand victims of the repression that played out from October 1793 to April 1794. Although undeniably brutal and summary, this repression was not blind. Most of those who were executed over that long winter had contributed to the defence of the city, at least according to the definition of resistance given in early December 1793 that indicted a range of professionals who had helped protect the city through their technical expertise. This rather mechanical appraisal may explain the large number of architects among the victims, including Morand.[18] It cannot, however, do justice to the passions of the time, nor does it account for their echo over the following century. On a first level, and for many generations, this bloody episode was seen by both Jacobin apologists and their opponents as a confrontation between republican and monarchist sides. From this perspective, Morand, once arrested, was unlikely to be spared because of his lifelong association with royal power and aristocratic circles in Lyon, as well as with high-level speculation. Few people in Lyon, and certainly few within revolutionary ranks, would have spoken for him under the circumstances. Morand's death can thus be said to reflect the choices he had consistently made and the enmities he had fostered thereby. However, the situation in Lyon was more confused than this categorical assessment suggests. Those who seized municipal power at the end of May 1793 went to great lengths, initially, to reaffirm their attachment to the Republic. They made repeated efforts to forge links with a handful of cities that were under less suspicion than Lyon of harbouring émigrés conspiracies, and Parisian envoys testified to their commitment to revolutionary ideals. Even the conservative rituals of the following century often strove to blend rousing accounts of a people's revolt on behalf of its king with subtler memories of a republican surge against dictatorship.[19] They did this for obvious political reasons but also because crucial ambiguities made it possible to argue that the great clash of 1793 had not been the inevitable result of a fundamental opposition between prorevolutionaries and counterrevolutionaries. Recent analyses have certainly viewed the "federalist revolt" that shook the young Republic as opaque. Paul Hanson has argued, for instance, that the intensity of the confrontation issued from the collision of traditional factors, namely, elite fears of the populace and

Parisian-provincial mistrust, with the entirely new and undecided matter of popular sovereignty.[20] This more reflexive analysis suggests that Morand was trapped in a struggle larger than himself, but certainly not by accident. He died neither for his convictions nor simply for his association with a bridge that automatically became a military asset, but rather because of the inescapably political nature of his prominence. He had spent much of his life in that very position, caught in the vortex of Lyon and Versailles politics.

Morand's trajectory in Lyon highlights many of the opportunities and obstacles facing entrepreneurs in the Old Regime. His initial steps remind us of how important geographical and social mobility were in the eighteenth century. One instance cannot add much to the knowledge of these phenomena built by serial studies. Yet it underlines the fact that well-trodden paths of migration still left room for personal circumstances and preferences. Morand's background was privileged, but only to a degree. His family was used to positions of influence, but his education was modest and short. After stepping away from a religious future that had perhaps been a family wish or an educational bid, Morands' tastes and talents allowed him to steer clear of the commercial and administrative occupations that attracted the majority of émigrés of his social standing.

Over the following years, Morand's career choices were guided by his encounters in Lyon and Paris. His personality naturally played a role. His correspondence indicates that he was outgoing enough to make contacts easily, but that few of his relationships were trouble-free. He was not easy to get along with. But such a temperament is timeless. More interesting is the array of people called upon, more or less successfully, to help advance his projects, and the fact that the timing of these encounters clearly mattered – some of the contacts made during his long sojourn in Italy could have taken him well beyond Lyon, but they did not; he was already rooted there. First on the list of Morand's supporters stands Soufflot, a celebrated artist through whom Morand met the elite of the Ponts et chaussées and several other institutions. The dynamic head of the Church of Lyon, first among equals as primat des Gaules, could also provide first-class introductions to countless people. Morand likewise befriended Bertin who, as intendant and

then minister, remained mostly well disposed towards him and
believed in the worthiness of his plans. Next on the list are several
important political figures in Lyon whose own agendas proved
compatible, at least temporarily, with Morand's plans. Through a
few aristocratic friends of regional standing, he was able to reach
more remote patrons who could put in a favourable word where it
mattered. Many people who escape our gaze would have played a
role in Morand's career. For instance, certain lenders, suppliers, and
artisans are repeatedly named among his papers. In an age when
personal trust compensated for the lack of institutional credit lines,
they lent a measure of stability to an otherwise volatile business
context, even if it could not be taken for granted.

Largely absent from the list of Morand's supporters is the core of
family relations that is central to many networks. Antoinette Levet
brought the only family ally of note evident in the record, her uncle
Machério. As the daughter of a notary, she was likely a source of
other contacts in Lyon; we noted the presence of silk merchants,
lawyers, and notaries at her side when she received her father's
estate.[21] They lie beyond our reach, however, and must have been of
secondary import. It is possible to say that Morand was always
something of an outsider in Lyon, an *étranger*. This meant that he
could not turn to relatives for assistance, and that his credit would
have been seen as fragile. Family networks could open doors and
provide assistance in various forms, but their visibility in a community also served as a reference point around which support beyond
their own circles could coalesce.[22]

If such networks are often difficult to sketch, surviving records
leave no doubt as to the crucial role played by Antoinette Levet in
Morand's career. Most evident, because they corresponded by mail
during his absences, is her ability to manage all levels of their affairs
when he was away. However, her familiarity with so many issues
was not activated only upon his departure and stored away at other
times: she was obviously engaged in their business dealings on a
continuing basis, even if the legal and cultural standards of the age
credited all such transactions to her husband, the "master of her
rights." A brief playful exchange after the birth of their first child
suggests that they wished to keep their family small. Their choice to
send both children to a wet-nurse at a time when the practice was
under attack among people who had a choice in the matter offers
further indication of Antoinette's desire to remain engaged in other

aspects of life.[23] On more than one occasion, she voiced a desire for a more peaceful, less driven way of life, yet she never stated a wish to leave business matters to her husband. She also always followed Morand's new ideas, at times even rather quickly. She seems to have been better able than he to prioritize the many issues facing them; she asked him, for instance, to reduce his demands when his plans for the Brotteaux were not advancing well. She never hesitated to advise her husband directly and firmly on the best course to follow with regard to a given issue, nor did she withhold her opinions when they disagreed. She concerned herself with all matters, whether narrowly technical or more broadly managerial, financial, social, or political in nature. All the pressures of business could be combined in a few words in her direct style. After having explained to Morand that an opportunity might present itself for them to lease several storefronts at the new theatre, she insisted that they would have to "grab them quickly" (*"agir vite et faire main basse sur les magasins"*) and immediately decried these pressures by concluding, *"Chiennes d'affaires."*[24]

Antoinette Levet's role ought to be seen as distinct from that of women who found themselves with the principal responsibility for businesses either because of unique personal circumstances or because the businesses were linked to the activities of their male partners. In the case of many small-scale ventures such as the manufacture of verdigris (copper acetate) in Montpellier, women ran operations that were, initially at least, secondary to a local industry – in this case the wine-making trade, which provided *marc de raisin*, the pressed grape skins that were the key ingredient in the necessary chemical process. In the exceptional case of the commercial and financial director of a major concern like Oberkampf's celebrated calico plant, we find a woman married to a man who wished only to be a passive partner in the venture. Most often, women came to the forefront of an enterprise when they were widowed. Generally, these examples testify to the ability of a minority of women to achieve some form of economic independence.[25] In the case at hand, we have an illustration of a tight partnership between spouses. Such partnerships were likely more common than economic leadership by a woman emancipated by the death of her spouse. Yet while the participation of both spouses in a trade might be expected among shopkeepers or home-based manufacturers (all cases documented in Lyon to the extent that such small or medium-sized operations have left records), it could also blossom within more dynamic economic sectors, or even among professional milieus where education reinforced male prerogatives.[26] Finally, because in this case the partnership was not driven by financial need, it is possible to suggest that it reflected personal choices based on a particular understanding of gender relations. Naturally, there was no context in that age for the formulation of such thoughts (and certainly not in terms that would suit a modern understanding), and Morand remained the public face of their partnership.

Morand was most often called an architect, a title that carried much prestige. He worked at a time when the profession was only just emerging in Lyon, where building contractors, often masons by trade, and a few renowned outsiders had generally dominated the field.[27] But it was also a time when the technical skills that would become the preserve of engineers were gaining in importance, notably through the rise of the Ponts et chaussées and the military corps of engineers trained at Mézières.[28] The increasing pace and scope of urban development also made room for the speculative ambitions of those who were able to assemble the financial and political clout necessary to any large-scale project; such people came to be known in the French context as *promoteurs*, or developers. It also attracted enlightened thinkers who dreamed of alleviating the ills of early-modern cities. At the same time, the profession of architecture was asserting itself and dividing along more specialized lines.[29] Morand refused to abide by the restrictions implicit in this last trend. His artistic leanings were certainly not revolutionary. Many of his drawings suited the rococo style in vogue in Lyon at the time, which he applied to generally simple, if not purely, neo-classical lines. Yet his Plan circulaire shows that he liked to think beyond the level of individual buildings. His technical competencies were undeniable. For lack of formal training, they rested on a deep interest and a keen eye, as well as a willingness to seek advice through publications and correspondence. (Here, we note again the importance of Italy as a source of inspiration for techniques and skills unknown in France.) Like other processes of professionalization, the emergence of modern architecture entailed a shifting blend of recognition, affirmation, and challenge. Morand's position in this contested field was made more uncertain by his lack of official credentials, by the tensions characteristic of a provincial city that was always uneasy with the trends of court and capital, and by his own attachment to a broad definition of his role.

Morand's professional choices were further complicated by the fact that, while his vision of a future left bank was most audacious, the economic interests behind his projects precluded grandiose or striking experiments. He wished to change the face of Lyon but proposed a self-effacing wooden bridge to do so. Similarly, even though the technical milieu in which he functioned was dynamic and open, his choices were consistently rather modest. Had he applied himself to the world of manufacturing, his talents and preferences would perhaps recall the pragmatic advances taking place in England, more than the prestigious investments often associated with the French context, to refer to a classic comparison.[30] Rather than flamboyant designs, it is his careful management of work sites, indeed, his rare ability to complete a large project on time and on budget, that distinguish him from many of his contemporaries.

Through his five decades in Lyon, Morand naturally pursued his own interests in a city that was familiar with the building of rapid fortunes. However, he was also responding to a deep-seated need for urban renewal, perhaps more evident in this crowded city than elsewhere, at a time when reflection on the nature of cities was laying the ground for what would eventually become the new science of urban planning. Morand's plans were favourably received in Paris, where they could be seen in their more abstract form without the impediments of a local context. Morand's self-taught competencies were quickly recognized in the capital, in part because the process of institutionalization that would later define the training and affiliations required of anyone likely to advance large-scale civic transformations was still incomplete. Yet Versailles did not always have the means to achieve its ambitions, and Lyon was not Paris, steeped in a long history of direct royal rule, nor was it a small provincial town where the wishes of the intendant reached above local divisions. Even Versailles's key reforms often appeared inconclusive when seen from Lyon. Indeed, Morand's many trips to Paris illustrate the often ambiguous nature of relations between central and regional forces under the Old Regime. The absence of a clear division and hierarchy of powers left him at the mercy of shifting alliances, delivering a characteristic mix of achievements and failures.

The great Hôtel-Dieu also placed its own interests first. Its financial woes, however, dictated a policy of retrenchment that was incompatible with the leading role that its place in the city's history and its near monopoly of real estate demanded in the opening of the left bank to urbanization. The traditional uncertainties associated with other local institutions such as the Sénéchaussée and the Cour des Monnaies were compounded by unfinished reforms that successively eliminated and recreated them in lesser forms. They could only offer shaky bases of power from which to oppose or support large-scale projects such as those proposed by Morand. The Consulat for its part, recognized its inability to lead any substantial transformation of the city but could not give up its ambitions to control local affairs. It could oppose, but never ignore, the actions of royal courts that offered an alternative path of promotion for local elites. It could resist, but ultimately not overrule, the informed opinions of the intendant, and it could delay, but never fully stall, direct ministerial interventions. To this mix must be added the voices of various religious figures and bodies, particularly that of the archbishop and the comtes of Lyon, always influential, yet increasingly challenged in the last decades of the Old Regime. The Villeroy family was yet another node of power. Far from wielding the kind of clout it had had a few generations earlier, it remained busy defending its myriad entrenched interests. Finally, one needs to recall that these many visible and vocal power bases were linked by personal, family, and business connections that were mostly hidden from the gaze of outsiders – and historians. Long-standing feuds and divisions could undermine apparent coalitions of interests, just as they could imperil the financial schemes indispensable to large-scale projects.

In this wealthy city, all of these institutions and the individuals who dominated them were powerful enough to stand their ground and advance their own claims, at least to a point. They were also always eager and able to challenge the claims of their rivals. To a great extent, such a multipolar structure of power suited the Crown, torn as it was between its centralist impulses and its fundamental respect for ancient institutions. A divided local political stage was likely preferable to a clear hierarchy that could eventually rally the kind of opposition coalitions that the Parlement of Paris was always eager to build. Similarly, the Consulat could only fear the creation of a more direct and powerful link between the city and Versailles. It welcomed the disappearance of the Conseil Supérieur that had embodied just such a risk between 1771 and 1774. While it certainly decried the limitations of its own powers, the Consulat knew that the overlapping and imprecise ways in which royal will was expressed in Lyon left room for the types of manoeuvres it excelled at. None of these factors were unique to Lyon, but in the kingdom's second largest city, the many institutions with a share of power were all strong enough to create a lively and unpredictable mix.

Morand's business strategies were fully attuned to the particularities of the society he lived in. They were focused on the grey area where public and private interests met, where freedom of enterprise and corporate privileges overlapped. His bridge was protected by a royal monopoly, he fought to keep a lifelong pension for his work on the theatre, and he sought subsidies for the Brotteaux as well as the privileges of the second order. As late as 1788, Morand (or at least his son) hoped that the new political circumstances, and particularly the creation of regional assembly, would offer him a new chance at being nominated surveyor of Lyon "for life."[31] If we add to this the fact that many of his private commissions emanated from public figures who themselves did not distinguish very strictly between their own purse and that of their institution, it is clear that Morand's sense of entrepreneurship and independence never ignored the lure of public institutions. No doubt he shared in the dual vision, the "*deux rêves*," exposed by J.-P. Hirsch; for all his actions suggest that he valued entrepreneurial freedom, as well as the order and relative security of a regulated corporate world. Or, to refer to a classic study of a significant contemporary of Morand's, he used privilege to build an enterprise – and vice versa.[32] However, the visible hand of royal power and institutions never precluded rivalries.

Morand's tenure of a royal monopoly would have been enough to bring him enemies, not only from the ranks of envious rivals but also because such *privilèges* were under attack, most notably in the wake of the Physiocratic movement. Increasingly, privileges were seen as antithetical to the freedom of initiatives that attracted the forward-looking minds of the age. Yet the monarchy was clearly not in a position to build on its own the infrastructure called for by economic development and, in particular, better communications – another physiocratic wish. This was not a problem for which an easy solution existed. Eventually, the revolutionary authorities regulated the granting of monopolies to reward innovations, but the demands of investors involved in large-scale public works remained problematic through many regimes. Most directly, the dispute between Morand and his associates regarding the final cost of the bridge reminds us that the Old Regime lacked the most rudimentary means to control such lucrative arrangements between the private and public sectors.

Discussions of the relative merits of private and public initiatives were further muddled by the fact that bids for royal support used a language familiar to the early liberal thinkers who had denounced such interventions as distortions of natural law. Morand, for his part, argued that his bridge was cost-effective, sound, innovative, and beneficial to the public. His supporters, from the intendant to the minister, recognized his right and that of his associates to substantial returns. Naturally, his opponents questioned all of these points, but the unique importance of the Hôtel-Dieu to the city allowed them to associate the interests of that institution with those of the public in general. They could also denounce the speculative nature of Morand's plans, because the hospital was the owner of a ferry monopoly that provided it with limited but secure returns that contrasted with the potentially large but uncertain benefits of the bridge. In the end, Morand's wealth was secured by a royal monopoly rather than speculation, while the Hôtel-Dieu managed its left bank properties so ponderously that what could have been a profitable speculative bubble was transformed into a century-long divestment that still did not solve its financial woes. For its part, the city was left with a well-used bridge; but no new neighbourhood emerged for several generations and key functions relocated across the Rhône only very slowly. All parties might have benefited from more daring and decisive initiatives. Any calculation to that effect, however, ought to take into account the shocks of an unexpected revolutionary decade that radically changed the city's demography and economy and made available *intra muros* lands long hoarded by religious institutions. In a matter as complex as urbanization, contrafactual history has little to offer.

In the end, Morand's endeavours are best understood when located within the multipolar power structure of the Old Regime, a dynamic system perhaps most evident from the perspective of a great and wealthy but nonetheless secondary city such as Lyon. The complexity of this world was illustrated, almost to the point of caricature, by the Hôtel-Dieu, obviously fully attuned to such imperatives, when it took care to have the letters patent it received in 1743 for its ferries across the Rhône registered by eleven distinct authorities.[33] Morand could certainly never have hoped to reach that level of consensus for his plans.

This composite power structure had several implications. It doomed many enterprises, even technically successful ones, to long delays and partial outcomes, involving many disparate parties in discussions that would today call for specialized and precisely organized expertise. To those engaged in such tedious and perilous struggles, royal fiat often appeared as the only higher recourse, although it could arouse deep-rooted objections and jeopardize local support. All of these patterns are reflected in some of the better-known dimensions of life and work under the Old Regime: the remarkable propensity to litigation; the burdensome, if logical, tendency to live off the returns of earlier investments rather than of enterprise (*rentier* investments); the vitality of countless networks of patronage; and frequent hesitations between respect for ancient contracts and genuine impulses toward thorough reforms. However, these essential characteristics of an age and a regime were never static pillars simultaneously guiding and containing entrepreneurs. Rather, they were dynamic forces meant to be manipulated, reassembled to suit a new project, a new partnership. They represented opportunities as much as obstacles. Eighteenth-century entrepreneurs did not wait for a golden age of market freedom. They played one institution against another, taking advantage of every influential voice to advance their plans.

Morand's proposals for a radical redesign of Lyon were certainly not ignored. They were heard and assessed at a time when the city was discovering the potential of its eastern and southern marches along the Rhône. Many voices were raised in support or in opposition, often in the name of powerful corporate bodies steeped in local politics. Each defended its own interests, but generally in a language that addressed contemporary concerns for the public good. Most striking, however, was the absence of a visible and effective hierarchy among the many poles of power when it came to an issue as radically new as expanding the city across the Rhône. Even ministerial might could not always cut through the shifting alignments triggered by Morand's initiatives among influential local institutions and individuals. Furthermore, neither in Paris nor in the city itself was there the kind of expertise that could have taken the debates beyond the level of particular interests or the broad concerns characteristic of the age. An influential science of urban planning was still many decades away. New priorities, such as those of the hygienist movement that inherited many of the intuitions of the aerist school familiar to Morand, had to grow into respected sciences before they could be institutionalized and entrusted with enough power. All of these factors were at work in many other contexts. In Lyon, all hopes and hesitations were organized and strengthened by the Rhône. Just as its new quays displayed tantalizing space to its crowded inhabitants, this powerful river concretized material and mental borders. It gave a focus to the fears associated with an understanding of the city as a circumscribed entity. Rival interests met inconclusively in this largely unpolarized field of public discussion. For lack of familiarity with the issue of expansion on the scale made possible by crossing the Rhône, Morand's propositions met with a field of mixed reactions that could not stop his initial plans, but ultimately undermined his greater vision. His new bridge led to a world of make-believe entertainment sites and *trompe-l'oeil* facades that were neither country nor city.[34]

Morand's plans were not irrelevant to the needs of the city, nor were they simply untimely. Neither were they stalled by a resurgent corporate opposition to an ambitious private initiative. Rather, they were eventually derailed by the absence of an authority able to manage and control, or at least coordinate and prioritize, the demands of all parties in the name of a legitimate, widely recognized system of reference relevant to what was, in Lyon, a radically new issue – projecting the city across the river that had always defined its eastern limit. The corporate order of the Old Regime and private initiatives, despite the tensions between them, were both legitimate to the players in the field, just as old and new conceptions of the city coexisted for many decades. Yet entrepreneurship is easily reified and sketched in opposition to its environment, while its dogged or inspired heroes are lionized, wittingly or not. Morand consistently decried the forces that frustrated his efforts; and in a city admittedly partial to failed or flawed heroes, his name (for naturally that of his partner is ignored) still stands for an enlightened but premature projection of Lyon across the Rhône.[35]

To recover a sense of the complementarity of the factors at work in this triangular joust among established institutions, enlightened ideas, and entrepreneurial tenacity, we must remember that historical agents faced neither eternal structures nor irresistible trends. All functioned within a conjunction of structures characteristic of their time, region, and field of action, a durable but not unchanging combination that shaped ambitions and was itself shaped by potent and pertinent initiatives. To place an enterprise fully within its context is to capture its roots and its uniqueness, its vulnerabilities and its transformative powers.

The calculations of all parties, however contradictory, were rational because they accounted for factors within their reach, implicitly or explicitly leaving aside what they deemed imponderable or unmovable at that moment. The resulting alignment of forces may seem, in retrospect, predictable, original, or merely confusing. To those who fought those battles, they were rewarding or disappointing, but never predetermined. Confrontations probed the relative weight of established and new interests, yielding a new combination of powers that prepared the ground for the next initiatives. Only this articulation of trends and events, structures and agents will account for the mix of confidence and trepidation that sustained any entrepreneurial trajectory.

Jean-Antoine Morand and Antoinette Levet were often disappointed and, perhaps, even bitter at times. However, they were never defeated; for their plans had an undeniable appeal rooted in the desire of the age for urban improvement. They had the support of many enlightened circles, and their rivals were, in their view, obstinate and short-sighted. Still, resistance to a dramatic perspective of urban expansion was real. Wealth and fame eluded the Morands until the end, and the promise of a better city remained just that, a key idea of the age unfulfilled. Nevertheless, their bridge proved very profitable for them and their associates, as well as for the city. Every weekend, thousands revisited the relationship between the crowded city and the open plain across the Rhône, merrily if unintentionally. Jean-Antoine Morand and Antoinette Levet had recast discussions of expansion in Lyon, showing that enlightened visions of urban renewal and growth would not simply add to the existing canvas. Their entrepreneurial zeal had revealed the radical dimensions of a project attuned to the sensibilities of the age. Their hard work had transformed the city, but it would take another age and a different context for the new Lyon to materialize. This was not their goal, and Morand himself was too tenacious a fighter to have been pleased with the ambiguous status of hero before his time. In fact, he was very much a man of his time – an age of powerful ideas, eager moves, and mixed results. That his name remains attached to a bridge may, in the end, be most appropriate. He took his willing compatriots to a new shore, but a modern city remained to be built. The importance of an enterprise is not simply related to the boldness of its vision, the fury of its rivals, or even the newness of its results. The measure of an enterprise lies in the relevance of its promises and the depth of the debates it triggers.

APPENDICES

Jean-Antoine Morand's Accounts (Business and Personal), 1748–1793

	Expenses	Key transactions, events, and undertakings	Revenues	Documented loans
Sept. 1748 – Dec. 1750	1,506 lt (business)		4,182 lt	
1751	1,621 lt (business)		3,836 lt	
1752	1,368 lt (household) + 1,117 lt (business)		3,139 lt	
1753	1,206 lt (household)		missing	
1754	1,837 lt (business)		4,498 lt	
1755	1,949 lt (household)		missing	
1756	13,038 lt (incl. or not 2,326 lt for household)		missing	
1757	29,532 lt	Purchase of first lot at Saint-Clair, beginning of construction.	missing	
1758	23,218 lt		6,487 lt (incomplete)	
1759	39,000 lt approx.	Marriage with Antoinette Levet (39,000 lt dowry)	38,633 lt (incl. payments for theatre)	
1760	37,000 lt approx.	Construction first house at Saint-Clair after two-year interruption. Italian travels.	43,923 lt (incl. 10,654 lt for work on theatre done in 1757)	19,200 lt
1761	65,834 lt		60,338 lt	
1762	55,703 lt		55,703 lt	

	Expenses	Key transactions, events, and undertakings	Revenues	Documented loans
1763	71,888 lt		74,631 lt	
1764	76,676 lt	Sale of first Saint-Clair house (207,000 lt). Purchase of second lot at Saint-Clair (28,680 lt); beginning of construction.	137,000 lt approx.	
1765	28,000 lt approx. (incomplete)	Purchase of land in Brotteaux, and sale of 2 lots (7,500 and 4,000 lt).	73,000 lt approx.	
1766	missing	Purchase of third lot at Saint-Clair (23,665 lt).	47,000 lt approx.	8,200 lt
1767	72,556 lt (until 3 March 1768)	Sale of second house, Saint-Clair (250,000 lt); Construction of third house at Saint-Clair.	162,327 lt	
1768	missing		90,000 lt (incomplete)	12,000 lt
1769	83,804 lt		87,438 lt	
1770	120,749 lt		119,288 lt	50,000 lt and 15,000 lt
1771	67,263 (incomplete?)		62,548 lt (incomplete)	
1772	101,897 lt	Beginning of bridge construction. Sale of lot, Brotteaux (15,000 lt).	99,884 lt	8,307 lt
1773	missing	Sale of one share in bridge.	100,909	4,200 lt
1774	108,348 lt (incl. 24,502 lt related to the bridge)		105,054 lt (incl. 23,515 lt from the bridge)	4,100 lt
1775	120,641 lt	Sale of a lot and house in Brotteaux (18,000 lt). End of bridge construction.	119,151 lt	
1776	62,147 lt		62,597 lt	25,156 lt
1777	71,445 lt		70,611 lt	

	Expenses	Key transactions, events, and undertakings	Revenues	Documented loans
1778	75,183 lt	Purchase of Machy estate (120,000 lt).	74,557 lt	18,030 lt
1779	132,161 lt	Sale of one share in bridge, exact date unknown.	132,192 lt	12,874 lt
1780	109,083 lt		112,324 lt	27,349 lt
1781	70,451 lt	Sale of lot, Brotteaux (6,000 lt).	128,950 lt	23,286 lt
1782	101,406 lt		136,995 lt	17,689 lt
1783	90,549 lt	Sale of lot, Brotteaux.	89,798 lt	2,887 lt
1784	104,883 lt	Sale of first part of La Paisible (33,000 lt).	103,700 lt	29,246 lt
1785	68,559 lt	Marriage of Antoine Morand; he notably received the Machy domain and one share of the bridge. Sale of lot, Brotteaux.	68,434 lt	
1786	59,717 lt	Marriage of Eléonore Morand, receiving 16,000 lt dowry, one share of the bridge, and the house inherited by her mother)	55,905 lt	
1787	75,058 lt	Sale of second part of La Paisible (17,000 lt).	75,120 lt	
1788	125,509 lt		62,663 lt	
1789	missing	Sale of 2 lots, Brotteaux (2,800 lt and unknown amount).	56,424 lt	
1790	missing		missing	
1791	67,309 lt		56,178 lt	
1792	100,501 lt	37,000 lt received from Machério estate. Sale of lot, Brotteaux.	89,521 lt	2,704 lt

	Expenses	Key transactions, events, and undertakings	Revenues	Documented loans
1793	67,107 lt or 86,423 lt and incomplete	Sale of la Rotonde and one lot in Brotteaux (16,000 lt + 15,000 lt).	92,720 lt for 7 months only	

Note. Revenues and expenses are drawn from 14 II 006 and 007; "Documented loans" figures refer to obligations listed most likely in 1792, 14 II 007; other transactions that are mentioned are referenced elsewhere in text. The date attached to an obligation is often only an approximation of the date at which the loan was effectively made, since the obligation could, after some delay, formalize a debt growing over the preceding months. Similarly, sales and purchases were not settled immediately, but often over several years.

Ownership of Saint-Clair Bridge (Number of Shares Held, 1786–1793)

1786	1789	1792	1793
J.-A. Morand (5) A. Morand (1; son)	J.-A. Morand (5)	J.-A. Morand (5)	J.-A. Morand (5)
	Paul-Bertrand Besson (1; son-in-law)	Besson (1)	
Ballet (1; bought 7 Apr. 1777 from Flachon)	Ballet (1)	Ballet (1)	Ballet (1)
Flachon brothers (8)	Flachon bros. (3)	Flachon bros. (8)	Flachon bros. (5)
de Bouffier (1) Minel (1)	de Bouffier (1)	de Bouffier (1)	de Bouffier (1)
Daffaux de Glatta (1.5)	de Glatta (1.5)	de Glatta (1.5)	de Glatta (1.5)
Mauro (1)	Mauro (1)	Mauro (1)	Mauro (1)
J. Adamoly (1.5; bought before 1784)	Adamoly (1.5)	Adamoly (1.5)	Adamoly (2.5)
J.-L. Boeuf de Curis (1; bought from Terrasse before 1783)	de Curis (1)	de Curis (1)	de Curis (1)
J. Alhumbert (1)	Alhumbert (2)	Alhumbert (2)	Alhumbert (1)
Veuve Dumenge (2)	Vve. Dumenge (2)	Vve. Dumenge (2)	Vve. Dumenge (2)
M. Bertrand (1; bought before 1784)	Bertrand (1)	Bertrand (1)	Bertrand (1)
*Finguerlin bros. (1)	Finguerlin bros. (1)	Finguerlin bros. (1)	
	de Pougelon (1)	de Pougelon (1)	de Pougelon (1)

1786	1789	1792	1793
	Veuve Jordan (1)	Vve. Jordan (1)	Vve. Jordan (1)
Hélié (1; Flachon's brother-in-law; bought 1778, from Terrasse)	Hélié (1)	Hélié (1)	Hélié (1)
Berlié (1; bought 21 June 1786)	Berlié (1)		
Richard (1)			
		Cambiaso (1)	Cambiaso (1)
	Chevandier (1)		
	Reveroni (1)		
	Delpeche (1)		
	Durand (1)		
			V.-P. Bertrand (1)
			Giraud (1; bought from Besson, 18 Apr. 1792)
			Savoy (1)
			Dumarest (1)

Source: From Book of Deliberations, 14 II 023 (see decision dated 29 May 1786; the sharp fluctuations of the number of shares under the name of Flachon suggest that some of their shares may have, at times, been under the names of relatives or associates).

* The Finguerlin brothers were Swiss bankers with a strong presence in Lyon.

Brotteaux Lands Sold by Morand (with Comparisons)

Date of Sale	Buyer	Surface	Price	Price per unit	Reference
9 August 1765	Jean-Etienne Laboré (to Flachon before 1772)	22,500 ft²	7,500 lt	6.7 sols/ ft²	3 E 9184, Not. A.-J. Caillot
10 August 1765	Fleurant et Perrache (to Guillin de Pougelon before 1778)	32,000 ft²	4,000 lt	2.5 sols/ ft²	Not. Fromental, 3 E 9709
29 Nov. 1772	Gilibert – sale cancelled		(15,000 lt)		14 II 018
20 May 1775	Antonio Spréafico	69,000 ft² (Barre)	18,000 lt (incl. build-ing)	5.2 sols/ ft²	14 II 018; Barre and Feuga
7 April 1777	J.-F. Pélisson	1,500 ft² – building?	2,000 lt	26.7 sols/ ft²	Not. Guyot, 3 E 5707
Up to agree-ment with H.-D.	4 sales	125,000 ft² = 11,34 bicherées	31,500 lt		
7 April 1781	Fillion and Mondet	15,000 ft²	6,000 lt	8 sols/ ft²	Not. J.-G. Berthon de Fromental, 3 E 5110
5 Sept. 1783	Michel Bertrand	500 ft²			14 II 018
30 Oct. 1784 and 22 March 1787	Descroix et al., for the Sagesse lodge	55,000 ft² (incl. house La Paisible)	33,000 lt + 17,000 lt	14.6 sols/ ft² (inc. bldg.)	14 II 019; Barre and Feuga

Date of Sale	Buyer	Surface	Price	Price per unit	Reference
4 March 1785	Joseph Padovany	15,000 ft²	8,000 lt	10.7 sols/ ft²	AD 69, 10 C 1240; Barre and Feuga
7 January 1789	Alexis Regnier	3,784 ft²	1,892 lt	10 sols/ ft²	Not. J.-B. Durand, 3 E 11132
22 March 1789	Vincent Bessière and ?	With building	17,000 lt		AD 69, 10 C 1291
24 January 1791	Albert and Pernoux	7,525 ft² (with small building)	2,800 lt	7.4 sols/ ft²	Not. J. Girard, 3 E 5265
11 August 1792	Rast de Maupas	14,875 ft²	10,000 lt	13.45 sols/ ft²	Not. J. Dussurgey, 3 E 4733
27 March 1793	Jean-Laurent Barbier	3,800 ft² (incl. new house, La Rotonde)	16,000 lt	84 sols/ ft² (incl. bldg.)	14 II 019
24 April 1793	Reigner and Challivet	45,000 ft²	24,000 lt	10.7 sols/ ft²	inv. 9 prairial an 6, 14 II 007 – Not. Devilliers; Barre and Feuga).
After agreement with H.-D	10 sales	160,484 ft² + unknown acreage	135,692 lt + unknown small sum		
Altogether	13 or 14 sales	285,484 + ? ft²	167,792 lt+		

Notes. Complementary information (as indicated) drawn from Barre and Feuga, *Morand et les Brotteaux*. The sale to Vincent Bessière (1789) is not mentioned anywhere beside its registration.

After the death of his father, Antoine Morand de Jouffrey sold 3,750 square feet to Claude Grimaud, carpenter, for 1,500 fr (it was specified that this sum was to be paid in metal currency, at the pre-1789 rate, amounting to an equivalent of 8 sols/ft²; 14 II 030, 29 Ventose, year 7, or 19 March 1799). A letter likely dated from the day before this sale mentioned a larger sale (7,500 ft²) to two buyers (a carpenter and a furniture maker), at the price of 10 sols/ft² but added that they would only pay three years later, although they would work for Antoine Morand, their bills to be deducted from the sums owed (14 II 035, Antoine Morand to Antoinette Levet).

Antoine's papers also contained an undated draft of a sale agreement with an unnamed buyer, to sell 22,500 ft² for 67,500 fr (i.e., 3 fr/f², or 60 sols/f²; the Lyon unit was used in this case; 14 II 030).

Estimate of area devoted to streets and square on Morand's land:
Grand Cours (east-west): 72 ft x 700 ft = 50,400 ft²
Place Morand: 122 ft x 86 ft = 10,492 ft²
Allée des Désirs (east-west): 36 ft x 700FT + 36ft x 86ft = 25,200 + 3,096 = 28,296 ft²

Allée des Soupirs (east-west): 36 ft x 700 ft + 36 ft x 86 ft = 28,296 ft^2
Rue Morand (north-south): 35 ft x 544 ft = 19,040 ft^2
Petit Cours (north-south): 40 ft x 544 ft = 21,760 ft^2
Supplement main square: 4 x 50 ft x 50 ft = 10,000 ft^2
  Total land reserved for streets and squares on Morand's lot: 168,284 ft^2

  Morand claimed to have set aside for such public use 146,502 ft^2 (1.72 ha), the difference likely coming from the fact that part of the land taken by the rue Morand and Petit Cours may have been taken from the holdings of the Hôtel-Dieu. The figure given by Morand amounts to thirty percent of the land he had originally bought (1.72 ha out of 5.6 ha). If a ratio of twenty-five percent is applied to calculate the acreage left to public use over the 43 ha scheduled for sale in 1781, some 32 ha were offered for sale by the hospital and Morand.

Lands Sold by Perrache or His Successors at the Head of the Compagnie Perrache

Date	Buyer	Surface	Price	Price/ft^2	Reference
9 May 1777	P. Adobé	2,500 ft^2	8,000 lt	64 sols/ft^2	3 E 5707, Not. O. Guyot
4 Oct. 1777	J.-M. Favier	2,448 ft^2	9,100 lt	74 sols/ft^2	3 E 5707, Not. O. Guyot
5 Nov. 1777	J.-B. Bonne	3,863 ft^2	17,383 lt	90 sols/ft^2	3 E 5707, Not. O. Guyot
27 Feb. 1778	C. Durand	3,081 ft^2	12,324 lt	80 sols/ft^2	3 E 5707, Not. O. Guyot
27 Feb. 1778	R. Tourau	3,525 ft^2	5,287 lt	30 sols/ft^2	3 E 5707, Not. O. Guyot
12 Sept. 1778	J.-M. Favier	646 ft^2	2,584 lt	80 sols/ft^2	3 E 5707, Not. O. Guyot
14 Sept. 1778	J.-F. Lomot	1,840 ft^2	7,360 lt	80 sols/ft^2	3 E 5707, Not. O. Guyot
15 Sept. 1778	C. Biolay	2,495 ft^2	9,972 lt	80 sols/ft^2	3 E 5707, Not. O. Guyot
1 Apr. 1779	de Laurencin	37,750 ft^2	37,750 lt	20 sols/ft^2	3 E 5708, Not. O. Guyot
11 Nov. 1781	Antoine Bertholon	1,080 ft^2	1,080 lt	20 sols/ft^2	3 E 4505, Not. P. Dubosols
25 Nov. 1781	Charles Giraud	493 ft^2	493 lt	20 sols/ft^2	3 E 4505, Not. P. Dubost
17 Nov. 1792	Dantin and Roset	44,100 ft^2	20,000 lt	9 sols/ft^2	3 E 4505, Not. P. Dubost
4 Mar. 1793	J.-B. Odobé	16,790 ft^2	27,200 lt	32.4 sols/ft^2	3 E 4505, Not. P. Dubost

The Cost of Real-Estate in (or near) Lyon From the Affiches de Lyon: Houses Sought or Offered for Sale in Lyon

Date of Advertisement	Price Quoted	Nature of Transaction; Location of Property
N. 16, 16 Apr. 1760	50,000 lt	Seeking loan to purchase property valued at [quoted values]
N. 1, 4 Jan. 1764	70–80,000 lt	Seeking house priced between [quoted values]
N. 8, 22 Feb. 1764	20,000 lt	Selling house, rented 1,000 lt and estimated at 5%
N. 11, 15 Mar. 1764	50,000 lt	Seeking higher offer over existing offer of [quoted value]; corner rue Longue and rue Rolland; rented 3,000 lt
N. 11, 15 Mar. 1764	20,000 lt	Seeking higher offer over existing offer of [quoted value]; corner rue St-Jean and place de la Baleine; rented 1,500 lt
N. 10, 6 Mar. 1765	30–40,000 lt	Seeking house priced between [quoted values]; rue de l'Enfant-qui-pisse
N. 10, 6 Mar. 1765	30,000 lt	Seeking house priced around [quoted value]; quai St-Vincent
N. 20, 15 May 1765	30–40,000 lt	Seeking house priced between [quoted values]; rue Tupin
N. 1, 3 Jan. 1766	20,000 lt	Seeking house priced around [quoted value]; rue St-Jean
N. 3, 15 Jan. 1766	20–50,000 lt	Seeking house priced between [quoted values]; in a "nice" neighbourhood, such as near St-Nizier church
N. 26, 26 June 1766	50–60,000 lt	Seeking house priced between [quoted values]; rues Grenette or Bois
N. 26, 26 June 1766	60–100,000 lt	Seeking house priced between [quoted values]; Ainay

Date of Advertisement	Price Quoted	Nature of Transaction; Location of Property
N. 3, 21 Jan. 1767	15–50,000 lt	Several houses for sale, priced between [quoted values]; in "good" neighbourhoods
N. 10, 11 Mar. 1767	80–100,000 lt	Seeking house priced between [quoted values]; rues Tupin, Grenette, Trois-Carreaux, or Mercière
N. 24, 17 June 1767	100–200,000 lt	Seeking house priced between [quoted values]; near place Louis-le-Grand
N. 28, 15 July 1767	80–100,000 lt	Seeking house priced between [quoted values]; rues Lafond or Puits-Gaillot
N. 1, 8 Jan. 1768	60–70,000 lt	Seeking house priced between [quoted values]; quais of the Rhône or the Saône, or near St-Nizier
N. 17, 13 Feb. 1771	108,000 lt	Seeking higher offer over existing offer of [quoted value]; rue Tupin
N. 8, 20 Feb. 1771	40–50,000 lt	Seeking house priced between [quoted values]; in "nice" neighbourhood
N. 8, 20 Feb. 1771	20,000 lt	Seeking house priced around [quote value]
N. 9, 27 Feb. 1771	60–100,000 lt	Several houses for sale, priced between [quoted values];
N. 9, 27 Feb. 1771	20–150,000 lt	Seeking houses priced between [quoted values]; near places St-Nizier, St-Pierre, Carmes, or Terreaux
N. 28, 10 July 1771	10–150,000 lt	Seeking houses priced between [quoted values]

From other sources. Among the figures that may be gleaned from the existing literature, the most meaningful are those associated with a detailed study of buildings. For instance, Olivier Zeller's study of the rental system characteristic of Lyon quotes the following prices for the Maison du Chameau (in fact, two four and five stories buildings, one fronting on the Saône): it sold for over 80,000 lt in December 1719, and for 139,735 lt only three years later (18 March 1723); in the 1780s, its owner valued it at between 147,000 lt and 168,157 lt. Early in the 1780s, the building next to this one had burned, and the empty land was valued at more than 82,400 lt for some 3,100 ft^2 ("A l'enseigne du chameau. Manières d'habiter, manières de gérer à Lyon au XVIIIe siècle," *Cahiers d'histoire*, 1993, n. 1, pp. 25–54). The same author also probed the estate of the Petitot family (Simon Petitot had been a well-known hydraulic engineer) when, late in the 1780s, two smaller houses were sold for 44,000 lt and 15,000 lt respectively ("Un exemple de gestion immobilière : l'administration du patrimoine foncier de la famille Petitot [Lyon, 1786–1790]," p. 257, in *Le sol et l'immeuble : les formes dissociées de propriété immobilière dans les villes de France et d'Italie [XIIe–XIXe siècle]*, edited by Olivier Faron and Etienne Hubert, 253–65, Lyon: Presses Universitaires de Lyon, 1995).

It would be most helpful to document the cost of building a house, but such data are rare. Most relevant to our study is no doubt the notarial contract signed in the summer of 1765 by J.-E. Laboré, a well-known Lyon entrepreneur (who bought land from Morand not long after), to have the architect Ratter thoroughly rebuild a house on the rue Buisson. The cost of the project was estimated at less than 30,000 lt, although it would only be determined after completion. The plans show a house some thirty-five feet wide, four stories above the ground floor, six rooms per floor on average (AD 69, 3 E 9184, Not. André-Joseph Caillat (répertoire), 20 June 1765).

Properties Sought or For Sale outside Lyon
(from the *Affiches de Lyon*)

Date of Transaction	Price Quoted	Nature of Transaction; Location of Property
N. 44, 3 Nov. 1763	30–60,000 lt	Seeking country home on the shores of the Saône, less than 9 kms from city
N 27, 4 July 1764	116,000 lt	Selling land – seigneurie, some 70 kms from Lyon, yielding 3,500 to 6,000 lt/year
N. 35, 29 Aug. 1764	300,000 lt	Sugar plantation and refinery for sale, land, machinery, and slaves, yielding 40,000 lt/year
N. 22, 30 May 1765	30,000 lt	Estate for sale, some 40 kms from Lyon, yielding 9,000 lt/year
N. 14, 3 Apr. 1766	12,000 lt	Seeking small country home near Lyon
N. 19, 7 May 1766	30,000 lt	Country house for sale, St-Germain-au-Mont-d'Or
N. 43, 22 Oct. 1766	80,000 lt	Seeking country estate, near Guillotière
N. 30, 24 July 1771	65,000 lt	Selling estate 15 kms from Lyon, house and 180 bicherées
N. 30, 24 July 1771	110,000 lt	Selling large estate in the Bresse, rented 4,200 lt
N. 30, 24 July 1771	65,000 lt	Selling estate in the Beaujolais

Notes

I have used the following abbreviations in the notes:

AML   Archives municipales de Lyon

14 II   Fonds Morand, Archives municipales de Lyon

AD 69   Archives départementales du Rhône

BMPD   Bibliothèque municipale de Lyon – Part-Dieu – Section ancienne

UNITS OF MEASUREMENT

1 14 II 010.

MONETARY UNITS AND PRICES

1 14 II 010; Cottin, "Le chantier du nouvel Hôtel-Dieu."

2 Young, Travels in France, 313–14, or the more complete *Voyages en France*, 800-4, 976; Mascoli, "Sur la route de Rome".

3 Coste et al., eds., *Un ingénieur des Lumières*. For a range of other figures, see Grenier, *Séries économiques françaises*.

INTRODUCTION

1 "Le voyageur [entrant dans Lyon découvre] de petites rues étroites, tortueuses, désagréablement pavées [qui] s'ouvriront peine pour le recevoir. Là, il ne voit le ciel qu'en échantillon. A travers les longs toits qui s'avancent en saillie, il n'en découvre qu'une étroite bande azurée. On penserait que ses anciens habitants craignoient de recevoir librement les bénignes influences de l'air et de la lumière ... Je respirais peine au milieu de ces petites rues." Letter from M. C*** de T***, Secrétaire du roi, to

his friend M. de Br*** in Paris (cited in Galle, "Lettres sur un voyage," 350).

2 "Les quais sont le plus grand ornement de la place. Celui du Rhône surtout est de toute beauté; il a près d'une lieue de long et au moins quatre-vingt pieds de large, avec un beau trottoir pour les gens de pied" (Marchand, *Voyage en France*, 161).

3 "L'étranger [forcé de traverser Lyon sans s'y arrêter] n'a rien vu des laideurs de la ville, de ses rues étroites, fangeuses, mal pavées et mal entretenues; mais son imagination ne perdra jamais le souvenir [de] cette cité aux constructions colossales ... où la nature mêle ses magnificences aux travaux des hommes ..." (Bernard, *De Lyon à la Méditerranée*, 1–2).

4 Many other visitors shared such mixed impressions of Lyon; see sidebar 4 for references to some notable texts.

5 For broad studies of the early-modern urban context, see Benedict, *Cities and Social Change*, and Saupin, *Les villes en France*. More focused references relevant to the themes introduced here will be found in the chapters where they are discussed.

6 See for instance Chouliaraki and Fairclough, *Discourse in Late Modernity*, notably chapter 2, 19–36: "Social Life and Critical Social Science."

CHAPTER ONE

1 "Le sieur Morand, Peintre, demeurant rue Tupin, dans la maison de M. Einard, vis-à-vis des Halles, fait toutes sortes d'ouvrages de peinture, tapisseries l'huile, paysages et figures, sujets d'histoire, renfermées dans des cartouches rehaussées en or; tapisseries en détrempe, coloré ou camaieu, dans quel genre que ce soit, paravents, fresques, vernis, et tout ce qui dépend de la peinture, excepté le portrait." *Affiches de Lyon*, no. 5, 4 February 1750.

2 "Je suis transporté par les ouvrages de Palladio." Letter, 14 II 004, Morand to Levet, 16 February 1760.

3 "Rome m'enchante toujours plus. Je visite tout ... Je te dirais cependant entre nous que la jalousie commence se manifester ... ils craignent de trop m'instruire !" Letter, 14 II 004, Morand to Levet, 22 October 1760.

4 See his *lettres de tonsure*, the certificate attesting to this initial ceremony marking a young man's entry into the clergy, in 14 II 005, dated 1 September 1741 (his father died two months later). Morand's origins are sketched in Dureau et al., *Hommage à Morand*, 18–23.

5 Dureau et al., *Hommage à Morand*, 42. In a letter to his wife from Rome, Morand recalled having spent over a year in Paris (5 November

1760, 14 II 004), while his two first documented trips lasted four months (letters from Morand to his mother, from 9 December 1753 to 28 March 1754, in 14 II 004; 14 II 010; and accounts from 11 January to 15 May 1758, 14 II 007).

6 See Morand's letters dated 9 December 1753 and 4 January 1754, 14 II 004. Briançon was a town of 2,000 to 3,000 inhabitants in a very modestly urbanized province: Favier, *Les villes du Dauphiné*.

7 *L'oeuvre de Soufflot Lyon*, 250.

8 Garden, *Lyon et les Lyonnais*, 586 and following; Benoît and Saussac, *Guide historique*.

9 See how artistic, technical, and commercial talents combined in the brilliant career of a contemporary of Morand's in Lyon, Philippe de Lasalle (Hafter, "Philippe de Lasalle").

10 To place Louis xv's Metz illness in its context, see Antoine, *Louis xv*, 372 and following. Dureau et al., *Hommage à Morand*, 42.

11 Unless otherwise specified, references to Morand's early works over the following pages come from surviving account books (starting 1 September 1748, in 14 II 010; other mentions of early works found in 14 II 007; and letters and other documents from this period in 14 II 002 and 004). See text and reference for his advertisement in the *Affiches de Lyon* at the beginning of this chapter.

12 For the context in which such figures must be placed, see preliminary note on monetary units.

13 Morand had also been taking care of his younger brother, whom he placed with a Lyon draper late in 1751 and then sent back to Briançon in the hope that he might obtain a position in the Ponts et chaussées. In 1761 he again tried to help when his brother was a low-ranking soldier (14 II 004, Morand to his mother, 30 December 1751, 9 December 1753; Pons to Morand, 10 March 1752; Morand to Chauvelin, 20 October 1761). In 1755 Morand also helped his sister Victoire to receive training in drawing, with the help of a gift of 2,500 lt from a family friend about whom little is known (14 II 004, copies of letters between M. Benoit, M. Cuisin, Morand, and his sister, dated 13 March 1754, 14 and 29 December 1755, and two undated letters). The settlement of the crippled estate inherited from his father took more than three decades (14 II 008, Levet to Antoine Morand, 11 November 1776; 14 II 004, Morand to Escalone, 20 January 1779); Morand's reflections on the matter were sketched out in a letter dated 27 September 1756, ii 325. For details of Morand's library and collection of artworks, see chapter 7 below.

14 Louis Tolozan de Montfort occupied that position at the head of the
Consulat, Lyon's highest municipal authority, from 1785 to 1790. For
the names and origins of migrants successful enough to become Bourgeois de Lyon, see the registers of the Nommées des bourgeois de Lyon,
AmL, BB 443–7 and 452–6. See also the examples cited by Trénard, *Lyon
de l'Encyclopédie*, 47–9. Chalier, Lyon's key revolutionary figure, also
came from near Briançon (he had also turned to painting for a while).
Brun de la Valette, "Louis Tolozan de Montfort."

15 For a thorough analysis of the place of immigration in Lyon's eighteenth-
century demography, see Garden, *Lyon et les Lyonnais*, part one, chapter
3, 79–80, who suggests that some 120,000 men and women, most of
them young, came to Lyon between 1700 and 1790. He also argues that
Lyon was the first industrial concentration in Europe at the time (Pinol,
ed., *Atlas historique*, 152). For a sketch of the socioeconomic structures
and dynamism of the city, see Gruyer, "La population active," and Poni,
"Mode et innovation."

16 Favier, *Les villes du Dauphiné*; Routier, *Briançon*.

17 See comments throughout the correspondence during his Italian travels,
in 14 II 004, for instance letters dated 15 November 1759, 2 February
and 4 October 1760. Laurence Fontaine has recast the history of Alpine
migration (*Pouvoir, identités*). See also Poitrineau, *Remues d'hommes*,
and, for a new perspective, Collins, "*Translation de domicile*."

18 Aubert de Tourny's offer to Morand of an annual salary of 5,000 lt is
mentioned in the biographical sketch written by his great-grandson, an
edited version of which can be found in Dureau et al., *Hommage à
Morand*, 45. For the transformations of France's great Atlantic port, see
Pariset, ed., *Histoire de Bordeaux*, or a brief sketch by Leroy Ladurie,
"Un urbanisme frôleur," 470–4.

19 14 II 04, Morand to Levet, 23 April 1777. Earlier, he had reminded her
that the Alpine origins of one of their hosts called for a "modest" reception (25 June 1760).

20 Architects commonly distributed engravings and even scale models to
advertise their successes (see Gallet, *Les demeures parisiennes*, chapter 2).
For an assessment of the decision to grant such a commission to an artist
who had yet to build anything, see *Soufflot et son temps*, notably p. 22.
Soufflot was born in 1713; the contract for the new Hôtel-Dieu was
signed on 28 June 1741.

21 See *Soufflot et l'architecture*, and notably Ternois, "Soufflot et Lyon"
and Roubert, "L'Hôtel-Dieu de Lyon"; also Ternois, "L'Hôtel-Dieu de

Lyon." Soufflot's nomination as controller is dated 9 October 1775 in
AmL, BB 341; details of his function in BB 342.

22 Pérez, "Soufflot et la société lyonnaise." Pérouse de Montclos,
Jacques-Germain Soufflot, 8–9.

23 *La formation architecturale*, passim. Letters from Morand to his mother,
in 14 II 004, from 9 December 1753 to 28 June 1754. See also Dureau et
al., *Hommage à Morand*, 71. At the time of Morand's visit, Servandoni
had embarked on a series of foreign assignments; later, he designed the
facade of the Saint-Sulpice church in Paris, and his house nearby; he had
worked in Lyon in 1738 (Braham, *The Architecture of the French
Enlightenment*, 24). Morand also spent the early part of 1759 in Paris,
although we know little of what he did during this trip (from 11 January
to 15 May 1759), besides spending 1,069 lt on books and engravings; see
14 II 007.

24 Letter, BMPD, fonds Coste, ms. 1133 n. 44, cited in *L'oeuvre de Soufflot
Lyon*, 255. The theatre opened on 30 August 1756, but work continued
long after.

25 AD 69, 1 C 202, letters between Bertin and de Courteille, 6 May and 25
June 1754. The petition to the duc de Villeroy is published in *L'oeuvre de
Soufflot Lyon*, 346–7. The Consulat's decision to build the new theatre is
in AmL, BB 321. See also Anezo, in *Soufflot et son temps*, 68.

26 A map was drawn indicating where coaches and chairs should park
(Charre, "Soufflot et l'urbanisme lyonnais").

27 The Loge des changes was built from 1748 to 1750, at a cost to the city
of between 120,000 and 140,000 lt, including 11,000 lt to Soufflot and
his partner, the Lyon architect Roche (AmL, BB 360, 27 August 1750; see
also *L'oeuvre de Soufflot Lyon*, 342). Since 1714, concerts had occasionally taken place in a rented tennis hall close to the site selected for the
new building. Gardes, "Le monument public français," 708; Clapasson,
Description de la ville de Lyon, 91.

28 See Soufflot's letter dated 17 May 1755, BMPD, fonds Coste, ms. 1133
(44). With this theatre, Soufflot introduced to France a truncated oval
design inspired by his Italian travels but improved through a progressive
opening of the room recalling antique amphitheatres. He also added an
experimental iron curtain as a fire-prevention measure.

29 Morand's yearly salary of one thousand livres tournois was later con-
verted to an authorization to build and run several small shops alongside
the Hôtel de ville. See AmL, BB 324 (deliberations, 1757) and BB 336
(deliberations, 1768). A fire brought this building down in 1826.

30 Mascoli, "Sur la route de Rome"; Anezo, in *Soufflot et son temps*, 68–72.

31 The theatre cost close to 1,300,000 lt to build (Zeller, *Une famille consulaire*, vol. 3, 289). See also Zeller, "Géographie sociale" and "L'intensification," chart, 213.

32 The monopoly covered all paying spectacles, from public dances to fireworks, from the display of rare animals to chemical experiments; many took place at alternative venues, but they all required an authorization from and payment to the holder of the monopoly. See Zeller, "En marge du privilège."

33 For references to the cost of subscriptions and related matters, see Zeller, "Géographie sociale." In 1787 admissions to the main theatre ranged in price from twenty to sixty sols. In Bordeaux, the theatre monopoly also transited through the hands of the governor, the duc de Richelieu (Pariset, *Histoire de Bordeaux*). See also a dispute in Nîmes along similar lines (AD 34, C 6820 and 6822).

34 The case is presented in Zeller, *Une famille consulaire*, vol. 3, 289–300. Soufflot had intervened in the affair, arguing that the new company planned to disfigure the theatre to expand its seating capacity (*Oeuvre de Soufflot Lyon*, 351, Soufflot's letter dated 3 April 1776). Meanwhile, Lyon's chief engineer pounced on the windfall, claiming it for one the city's ongoing projects (AD 69, 1 C 115, de Lallié to the intendant, 4 March 1776). The bribing of Turgot's secretary contributed to the fall from power of the reformist minister.

35 See Morand's marriage contract dated 15 January 1759, in 14 II 05. To place this figure in its context, see Garden, *Lyon et les Lyonnais*, 213–23, 356–98: only 9.6 percent of marriage contracts registered during 1780–89 brought more than 10,000 lt, and the average contribution among professionals and legal officers ranged between 32,700 and 41,700 lt; two generations earlier, between 1728 and 1730, only 3.6 percent of contracts registered more than 10,000 lt, a proportion that had risen to 4.55 percent between 1749 and 1750. Etienne Levet practised from 1721 to 1753, after his father Jacques Levet's long career (1676–1720). He was syndic of the notaries (designated administrator and representative) in 1752 and sold his office on 21 March 1754 for 12,000 lt; his files are in AD 69, 3E 6150 to 6165.

36 I mention details of Machério's financial contributions to the family throughout this text.

37 14 II 008, "*Levée des scellés*" (Breaking of the seals), 30 September 1755.

38 For a dated but detailed study of the links between France and Parma after the treaty of Aix-la-Chapelle, see Bédarida, *Parme et la France*. For a more focused assessment, see Dureau et al., *Hommage à Morand*, 71–8.

39 Dutillot likely followed a recommendation extended by Simon Mangot, brother-in-law of Rameau, who had left the direction of the Lyon music academy for Parma in 1756 (letter from Dutillot to Mangot, 9 June 1759, in Hours and Nicolas, *Jean-Antoine Morand*, 45). Dutillot was familiar with such transalpine hirings. Only a few years earlier, to rebuild the duke's palaces and gardens, he had recruited Ennemond-Alexandre Petitot, the promising son of a Lyon architect remembered for his hydraulic machines.

40 See for instance "Le rôle de Lyon," in *Cahier de l'Institut*.

41 Dureau et al., *Hommage à Morand*, 78.

42 Letters between Morand and Levet, 14 II 004, dated 19 January, 8 March, 4 October 1760. A few years later, someone advertised the secret of an "imitation marble better than currently known stucco" (*Affiches de Lyon*, no. 2 (12 January 1763).

43 References to the techniques and products as well as other observations mentioned in the following two paragraphs are found throughout his travel log and his correspondence with Antoinette Levet (respectively in 14 II 005 and 004). See also Daniel Roche, *Humeurs vagabondes*.

44 See comments by Antoinette Levet to Morand on 18 September 1760, 14 II 004.

45 Correspondence between Morand and his wife, 14 II 004: 13 December 1759, 2 February, 5 May, 20 September, 11 October 1760. François Claude de Chauvelin, a career soldier and son of a future minister, had literary aspirations and many connections in the world of letters, most notably Voltaire. After serving in Corsica, he became envoy at Genoa, and then ambassador at Turin with important missions to Parma (he was a personal friend of Dutillot's).

46 See correspondence between Morand and his wife, 14 II 004, 19 February 1760 and an undated letter soon after the birth of his son, in March 1760; also, 6, 20, and 29 September, 4, 9, 11, and 29 October 1760, and the final sum in 2 December 1760.

47 Almost all letters between Morand and his wife during his visits to Italy contain references to such assessments (14 II 004). For instances of "double-letters," see those dated 19 January, 16 August, 22 and 29 October 1760.

48 References to the information mentioned in the following paragraphs come from the dense exchanges between Morand and his wife during his

absence; see 14 II 004, letters numbered 28 to 237, dated from 9 November 1759 to 27 December 1760).

49 Dated 6 November 1759, 14 II 005.

50 The granting of the *"Privilège des fiacres pour Lyon"* to another bidder was made public in the *Affiches de Lyon*, 26 November 1760, but Levet was coping with the setback a week earlier (letter n. 105, dated 20 November 1760, in 14 II 004). Financial failure was a real threat in the construction industry, and perhaps even a common occurrence, leading, on at least one occasion, to a plea for funds in the *Affiches de Lyon*; see no. 19 (11 May 1763).

51 Garden, *Lyon et les Lyonnais*, 116–40.

52 In notes intended to be the start of an autobiography, Antoine added that he had been luckier than his sister, whose wet nurse provided such poor care that she was still not walking at the age of four (14 II 028, "Principales époques de la vie d'Antoine Morand de Jouffrey," begun 1 May 1788). To facilitate her many tasks, Antoinette Levet lived across from her construction site.

53 14 II 004, Morand to Levet, 5 November 1760.

54 14 II 004, Levet to Morand, 14 November 1760.

55 Lespagnol, "Femmes négociants," 463–70. Upon encountering a widow at the centre of an important enterprise, Paul W. Bamford was "tempted to attribute ... business acumen and independent spirit to her or to imagine that she was encouraged ... to perform business chores, to work with [her husband], even to travel for him and learn the business," but he refused to speculate beyond the lack of evidence (Bamford, *Privilege and Profit*, 21.

56 14 II 05, Declarations, 1762 and 7 October 1772. Comments on the importance (and fiscal value) of this *Droit de bourgeoisie* in AML, BB 249, 1691, BB 260, 1702, and BB 296, 1732. See also the Consulat's sharp reaction to a rumour that the royal state was thinking about doing away with this privilege (BB 361, 26 September 1772).

CHAPTER TWO

1 "J'ai hâte de voir votre maison, et la seconde que vous m'annoncez ... mais en serez-vous propriétaire, des deux ?" 14 II 004, letter from Cuisin Devernambon to Morand, 20 March 1761.

2 "A louer, appartement de 14 pieces de plain-pied, vue sur le quai du Rhône, sur la rue Royale, et la rue Dauphine, avec caves et greniers,

dans la maison de M. Pitiot, à louer ensemble ou séparément : s'adresser
à M. Morand, architecte, rue Royale." *Affiches de Lyon*, no. 18, 2 May
1770.

3 "A louer, très joli appart., meublé, 6 pieces de maître, chambres pour
domestiques, cuisine, au deuxième étage de la maison de M. Morand,
avec cave et grenier." Ibid., no. 48, 25 November 1772.

4 "Un particulier souhaite acheter une maison en cette ville, du prix de 70
à 80 mille livres ..." Ibid., N. 1, 4 January 1764.

5 At the time, only four bridges spanned the Rhône, and even today only
seven cities spread to both shores over its 543 kilometres beyond Geneva
(Châtelain, "Les ponts du Rhône"). The Dauphiné, south-east of Lyon,
had joined the kingdom of France in the fourteenth century, but the two
provinces of Bresse and Bugey, immediately north-east of the city, only
did so in 1601. The Franche-Comté, less than one hundred kilometres
to the north-east, became French even later, in 1678, while the border
with the duchy of Savoie to the east was even closer (and would stand
until 1860). All these lands were often still referred to as lands of the
Holy Roman Empire (*Terres d'Empire*) long after they had lost that
status.

6 Calculations from the 1735 Séraucourt plan suggested that the city controlled 363 hectares, but that the river and fortifications left 241
"usable" hectares ("Mémoire sur la nécessité d'agrandir la ville," AmL,
DD 274, likely 1742). Private interests shared in this hoarding of lands
within the city, and steep slopes often prevented construction. A small,
but unknown, percentage of people lived outside the walls. For detailed
studies of the city's demographics, turn to Garden, *Lyon et les Lyonnais*,
part one, chapter 2, and Bayard, *Vivre à Lyon*, 105–11; for an earlier
age, see Gascon, *Grand commerce*, 341–51. See also Saupin, *Les villes en
France*, 17–8.

7 Marcel Roncayolo offers comparisons that leave little doubt that Lyon's
90,000 to 100,000 inhabitants per square kilometre stands above
densities found in most other European cities, then or now (*La ville et
ses territoires*, 36). The *"mur des Fermiers Généraux"* built from
1784 to 1791, enclosed some 600,000 Parisians within some 3,350
hectares. For a sketch of urban growth during the eighteenth century,
see Emmanuel Leroy Ladurie, "La démographie des Lumières,"
295–310.

8 The records generated by the requirement of *alignement* suggest that
between 1753 and 1762, 3.5 percent of Lyon's housing stock was rebuilt

(Garden, *Lyon et les Lyonais*, part one, chapter 1, and part three, chapter 1). The rate of reconstruction accelerated throughout the century.

9 François de la Rochefoucauld, early 1780s, in Marchand, *Voyage en France*, vol. 1, 161.

10 Bayard, *Vivre à Lyon*, includes a list of such initiatives (216–18); see also Garden, *Lyon et les Lyonnais*, 473–5. For the characteristic arguments surrounding, for instance, the 1738 sale of land by the abbot of Ainay, see AmL, DD 278, 16 September 1738. The 1779 sale of the Célestins convent opened a last round of such speculation (see chapter 7, below).

11 "Mémoire instructif sur l'agrandissement ...", AmL, DD 274. On 16 April 1765, the Reverend Fathers of the Oratory offered land to build on the southern flanks of the Croix-Rousse, the duration of the lease to be discussed, in the *Affiches de Lyon*, no. 16.

12 See Zeller, "A l'enseigne du chameau"; Lozancic, "Le logement à Lyon." The figure of 4,000 houses had been cited by the intendant at the end of the seventeenth century (Gutton, ed., *L'intendance de Lyonnais*). The "Mémoire sur la nécessité d'agrandir la ville" was more precise, recording 3,842 houses, but another memorandum submitted to the city in 1789 again used the round figure of 4,000 (AmL, DD 274, and DD 308, "Mémoire sur les inconvénients ...," 30 pp.). Messance's *Recherches sur la population* tallied 4,770 houses (p. 42). For comparisons with other French cities, see Meyer, *Etudes sur les villes*, vol. 1, 135–6. In Nîmes, another crowded city, close to 1,400 small houses sheltered some 376 inhabitants per hectare on some thirty intra-muros hectares (Teisseyre-Sallmann, "Urbanisme et société").

13 Bayard, *Vivre à Lyon*, 234; Zeller, "A l'enseigne du chameau"; Lozancic, "Le logement à Lyon," notably graph p. 556; Perrot finds a similar situation in Caen (*Genèse d'une ville moderne*, 779); Leroy Ladurie, "Un urbanisme frôleur," 481.

14 For the case of Lyon, see Garden, *Lyon et les Lyonnais*, part two, chapters 2 to 5.

15 Zeller, "Un mode d'habiter à Lyon."

16 Leroy Ladurie, "Un urbanisme frôleur," 481. All studies of Lyon's real estate market mentioned in the previous notes refer to returns within the three to five percent range. This sixty-one-page "Rapport d'expert" is found in AD 69, BP 2561, dated 1759–61.

17 Papyanis (*Planning Paris*) places the key principles of urban reform in their most important context, that of the late eighteenth and early nineteenth century. Cleary (*The Place Royale*) offers a straightforward survey

of the age's key ideas, as well as a catalogue of the main initiatives across France. Garrioch (*The Making of Revolutionary Paris*) presents a lively sketch of the problems facing a (very large) early-modern city, as well as the great range of reforms undertaken (and some of the reactions these initiatives triggered). For a classic survey of the French context, see Harouel, *L'embellissement des villes*, or the glossy Michel Le Moël and Sophie Descat, eds., *L'urbanisme parisien*. For a short assessment of the field, see Christine Lamarre, "La physionomie des villes." Her *Petites villes* illustrates the reach of the movement beyond larger cities. See also Saupin, *Les villes en France*.

18 Pardailhé-Gallabrun, *The Birth of Intimacy*, 40–72. Guillerme, *Bâtir la ville*.

19 The introduction to *Cahiers d'histoire* 44, no. 4 (1999), a special issue devoted to urban history, argues that the word "segregation" overstates the trends characteristic of the eighteenth century (p. 511). Nevertheless, such trends are clear in Paris, with the decline of the Marais and the emergence of fashionable quarters at the west end of the city around new public buildings and thoroughfares; Leroy Ladurie, "Un urbanisme frôleur," 465–70; Le Moël and Descat, *L'urbanisme parisien*.

20 See Garden's geographical analysis of the hierarchy of wealth at the end of the Old Regime (*Lyon et les Lyonnais*, 175–210), and Bayard's more succinct reflections on the nature and evolution of spatial segregation (*Vivre à Lyon*, 238–44). In Lyon's high buildings, the better apartments were on the lower floors — but not the ground floor, and the quality of the apartments tended to diminish as one climbed toward the fourth and fifth floors, to accommodate a range of social groups. Social distinctions between neighbourhoods were certainly clear to eighteenth-century residents, although they remained less pronounced than they were a century later.

21 See the Consulat's deliberation relative to the construction of this new riverfront in AML, BB 301 to 305, 1736 to 1740.

22 AD 69, 1 C 114, fo. 119–20, letter from Lallié to Boileau; and AML, AA 19 fo. 25, BB 343, Délibérations – 1775 – payment of 49,135 lt upon completion of the new quay by Rigod de Terrebasse. Bayard and Cayez eds. *Histoire de Lyon*, vol. 2, 10.

23 AD 69, 3 E 7019, notaire Perrin, 12 December 1742, land sale to Breton, Desraisses, Millanois, and Soufflot. Three houses were quickly built just north of the lands to be reclaimed (Pérez, "Soufflot et la société lyonnaise"). Decision from the Consulat, 22 October 1749, in AD 69, 27 H

428, and in AmL, BB 315 and DD 256. The new road to the Bresse was completed by 1780 (AD 69, 1 C 115, letters from de Lallié to the Consulat, 26 September 1775 and 16 December 1780; a competing project briefly emerged in 1764 – see *Affiches de Lyon*, no. 20 (16 May 1764).

24 In his memoirs, R.-C. [Ricard-Charbonnet] recalled the power of the trend that "forced" his father to relocate (from the old Saint-Georges neighbourhood) to the shores of the Rhône where "his kind" (business people) gravitated (R.-C., *Mémoires d'un Lyonnais*, 5).

25 Among those who invested in or at least moved to this neighbourhood were many members of the Consulat as well as architects and builders. Besides Morand, there were Rater, Roux, Munet, Loyer, Drivon, Lombois, l'Habitant, Viehle (see names and addresses in the *Almanach de la ville de Lyon*, mid-1760s, entry *"architectes"*; Charre and Servillat, "L'entreprise du quartier Saint-Clair," 21–6, in *L'oeuvre de Soufflot à Lyon*). See also Garden, *Lyon et les Lyonnais*, 208–9, and diagrams 3 to 10, 692–9. A similar pattern has been noted in Bordeaux: the new boulevard (later known as the Allées de Tourny) attracted a great number of the city's architects (Pariset, *Histoire de Bordeaux*, 557–9).

26 Charre and Servillat, "L'entreprise du quartier Saint-Clair," notably 24. The partners also built houses on the site.

27 14 II 017, lot at 12 quai Saint-Clair, purchased on 25 February 1764 from J.-F. Genève, who had bought it four years earlier for 16,000 lt; house sold on 15 September 1767 to Pitiot. 14 II 015, lot at 16 quai Saint-Clair, 4,770 square feet purchased on 24 March 1757 from Soufflot and associates; to the initial cost of the lot should be added the 600 lt paid to register the sale with the Contrôle des Actes (public registry of notarized acts), 153 lt to the notary, and a gratuity known as *épingles*; house sold, on 3 July 1763 and 1764 (see also AmL, *Mémoire*, 1779, 0001 C 704 336). 14 II 007, lot at 4 quai Saint-Clair purchased on 29 March 1766 from Munet; comments on value of house (175,000 to 200,000 lt) in 14 II 004, Morand to Levet, 14 and 21 April 1777, estimating the mortgages bearing on that house at 175,000 lt; this building brought in 7,705 lt in rental income in 1777.

28 Records of rental income in AmL 14 II 006 and 007. The Pré Deschamps was bought on 3 July 1765 (see chapter 3, below). Morand designed the house of his physician, Dr Grassot, and that of Millanois; the drawings and plans are in Hours and Nicolas, *Jean-Antoine Morand*.

29 For a fresh perspective on the wealth of advertisements in the *Affiches*,
see Jones, "The great chain of buying."

30 Garden, *Lyon et les Lyonnais*, 12–24, 691. If only ten percent of houses
were assessed at more than 100,000 lt in the city, the proportion rose to
twenty-five percent for the north-east district. Smaller houses were often
found on the hillsides where the geography did not permit larger buildings. Naturally, one also met the occasional "*hôtel particulier*" suited to
the needs of very wealthy aristocrats, although Lyon's elite more often
built their dream houses outside the city, in the Italian fashion.

31 The construction of the place Louis-le-Grand exemplifies this approach
to urban development. Almost a century earlier, an imposing Hôtel-de-
ville (whose construction began in 1645, and which was rebuilt after a
fire in 1674) and the Benedictine convent (today's Palais Saint-Pierre,
begun in 1659) had similarly brought the Terreaux to the attention of
wealthy residents.

32 Over the previous decades, municipal authorities discussed the need for a
north-south artery, new crossings of the Rhône, better water supplies,
and the relocation of noxious trades; they had justified the purchase of
an island at the southern end of the Presqu'île by the "eventuality that
the expansion became necessary." See a long series of council decisions in
AmL, BB 282 and following for the years starting in 1720. For these matters, see previous references in note 17 as well as Perrot, *Genèse d'une
ville*.

33 Leroy Ladurie, "Un urbanisme frôleur," 473. In Bordeaux, Gabriel
argued that the construction of the facades of buildings lining a proposed
boulevard would give the public a positive image of the future street and
encourage investments (Pariset, *Histoire de Bordeaux*, 538).

34 22 October 1749, *Registres des actes consulaires*, AmL, BB 315 and DD
256, and AD 69, 27 H 428. Two years earlier, Soufflot had drawn plans
for a new port in the area and delivered a "Mémoire sur les maisons à
pilotis de la Saône," a technique that would be needed for reclamation
work; AmL, BB 313, 1747; presentation to the Lyon Academy on 24
January 1747, *L'oeuvre de Soufflot à Lyon*, 251.

35 Morand–Levet correspondence, 14 II 004, dated 10 and 19 January, 2, 7,
14, and 16 February, 8 March, 1 and 14 August, 18 and 29 September,
and 9 and 29 October 1760.

36 The unit was not defined in the original contract (in AD 69, 27 H 428);
subsequently, Soufflot and his partners were careful to add the words

pieds de Roy in their rendering of this contract (see for instance sale dated 26 July 1760 in AD 69, Not. Dalier, 3 E 3868). An undated note in Morand's papers detailed the differences between the two sets of units (14 II 010; see introductory notes). In a world of countless unit systems, such errors were frequent (see for instance the discovery, in the 1730s, that the weight of stones used in the construction of the port of Agde over some fifty years was erroneous; AD Hérault, C 4271). For details about these and other units, see my notes on units of measurement, p. xvii.

37 The first regulation of this ratio between the width of a street and the height of buildings dates from 1783 in Paris (Harouel, *L'embellissement des villes*, 228–9).

38 These problems are mentioned in the correspondence between Morand and Levet, 14 II 004: 21 February and 8 March, regarding structural weight bearing; 15 December 1759, 25 June, 1, 7, 21 August, and 18 September 1760, the digging of the foundations, driving of the house-bearing posts, and walling of the riverside; 12 September 1760, shared walls; 23 September 1759, 28 March, 18 September and 24 October 1760, supplies; and 28 August 1760, labour.

39 Charre and Servillat, "L'entreprise du quartier Saint-Clair."

40 This list of payments is found in Hours and Nicolas, *Jean-Antoine Morand*, 6 (one of the payment, for the sum of 5,280 lt, went to a person not identified as a supplier or a lender). The data are in 14 II 015 – 017. We know of at least one other loan contracted by Morand on 15 April 1767, for 4,000 lt from Antoine Durand, jeweller (14 II 008).

41 This land was sold for 50,000 lt (15,000 lt cash, the rest at five percent), but the sale only became effective after a two-year delay, bringing the buyers a 1,500 lt rebate; two of the original buyers pulled out of the deal in 1745 (AD 69, 3 E 7019, notary Perrin, 12 December 1742; 27 H 256, 4 September 1744). The sale was advertised and other offers entertained, but Soufflot had the support of the archbishop of Lyon.

42 These rates are spelled out in the Consulat's grant to Soufflot and associates, 22 October 1749, in AD 69, 27 H 428, and AmL, BB 315 and DD 256. Across France, rates ranged from one-third to one-fiftieth of the property's price. In many places, seigneurs were ready to cut their rates in order to promote sales and encourage their reporting, but in other areas, they felt strong enough to add a *droit de retrait* (seigneurial right to claim back a property) to the traditional fee (Bély, ed., *Dictionnaire de l'Ancien Régime*, entry "Droits féodaux et seigneuriaux"). To this substantial levy was added the more symbolic annual *cens et servis* (seigneurial quit rents

and dues; three sols per year in the case of the Saint-Clair lands). This matter has received only limited attention: see Nagle, "Un aspect de la propriété seigneuriale," and Noël, "Seigneurie et propriété urbaine."

43 All documents relative to this dispute were gathered under the title "Titres distinctifs de la rente noble de Madame l'Abesse de Saint-Pierre ...", in AD 69, 27 H 428 (39 p.). The Rhône islands were notorious for their changing shape.

44 Such a grant was certainly not unprecedented. In 1666 Pierre-Paul Riquet, creator of the celebrated canal des deux mers, was granted all seigneurial rights over the canal and adjacent lands (André Maistre, *Le canal des Deux mers*, 263–5).

45 14 II 004, Morand to Levet, 18 and 26 January and 16 February 1763.

46 AML, BB 330, 331, 341, 5 May 1746, 24 April 1769, 28 May 1770, 19 December 1772.

47 AML, DD 330 and DD 55. The dispute was mentioned in a letter from Soufflot to Morand dated 1 October 1764 (published in *L'oeuvre de Soufflot à Lyon*, 288).

48 Zeller, *Une famille consulaire*, vol. 3, 216–17. For evidence of Munet and Morand's earlier association, see the many references in the correspondence exchanged between Morand and Levet during his sojourn in Italy (14 II 004).

49 *Soufflot et son temps*, 38.

50 See the many letters exchanged between Morand and his wife on this affair in 14 II 004. In 14 II 016: proposition by Millanois (1 April 1763); memorandum for Tolozan (31 May 1779); order to resume work (9 August 1758); letter from Morand and Levet to the premier président, Parlement of Paris, no date; manuscript presentation of the case by Morand (29 March 1779); printed survey of the case (1779). See also reference to the matter in 14 II 003 and 14 II 005 (5 July 1779), and the comments made in 1854 by Morand's great-grandson in Dureau et al., *Hommage à Morand*, 48–9. There are also mentions in the Consulat's Deliberations, for instance AML, BB 361, 26 January 1764.

51 *Soufflot et son temps*, 38. Poidebard, "Etablissement de la place Tolozan."

52 Because of the recognition he received for his role in the construction of the new theatre, letters were addressed to Morand as "*Architecte pensionné de la ville*" (stipendiary city architect; 14 II 004, Levet to Morand, 17 January 1760, and Cuisin de Vernambon, 20 March 1761).

53 *La formation architecturale*; Carvais, "La force du droit." The first list of Lyon architects appeared in the 1750 *Almanach*, but a 1744 landslide

had led the Consulat to commission three architects (including Soufflot) to regularly visit all potentially dangerous buildings (Cottin, "L'architecte à Lyon"). It was only in 1780 that the still fledgling École royale gratuite de dessin opened a first section teaching architecture in Lyon; however, prominent architects had been called to the Lyon Academy for several decades (Morand was never invited; Marie-Félicie Pérez, "Soufflot et la création de l'école").

54 Picon, *French Architects*.

55 See the comments of Perrot, *Genèse d'une ville*, 7–27. For the particular role played by Soufflot in this transformation in the context of Lyon, see Charre, "Soufflot et l'urbanisme lyonnais."

56 Cottin, "L'architecte à Lyon." For the rise of Lyon's *profession libérales*, see Garden, *Lyon et les Lyonnais*, 381–7.

CHAPTER THREE

1 "Depuis 1764, [Morand] ne s'est occupé que de l'embellissement de la ville de Lyon. Il avait projeté son accroissement en forme circulaire [... rapprochant] le plus possible toutes les distances [et offrant] l'agrément de renfermer le Rhône et la Saône dans ... la ville ... il a fait le sacrifice de six arpents d'un terrain très précieux [et] formé des allées plantées d'arbres ..." "Au Roy," Morand's 1789 plea for the Order of St Michel (14 II 003).

2 "Il s'est formé une Compagnie pour l'exécution du projet de M. Perrache, qui a mérité ... l'approbation du Consulat et des Notables ... et celle du Roi ... La Compagnie se propose de vendre des actions sur l'entreprise générale ..." *Affiches de Lyon*, no. 46, 14 November 1770.

3 "Perrache se fait architecte!" François-Régis Cotton, "L'abbé Duret," 74.

4 Mentioned in a memorandum presenting Morand's position in his dispute with the Hôtel-Dieu (see below). The project never materialized (see 14 II 018, memorandum, 11 August 1765).

5 14 II 004, Morand to Levet, dated 16 February 1763. Morand's papers contain drawings of a never-built canal intended to link the quarries of Couzon to the Saône River (Hours and Nicolas, *Jean-Antoine Morand*, 29). The Paris gardens project, discussed with Victor Louis and M. Monet, was inspired by a precedent in London (14 II 018, memorandum, 11 August 1765).

6 Copy of the sale contract in 14 II 020 (3 July 1765; the seller was Michel Deschamp, a merchant from la Guillotière). Morand also paid 2,000 lt to

the Saint-Jean chapter and received the *lods* for all first sales of any part of this meadowland for a twelve-year period (with a five percent cap on the second transactions; AML, DD 308, 8 August 1765). The comtes de Lyon added a provision to the contract preventing sales of all or part of this land to any institution falling under the jurisdiction of mortmain; such institutions were not allowed to sell land, thus seriously limiting the profits that the chapter could expect from further sales.

7 14 II 018, contracts dated 9 and 10 August 1765. The memorandum of 11 August 1765 (same file) suggested that the public space planned for this development would total 13.25 bichérées, i.e., over a quarter of the field bought by Morand.

8 See "Nottes relatives au Broteau," starting 24 July 1766, in 14 II 005.

9 Records of the measures taken in the eighteenth century in AD 69, 1 C 114, 161–3. See also frequent discussions of these matters in the Consulat's deliberations, for instance in BB 324 (1757), BB 330 (1762), BB 331 (1763), etc. As usual, the work campaign of the 1760s was marred by substantial cost overruns and sharp disputes between individuals and agencies.

10 Documents in 14 II 018 and 020, and relevant deliberations of the Consulat in BB 335 (20 May 1767). The printed abstract is dated 20 January 1767. Morand's record suggests that he was heard by the council on 10 July 1766 and that he made a submission to the comtes de Lyon in April 1768 (AML, DD 308).

11 Morand's Plan circulaire was for instance used again in Duby, ed., *Histoire urbaine de la France*, vol. 3, 441. For a close reading of Morand's publication strategies, see Chuzeville, "Publication et publicité."

12 Burnouf et al., *Le pont de la Guillotière*.

13 AD 69, 1 C 163, memorandum, Deville to the Consulat, 7 March 1733, and "Supplication des Recteurs de l'Hôtel-Dieu," no date.

14 Both documents in 14 II 020; the first bears the date 1754, the second is undated but refers to the establishment of the ferries, "15 or 16 years earlier." The first speaks in the name of the hospital's directors; the second is more anonymous, more publicly styled. The Consulat had approved the ferry monopoly three years before the letters patent (AML, DD 308, fo. 125, 30 August 1740; 14 II 020, doc. 1, 28 March 1743).

15 De Lallié's plans are mentioned in the short biographic sketch found in *Forma Urbis*; Barre suggests that Morand's first presentation was initiated by the rectors ("La formation des quartiers lyonnais"). There is mention of a 1762 proposal for a bridge in Cottin, "L'abbé Duret," 73.

16 14 II 20, folder "*Préalables, 1754–1769*," doc. 2, dated 20 January 1767.

17 In a later summary of the negotiations that followed this presentation, Morand identified the prejudice that had, for centuries, made people in Lyon fear the Rhône while they thoroughly integrated the Saône into their living space (14 II 020, "Observations sur la dernière réponse ...," 14 August 1769, notably p. 2, out of 19 pp.).

18 Not much later, a dearth of firewood seemed to boost Morand's cause (14 II 020, 27 November 1770).

19 Congestion on the old bridge always brought back memories of the accident that killed 238 people in 1711, when the overturning of carriages created panic among the thousands returning from a festival in nearby Bron (see AmL, BB 272, 1711; the same series documents the maintenance of this ancient bridge).

20 References to both documents are given in note 14 above.

21 There are many mentions of sums paid to Louis-Michel Perrache (1686–1750) in the the city's deliberations; see for instance, AmL, BB 282, 1720; BB 265, 1705; BB 294, 1739, etc.

22 See for instance, AmL, BB 325, 1758; BB 327, 1760 and 1761; BB 332, 1764; 14 II 018, sale dated 10 August 1765, from Morand to Fleurant and Perrache.

23 Hardouin-Mansard envisioned an administrative city and ornamental gardens that called to mind a "small Versailles" to the south of today's Bellecour (Gardes, *Lyon, l'art et la ville*, vol. 1, 48). For a general and detailed overview of Perrache's enterprise, see Rivet, *Le quartier Perrache*. Two contemporary analyses are found in AmL, 49 II 3 (Fonds Fleurieu). Perrache had also presented to the Académie des sciences, belles-lettres et arts plans for a canal on the Rhône for the operation of mills (*Affiches de Lyon*, no. 17, 23 April 1766).

24 The purchase, dated 20 December 1735, and subsequent long-term leases can be found in AmL, BB 305 ("Etude attentive du terrain de l'île Moignat acquise ..."), 317, and 321. Purchase of the jardins d'Ainay from the abbey of the same name is dated 16 September 1738 (DD 278; several leases followed). For Delorme's plan, see AmL, DD 275, docs. 1 and 6; see also 29 December 1740, BB 305; and Burdy, "Guillaume-Marie Delorme.") Several memoranda were then written in favour of expansion (DD 274 and 278).

25 Delorme's calculations of the respective levels of the two rivers had also been flawed, and it is not clear whether Perrache performed his own measurements or followed this earlier authority (Burdy, "Guillaume-Marie Delorme," 188).

26 Perrache also expanded his project, calling for a stone bridge rather than the wooden one originally planned, and quays alongside the Saône and the left bank of the Rhône (AmL, 49 ii 21).

27 In May 1768 Morand visited the new gardens at Saint-Cloud, opened to the Parisian public at the (steep) cost of twenty-four sols tournois per visitor (14 ii 020, Flachon – Morand, 22 July 1768). A revenue-producing bridge was also to be the first step in the expansion of Bath, in England (Gresset, "Un projet d'extension").

28 14 ii 020, "Observations sur la dernière réponse ...," 14 August 1769, p. 5 (of 19 pp.): Morand claimed to have faced that objection when he presented the Consulat with a project to link the île Moignat with the Presqu'île.

29 AmL, BB 335, 20 May 1767, and BB 366, fos. 8 and 9. A panel of eight experts that had been named on 21 June 1766 to assess Perrache's submission most likely considered both proposals.

30 AmL, AA 132, "Correspondance reçue par la commune, 1773–1777" – "Modifications apportées par Soufflot au plan de A.-M. Perrache ..."; BB 338, Consulat's approval of Perrache's project, 1770; approval in Royal Council on 13 October 1770 and letters patent registered in the Conseil Supérieur on 20 December 1770 (AmL, 49 ii 3); the company went public in the *Affiches de Lyon*, no. 46 (14 November 1770), and no. 52 (28 December 1771).

31 14 ii 020, schedule of meetings drawn by Morand, mid–1768.

32 14 ii 20, "Devis," "Propositions," and "Réponse du Chapitre," docs. 4, 5, and 9B of twenty-four documents forwarded to Bertin. AmL, DD 308, April 1768, "Mémoire présenté à MM. les Comtes de Lyon." They wished to retain control of the level of the lods and insisted that the hospital sell rather than lease its lands, terminating their mortmain status.

33 14 ii 020, doc. 7, deliberation, Bureau de l'Hôtel-Dieu, 25 May 1768 (and doc. 6, an intermediary step); the comtes de Lyon were clearly disappointed by this answer (Durand to Guillin du Montet, 28 May 1768).

34 After serving as intendant at Lyon (1754–57), Bertin was called to the positions of lieutenant general of the Paris police and controller general (1760–62). He then occupied, until 1780, a unique secretaryship of state concerned with various financial and economic matters, with a particular interest in Lyon. He (and his secretary M. de la Barbérie) were notably interested (and had interests) in the coal-mining efforts in the Cévennes (Lewis, *The Advent of Modern*). Although associated with the Dévot party, Bertin was a pragmatist, devoted to the monarchy and well aware of the need for reforms.

35 14 II 020: docs. 8 and 13, Morand to Bertin, 18 June 1768, and Bertin to
    La Verpillière, 27 July 1768. That the hospital was aware of the brothers'
    poor reputation is evident in several files in A 19, Archives des Hospices
    Civils de Lyon. In 1768, after the son of a good family (the Lombois,
    neighbours of Morand's at Saint-Clair) fell off a ferry boat, the brother
    piloting the craft had refused to rescue him, arguing that there were too
    many children in the city. Not only did the hospital not punish him but it
    threatened to sue a witness to silence him (Flachon to Morand, 5 July
    1768). See also, in the same file, May – June 1768, letters from la
    Verpillière (prévôt des marchands), Gendrier, Bouchet (both from the
    Ponts et chaussées), and others to Bertin and Trudaine.
36 14 II 020, doc. 12, 26 June 1768, Bureau de l'Hôtel-Dieu to Bertin.
37 14 II 005, for the accounts for this trip (during which 4,831 lt were
    spent). Details of Morand's activities are found in letters between
    Morand, Guyot, and Flachon, between 31 May and 6 August 1768, 14 II
    020.
38 14 II 020, Morand–Guyot exchange, 23 June and 4, 23, and 27 July 1768.
39 14 II 020, Flachon to Morand, 5 July 1768.
40 14 II 020, Flachon to Morand, 5 and 22 July, and 4 August 1768. By
    1770, Saint-Clair residents and the Bresse province had supplied 50,000
    lt toward this project; another 70,000 were needed; the road opened a
    decade later (AD 69, 1 C 114, de Lallié to intendant, 29 January 1770; 1
    C 115, de Lallié to the Consulat, 16 December 1780). See also Barre, *La
    colline de la Croix-Rousse*, 89–92.
41 14 II 020, doc. 14, "Second Propositions, Company to the Hôtel-Dieu,"
    21 February 1769.
42 14 II 020, doc. 15, memorandum from the Hôtel-Dieu to the prévôt des
    marchands, 7 August 1769, and "Observations sur la dernière réponse
    ...," 14 August 1769. Zeller analyzed the struggles in which Brac was
    involved in *Une famille consulaire*, vol. 3, 216–22, 227–34.
43 14 II 020, doc. 16, Morand's undated reply to the hospital's memo dated
    7 August 1769; "Observations sur la dernière réponse ...," 14 August
    1769; letter from unknown person in Paris to Morand, 13 September
    1769; Morand to Guyot, 15 December 1769.
44 There is a list of meetings in Paris, November and December 1769,
    undated, in 14 II 020. Expenses for this trip reached 1,172 lt from 18
    November to 21 December 1769 (14 II 005).
45 14 II 020, la Verpillière to Morand, 25 December 1769; Flachon to
    Morand, 2 February 1771.

46 14 II 020, Bertin to de Flesselles, 15 January 1770. AD 69, 1 C 114, fo. 113 verso, 29 January 1770 (Morand's last proposal was a response to the Hôtel-Dieu refusal of 7 August 1769).

47 14 II 020, docs. 18 and 19, 31 May and 6 June 1770, or Archives des Hospices Civils de Lyon, A 19, May 1770. AD 69, 1 C 114, fo. 116, 117, 119, and 120.

48 14 II 020, doc. 20, *Avis de l'intendant*, 30 July 1770, and Morand's reply, doc. 21.

49 14 II 020: Archbishop to Morand, 4 June 1770; Martin–Morand correspondence, 12, 27 September 1770; Barbérie–Morand correspondence, 18 September, 4 November 1770. Morand's note on the de Lallié incident is found in 4 November 1770 (published in Hours and Nicolas, *Jean-Antoine Morand*, 43).

50 14 II 020, docs. 23a and 23b, 2 December 1770.

51 14 II 020, docs. 23c and 23d, 6 December 1770; Martin to Morand, 4 December 1770; for references to the political tensions of the moment and the Maupeou reform, see note 55 below.

52 Details of this meeting are in "Note essentielle du 9 January 1771"(14 II 004; in same file, see also Morand to La Verpillière, 8 February 1771). The position of "voyer de la ville" went to François Grand, for whom Morand had little respect (14 II 005, 1770, Mémoire pour le poste de voyer ...). Initial work on this house went back to 1765, reminding us of Villeroy's somewhat removed knowledge of Lyon's affairs (see chapter 4 for details on this affair).

53 14 II 020: doc. 24 (Bertin's report to royal council, relying on the intendant's report); Arrêt and Lettres-patentes, 4 January 1771; Martin to Morand, 15, 22, 31 March 1771, 1, 4, 7 April 1771.

54 The monopoly given to the Hôtel-Dieu in March 1743 had been registered by the Parlement of Paris in May, the Lyon Sénéchaussée in June, the Maîtrise des Eaux et Forêts in September, and the Bureau des Finances in December of that same year (as well as by seven other authorities; Archives des Hospices Civils de Lyon, A 19, 1743).

55 Maupeou's reforms aimed at definitively curbing the opposition of the parlements are given much attention in all studies of the end of the Old Regime (see for instance Antoine, *Louis XV*, 927–40). For the particular context in Lyon, see Paul Metzger, *Contribution à l'étude*. 14 II 020: *Lettres de relief d'adresse* to the Conseil Supérieur, 24 October 1771; Martin advised Morand to "give consistance" to his project (23 April 1771). The new court had been inaugurated on Monday, 11 March 1771, with de

Flesselles as its first president; see the account given in the *Affiches de Lyon*, no. 11 (13 March 1771).

56 14 II 020, Flachon to Morand, 17, 22 February 1771; Morand to Martin, 13 April, 8, 24 June 1771. AD 69, S 1338, Report, Ponts et chaussées, 1882–83; visitors noted that the bridge hid the river's far shore (Mascoli, "Sur la route de Rome"). 14 II 020, Flachon to Morand, 19 May 1772; 14 II 021, note by Morand, 28 October 1774. Soon, the arrival of supplies needed to build the bridge created new conflicts (see for instance 14 II 020, Tolozan to Morand, 21 May 1771).

57 14 II 020, letters between Martin, Bourdin, Morand, 4, 5, 7, 13, 23 April, 6, 8 June, and 12, 16, 27 November 1771. The royal seal, the "Marc d'or," carried a steep price – 1,300 lt in this case; Martin also claimed 1,200 lt for his services.

58 For a sketch of the role of these inquiries, see Reynard, "Public Order and Privilege." 14 II 020, Morand–Martin correspondence, 11 May, 8, 14, 24 June, 31 July 1771; Flachon to Morand, 17, 22 February, 17 November 1771; and "Enquête de commodo-incommodo pour le pont en bois sur le Rhône" (36 pp.). A similar inquiry was held for the 1743 ferry monopoly (8 April 1743; AD 69, BP 3603); another considered Perrache's project and, a few months later, Etienne Laboré's monopoly for the cleaning of cesspools (Metzger, *Contribution à l'étude*, 306).

59 Christin, "*Ancien Régime* Ballots."

60 Beside the inquiry's transcripts, see Morand's notes on the testimonies, AmL, ii 317.

61 AmL, BB 339, Avis du Consulat, dated 19 December 1771 (following a request from the Conseil Supérieur, 28 November 1771); DD 308, "Observations du Sr Morand," dated 21 December 1771.

62 Antoinette Levet explained to her son, who was away at college, the welcome news of the nomination of the marquis de Bellecise as Lyon new first magistrate (14 II 008, 19 December 1771). Bellecise was indeed one of the first to congratulate Morand on his success (14 II 020, 9 January 1772). Morand acknowledged the intendant's role in 14 II 020, letter to Martin, 6 January 1772. Printed copies of all these documents are in 14 II 020.

63 Only a few years later, a brutal reversal showed how insecure a project could remain until the last minute. The brothers Brançion had formulated and carried forward plans for the opening of a canal between the Saône and Loire rivers, a multimillion-livres tournois venture. They appeared to have secured all necessary permissions when, at the very last minute, it was decided that the canal would indeed be built, but under the direct

control of the Estates of Burgundy and without their participation (Coste et al., eds., *Un ingénieur des Lumières*, 89–108).

64 AmL, DD 308, Requête to the Conseil Supérieur, 12 February 1772, 30 pp.; "Précis pour les Recteurs …," 22 pp.; "Observations du Sr Morand …"; "Réponses pour servir aux Administrateurs …"; and "Notes des Administrateurs sur les Observations …," 31 pp. See also a copy of the rector's arguments given to Morand by the secretary of the Conseil Supérieur, AmL, ii 317, 20 December 1771. Many of these same documents are also available under the catalogue numbers 706.344, SM 490, SM 491, 704.439, library of AmL.

65 14 II 020, Morand–Soufflot correspondence, 20, 28 February 1772. Morand called for a search of the relevant records to dispel the rumour of separation, and a certificate was issued to that effect by the clerk of the Lyon Sénéchaussée (14 II 005, 21 February 1772). Morand also noted that the hospital was ready to offer him a life annuity of 4,000 lt if he withdrew from the whole affair.

66 14 II 020, Morand to Soufflot and Bertin, 28 February 1772; Flachon to Morand, 23 January 1772.

67 14 II 020, Morand to Bertin, 28 February 1772; Morand de Longchamp to Morand, 26 February 1772.

68 14 II 021: Trudaine to intendant, 20 March 1772 (complaint from the Fermiers généraux); Consulat calling for further investigations (18 April 1772). 14 II 020: Morand to Soufflot (27 March, 25 April 1772); Morand to Flesselles (2 April 1772); report from Brac and Servant to the Consulat (17 pp., 15 April 1772); Morand to Consulat (28 April 1772). DD 308, 3 April 1772 (timber merchants). Archives des Hospices Civils de Lyon, A 20, 14 June 1772 (petition, la Guillotière).

69 DD 308, de Lallié's report, 16 pp., 18 May 1772, and two further reports from the Bureau de l'Hôtel-Dieu (17 pp., 27 May 1772, and 9 pp., 14 June 1772); Morand to Flachon, 14 II 020, 6 June 1772. Morand related de Lallié's enmity to earlier confrontations over the new theatre – and to the fact that he stood to lose some 8,000 to 10,000 lt if he was not chosen to inspect the bridge (Morand to Soufflot, 14 II 020, 25 April 1772). To defend the integrity of his measurements, Morand hesitated between arguing that there had been shifts in the river floor or an error in the copying of his map (14 II 020: Morand–Soufflot correspondence, 22 May, 15 June 1772; Morand–Flachon correspondence, 12, 14 June 1772).

70 14 II 020, Martin to Morand, 14 January 1772; Morand to Soufflot, 27 March 1772. Flachon spent the spring in Paris and frequently reported

on growing exasperation among officials with the obstinate attacks from the hospital and the Consulat (14 II 020, Flachon to Morand, 1, 6 April, 2, 8, 11 May, 9 June 1772, etc.; his letter of 26 March 1772 noted that the duke of Uzès himself had recently lost a similar case when a bridge replaced a ferry boat of his).

71 14 II 020, 26 February 1772, Morand to unknown correspondant who had sold his interest in the bridge and was spreading negative news (perhaps L. Roux); 7 April and 20 May 1772, sale of Audiffret share to Minel; 27 June 1772, one de Glatta share sold to Guyot. 14 II 018, 25 March 1772, G. Gaudin sold his share to M. Terrasse. Even more telling was the statement signed in March by Morand and Flachon that de Glatta would be fully reimbursed should the hospital succeed in overturning the letters patent – this paper was to be burnt if all was well by 1 November 1772 (14 II 022, 21 March 1772).

72 14 II 020: Morand to Bellecise, 10 June 1772, and undated draft of a letter from Morand to the hospital; Morand to Bertin, 28 February 1772; Flachon to Morand, 15, 19 May 1772; see also Flachon to Morand, 15, 19 May 1772 (and an undated, unsigned letter likely from Flachon reporting the intendant's opinion that a new offer would reflect badly on the minister's decision).

73 14 II 020, Morand to intendant, 2 April 1772, and exchanges between Morand, Flachon, and Soufflot: 30 April, 2, 5, 7, 9, 11, 14, 19, 22, 25, 27 May, 8, 16, 19 June 1772. On 19 June 1772, Morand told Flachon not to erase the pencil marks on a plan, for they were in the hands of Perronet and reflected well on his design; the same letter makes reference to the positive comments made by the engineer Chavenant, and we have an undated and unsigned copy of a letter by another engineer. Morand also recorded the slope of the access ramps of all bridges in the city to show that his fell within this range. Maurice Gallet (*Les demeures parisiennes*) mentions the frequent use of scale models.

74 14 II 020, 4 August 1772, company deliberation; undated, unsigned letter from Paris to Morand (February or March 1772) reporting on Soufflot's confession to Bertin (14 II 020).

75 14 II 020, letters dated 13 May, 11, 16 June 1772; Flachon to Morand, 9 May, 2 June 1772 (Minel had just bought a share of the bridge). Three years later, d'Audiffret asked Morand to put in a good word with "his friend Bertin" to support his son's claim to a cavalry regiment (14 II 007, 4 December 1775).

76 14 II 020, two letters to communities across the river dated 14 May 1772; Morand to Soufflot, 25 April 1772 (making the link between the

opposition raised among timber merchants and M. Henri, a rector who also happened to own a shipping privilege on the Rhône); two months earlier, Morand had identified a M. Tournachon as the link between the difficulties he was encountering with regard to the theatre and opposition to his bridge (Morand to Soufflot, 20 February 1772).

77 14 II 020, Morand to Flachon, 11, 12 June 1772; Morand to Soufflot, 15 June 1772.

78 Zeller, *Une famille consulaire*, vol. 3, 227–34. The matter was decided in the Conseil des Dépêches (royal council of dispatches) held on the 16 or 17 June 1772 (14 II 020, Flachon to Morand, 15, 16 June 1772, and 14 II 021, letter to Morand, 17 June 1772). Archives des Hospices Civils de Lyon, E 1597, Recteur to the Contrôleur général, 11 November 1772.

79 14 II 021, documents dated 17 June, 1, 16, 23, 29 July; and undated memorandum (summer 1772) from Morand, "Réfutation des principales objections ..." (12 pp.).

80 14 II 020, exchanges between the Consulat (or prévôt des marchands) and the company (or Morand), 2, 4, 7, and 9 August 1772.

CHAPTER FOUR

1 "Ce lundi Onze mars, à neuf heures du matin, tous les Magistrats pourvus d'offices pour former le Conseil Supérieur, créé par l'édit de février dernier, pour la ville de Lyon, s'étant rassemblés en l'hôtel de l'intendant, premier président, en sont sortis à neuf heures trente, pour se rendre au Palais de justice. Les rues, les ponts et les places étaient bordée des deux côtés d'une haie de la Milice Bourgeoise ... qui voulait témoigner de sa joie vu les avantages que la Ville de Lyon acquiert par cet établissement ... Tout s'est passé avec dignité, et sans autre éclat que celui de la joie publique." *Affiches de Lyon*, no. 11 (13 March 1771).

2 Archives des Hospices Civils de Lyon, archives de la Charité, B 343. In 1762 both hospitals had bid for and received some of the properties of the Jesuits expelled from the kingdom.

3 This was a hotly defended privilege: in 1786 Brac went to court to protest the fact that he was denied the right to sell his wine *"bourgeoise-ment,"* on the ground that he had not been born in the city (and presumably had not acquired the title of bourgeois de Lyon, under the belief that he had automatically inherited it from his father; see pamphlet 117 749, BMPD).

4 14 II 021, Trudaine to intendant, 20 March 1772; 14 II 004, Morand to Levet, 8 June 1779; and "Mémoire sur les inconvénients ...," DD 308,

1788. The Consulat had bought the justice rights to La Guillotière and Moignat island earlier in the century (AmL, BB 360, 23 and 24 September 1705; DD 274, 29 December 1740). To assess the role of the *Ferme générale* in French fiscal matters, see Bosher, *The Single Duty Project.*

5 For a recent if broad assessment of Lyon's economy during this age, see Bayard and Cayez, *Histoire de Lyon*, vol. 2, ch. 5, notably 127–8; Louis Trénard speaks of protracted crises starting in the early 1770s (*Lyon de l'Encyclopédie*, 22–42). We know of at least two episodes of grain short-ages: a new charity initiative distributed 20,000 "economic soups" to unemployed workers over the first half of 1771, and the expenses incurred by the Consulat during the 1775 crisis led to the definitive clos-ing of the *Abondance* grain-stocking institution established in 1643 (see Zeller, "Politique frumentaire"). Morand's correspondence mentions many serious financial difficulties as early as 1759 (14 II 004, Levet to Morand, 15 December 1759). *Affiches de Lyon*, nos. 4 and 5 (28 and January, 4 February 1767). A year earlier, the *Affiches* reported the gen-erous gesture of M. Jars, directeur of nearby mines, who offered to sell coal at cost to help the city through a miserable winter; no. 5 (20 January 1766).

6 Joël Félix, "Les finances urbaines." Among Lyon investors of note were Montribloud, de Masso, de Grollier, Genève, Morin, de Laurencin, etc. (AmL, 49 II 10). By the time of his bankruptcy (1778), Montribloud's stake in Perrache's venture had doubled from an original commitment of 200,000 lt to 442,964 lt, an indication of this company's need for capital (AD 69, 1 C 225–6, inventory).

7 Durand, *Le patrimoine foncier de l'Hôtel-Dieu*, passim and notably ch. 3; Barre, "La formation des quartiers lyonnais." Extant records of the hospital titles to and management of its lands are in the series B of the Archives des Hopsices Civils de Lyon.

8 Félix, "Les finances urbaines."

9 AmL, BB 322, 1755, and BB 360, 27 May 1755. In 1755, for instance, the hospital received from the city a meagre 5,000 lt toward yearly carrying charges. Details of the hospital accounts in series E, Archives des Hos-pices Civils de Lyon. Croze et al., *Histoire du grand Hôtel-Dieu*; Durand, *Le patrimoine foncier de l'Hôtel-Dieu*, 228–9; see also Roubert, "L'Hôtel-Dieu de Lyon," 137. Correspondence with the intendant in AD 69, 1 C 297. The hospital remained in a defensive mode until the 1820s.

10 In the early 1760s the dike protecting the Tête d'or estate had cost well over 200,000 lt. Discussions in AD 69, 1 C 163; Archives des Hospices Civils de Lyon, E 15, and E 17, Deliberations, 4 May 1763.

11 The hospital also asked the city to tighten its regulation of the banks of the Rhône. Morand's position in the dispute was summarized in a memorandum, 11 August 1765, 14 II 020; the bureau's stand was formulated in sharp terms on 21 July 1765 (Archives des Hospices Civils de Lyon, E 17). Munet, with whom Morand had clashed at Saint-Clair, designed this house.

12 Archives des Hospices Civils de Lyon, E 17, Deliberation, 31 December 1766.

13 Various figures relative to the operation of the three ferries are found in Archives des Hospices Civils de Lyon, A 19, "Recettes et dépenses des trailles, 1758–1768"; 14 II 20, "Produit annuel des possessions ..."; 14 II 20, "Recette des trailles." These documents, however, emanate from opposing sources (the records of the hospital and that of Morand) but also refer to different time periods and never make clear what types of expenses were included or left out of calculations. These contradictory estimates of the profits generated by the ferries range between 6,000 and 18,000 lt.

14 Indeed, when the hospital sold land in the Brotteaux in the 1780s (see below), the intendant complained that the rectors were applying the returns from these sales to their current operations rather than paying down their enormous debts (AD 69, 1 C 297, 21 February 1786).

15 For a detailed study of this dual institution, see Metzger, Contribution à l'étude.

16 See below for further comments on the context and implications of this reform. Garden, Lyon et les Lyonnais, 500–9. Bordes, La réforme municipale.

17 AmL, BB 338, 365; and Archives des Hospices Civils de Lyon, "Procès Pupil de Myons," B 482–3, and notably, Deliberations, 23, 27, 30 March 1768; Metzger, Contribution à l'étude, shows that de Myons's manoeuvres were only one dimension of a range of bitter conflicts across the range of Lyon's highest institutions (see below).

18 14 II 020, list of meetings, potential partner, late 1767 – early 1768; trip to Paris in late December 1770 documented in 14 II 005; Morand to Martin, 24 June 1771. Cottin, "L'abbé Duret," 69; 14 II 020, doc. 12., Rectors to Bertin, 26 June 1768.

19 Metzger, Contribution à l'étude, passim, and De Myons's Petition to the Parlement of Paris (1770, BmPD, factum 115 629), in which he acknowledged having fought with many or most of his peers but blamed these bitter struggles on jurisdictional overlaps in the city.

20 Nivet, "Prost de Royer."

21 Archives des Hospices Civils de Lyon, Deliberations, A 19, 26 October 1821.

22 Cobb, *Reactions*, 56.

23 Zeller, *Une famille consulaire*, vol. 3, 241, and "Enjeux d'urbanisme." More generally, see Garden, *Lyon et les Lyonnais*, part 3, chapter 3 (notably 515–22), and, more briefly, Bayard and Cayez, *Histoire de Lyon*, chapter 4.

24 As late as 1786, officers of the Sénéchaussée felt unjustly denied access to municipal offices (AD 69, 1 C 142).

25 La Justice Royale a toujours revendiqué, avec raison, la supériorité qui lui est due; elle lui a toujours été contestée par le Consulat, espèce d'administration plus républicaine d'une part que municipale; et de l'autre, plus despotique encore, peut-être, que républicaine, reste des siècles de barbarie et de confusion, dont une infinité de réglements sages promulgués depuis n'ont pu détruire l'esprit; de là, des disputes, des querelles et des procès sans fin. De Myons, Petition to the Parlement of Paris, 1770, BMPD, factum 115 629, pp. 23–4.

26 Jones, *Reform and Revolution*.

27 Garrioch, *The Making of Revolutionary Paris*, particularly chapters 9 ("Urbanism or Despotism") and 10 ("The Integration of the City").

28 Kleinclausz, *Histoire de Lyon*, 220–8.

29 The trésoriers de France gave the alignment for the new Saint-Clair constructions (14 II 015, 6 February 1764).

30 The matter, however, continued over the following years. These disputes are documented in AD 69, 8 C 429, 430, and 10 G 3814, 3815 (as well as 10 G 717 to 721 for records going back to the fourteenth century). See also Bayard and Cayez, *Histoire de Lyon*, ch. 4. Matters related to the uses of water also fell under these claims.

31 François Grand, surveyor of Lyon (a position for which we saw Morand unsuccessfully compete, some five years earlier), submitted his report on 3 April 1775. Three days later, the city opened the bridge to pedestrian traffic. However, the Bureau des Finances had already communicated to the minister the results of its own inspection, some time in March (AmL, DD 308, 6 April 1775; see also BB 343; Bertin to de Flesselles, 14 II 020, 29 March 1775). Riders, carriages, and beasts of burden were admitted a year later (AD 69, 8 C 430, 13 March 1776). 14 II 022, letter from Morand, 23 February 1775. Cottin, "L'abbé Duret," and "Le carrefour de Lyon." To an order from the Bureau des finances to modify a street alignment, the local Ponts et chaussées engineer replied that he only took orders from a royal council (AD 69, 1 C 115, de Lallié to the intendant,

12 May 1781). Ordinance dated 4 September 1776, in *Almanach de Lyon* (and same ordinance in 1778, 1779, 1780, etc.). Similar tensions surfaced when it came time to give the intendant jurisdiction over all disputes related to the bridge and when the Commission des péages had to record the schedule of tolls (see Morand's manuscript note on these matters at bottom of p. 16 of a copy of his bridge privilege, "Extrait des Registres du Conseil du Roi du 4 Janvier 1771," 14 II 020).

32 The diary of a prominent legal officer of the Bureau des Finances offers insights into these struggles over the period 1715 to 1744; see the brief comments by Cuer, "Léonard Michon."

33 Bossenga, "City and State."

34 Bossenga, "City and State," and Horn, "The Limits of Centralization."

35 For more details on this protracted struggle, see Garden, *Lyon et les Lyonnais*, 517–20, and, again, Metzger, *Contribution à l'étude*. Montribloud was a financial backer of Morand's and Perrache's (14 II 022, Morand to Montribloud, 12 June 1773, and appended draft of thank-you note; see also the list of creditors drafted by A. Levet, 14 II 004, 5 June 1777. AD 69, 1 C 225–6).

36 Zeller, "Politique frumentaire"; in the process, Perrache found his enterprise accused of undermining the productivity of the mills at the Quarantaine; it took a ministerial intervention to cancel the Consulat's decision to stop his work (AmL, BB 343, 14 June 1775).

37 AD 69, 1 C 142. Among other fights during the brief tenure of the Conseil Supérieur, Paul Metzger mentions clashes over the fate of Lyon's agents de change, its guild system, the city's college (vacated by the expelled Jesuits) and jails, the labour rates of silkworkers, etc. (*Contribution à l'étude*, 162–86).

38 In a supplement to the *Affiches de Lyon,* no. 16 (10 April 1769), the Hôtel-Dieu launched a competition to generate new ideas to support the city's poor.

39 The Brac family has been the object of an exceptionally comprehensive study, thanks to a trove of family archives (Zeller, *Une famille consulaire*). For the *"Bail* Stuntz" affair, see AD 69, 1 C 142, 1775–7.

40 Indeed, how many of the key moves and key players in these struggles can we know at all with any measure of certitude? Explicit mentions of names, both in support and in opposition to Morand's project, are relatively rare in the documents that we have. All parties knew that committing names to record would only make concessions and retractions more difficult. Private scribblers, for their part, always worried about the security of their mail. Often, allusions to friends or foes that would have been

clear to contemporaries remain vague to us, if entertaining. In Morand's letters, opponents to his projects are referred to as "*ces messieurs*," "our adversaries," "those fanatics," "*l'homme en noir*," "that stubborn small gang," "*celui que vous savez*," or, in the case of one particular opponent (likely Brac), someone "as crazy as his name." The most telling reference made in the exchanges that have reached us was to the inability of "*les Perruques*" (the Wigs) to move "the people." This is likely a transparent allusion to the fact that opposition to the project was in part centred around officers of judicial courts, and to the importance of public opinion in the matter. See 14 II 020, Flachon de la Jomarière to unnamed, 26 February (or March) 1772; Flachon de la Jomarière to Morand, 2 May 1772; Martin to Morand, 14 June 1771; 14 II 021, Morand to Soufflot, 8 June 1772; 14 II 022, Machério to Morand, 19 October 1775.

41 Beik, "Louis XIV and the Cities," and Kettering, "State Control."

CHAPTER FIVE

1 "[Le pont Saint-Clair] est des plus magnifiques ... [C']est une miniature, pour ainsi dire, quoiqu'en grand, d'une grande propreté, d'une structure et d'un assemblage de charpenterie des plus justes et en même temps des plus solides. Il est tout vernissé à huile en rouge, en sorte qu'on ne voit ni les jointures, ni les chevilles de l'assemblage. La foulée est partagée en trois. Le milieu, bombé et terminé à côté par des bancs aussi vernissés et des rigoles pour écouler les eaux, est pavé de petites pierres très propres; les deux à-côtés, en forme de trottoirs entre les dits bancs et les garde-corps du pont, sont proprement carrelés. Les gens de pied y passent, les équipages, cavaliers, voitures, etc. passent au milieu. A chaque extrémité du pont est une porte en arc de triomphe, en belles pierres de taille, ornée d'architecture, etc. et un bureau avec un commis pour la perception du péage." Duranton and Lauvergnat-Gagnière, *Journal d'un voyage*, 179–80.

2 A few decades earlier, the architect and engineer Guillaume-Marie Delorme had recalled the local prejudices towards the Rhône. See Burdy, "Guillaume-Marie Delorme," 188.

3 Nicolas Reveyron, "Influence de la charpenterie." Four of Lyon's seven bridges were wooden bridges well into the nineteenth century. For a survey of Lyon bridges before the new age of iron, see Sarocchi, "Les précurseurs."

4 AmL, BB 255, 270; BB 252, 1694. BB 293, 1729, for considerations of boat-bridges.

5 AmL, BB 363, 1782–89, file "Pont de Serin."

6 A combination of stone piers and wooden arches was also considered for the pont de l'archevêché, in the 1770s (AmL, BB 339, Délibération du Consulat, 30 August 1773, and estimate, BB 341, 1773). Burnouf et al., *Le Pont de la Guillotière*, 84–91.

7 Exchanges between Morand, Martin, Flachon, and Soufflot, 14 II 020, 8, 14 June 1771, 30 April, 14, 27 May 1772 (including a separate technical note); DD 308, printed report, 21 December 1771.

8 For the evolution of techniques, see Picon, *French Architects*, 156–68, and Mesqui, *Le pont en France*.

9 The heavy maintenance requirements of wooden bridges are easily documented. The Bellecour bridge, rebuilt in 1711, was in serious need of repair by 1732 (cost unknown), in 1749 (81,347 lt), 1759 (105,400 lt), and 1769 (31,048 lt; AmL, BB 296 and 360). The bridges at Saint-Georges (Ainay) and Serin, built after 1744, required some 72,360 lt of repairs barely twenty years later (Archives des Hospices Civils de Lyon, Archives de la Charité, B 325 and B 124; see many other figures related to repairs of these bridges in B 126).

10 14 II 022, comments on the events of 14 January 1789, and *Journal de Lyon*, 5 February 1789. Stones were loaded on the bridge in preparation for the shock (BMPD, MS Coste 1129, and AmL, BB 348, "Préparations pour la grande débâcle imminente ...").

11 AD 69, S 2023, 4 February 1823 and 8 May 1827. In 1867 the Service Spécial du Rhône worried about finding posts of a diameter similar to what Morand had used, and another report drawn at that time argued that a wooden bridge, while necessitating more maintenance, could never be as solid as an iron or stone bridge (AD 69, S 1376, 23 March, 31 May, 17 July 1767).

12 The work of Perronet himself can be seen as bound by tradition, notably in his rejection of metal (Malverti, ed., *L'idée constructive*, 87).

13 Coste et al., *Un ingénieur des Lumières*, 207–36 (see also related articles in Malverti, ed., *L'idée constructive*).

14 14 II 020, note, 4 November 1770, recounting Morand's meeting with de Lallié on 15 September 1770; 14 II 012, Morand to Soufflot, 8 January 1778.

15 Anonymous, undated pamphlet inserted in AD 69, 1 C 156 (the second reference is to Morand, the third to Perrache, and the last to Zacharie – the first remains uncertain). Ironically, this text was intended to defend the comte de Laurencin who had taken over the company created by Perrache but had little training himself in these matters.

16 The limitations of the tools at the disposal of engineers trying to assess the cost of a project are evident in the case of a Burgundy canal: Coste et al., *Un ingénieur des Lumières*, 123–36.

17 We know of at least one upward revision suggested by le Gendrier and Soufflot for some 40,000–60,000 lt (14 II 020, Flachon de Barey to Morand, 17 November 1771).

18 Estimates for the Ainay and Serin bridges (respectively 234 feet and 280 feet, for nine and seven arches; Morand's seventeen arches spanned 636 feet) ranged from just over 240,000 lt to 288,562 lt (Archives des Hospices Civils de Lyon, Archives de la Charité, B 325 and B 126, or AmL, BB 308, 1742, BB 310, 1744). An undated "Devis sommaire ... pour la route de Lyon en Languedoc" called for a bridge over the Saône at a cost of 198,000 lt (AmL, 49 II 21); on 19 February 1777, Perrache argued that de Lallié had added 100,000 lt to his estimate (AmL, DD 276).

19 This was a private project that never materialized (Perronet, *Construire des ponts*). This text provides several estimates of the cost of more expensive stone bridges.

20 14 II 022, Morand to Flachon and Guyot, 12 August, 25 November, 9 December 1775; Note, to the date of 1 May 1776. 14 II 023, "Registre des mandats." Part of the difference between such a figure and the 360,000 lt called from the associates came from the benefits drawn from the operation of the ferries during that period (estimated at over 52,000 lt in the document mentioned in chapter 6, and found in 14 II 21, "Recette des trailles").

21 14 II 020, "Arguments pour être dispensé des vingtièmes ...," no date. 14 II 022, Flachon to Morand, 12 August 1775. Morand also recognized that the original books were needed to resist pressures from workers and contractors, not to mention attacks from his partners

22 14 II 020, Morand to Soufflot, 28 February 1772. The original plans called for eleven posts for each pier, plus three in front of each pier, but Perronet had called for three more posts per pier (see note in 14 II 024, relative to a bid for a tax exemption); plans drawn in 1867 show seventeen posts (AD 69, S 1376). Posts were meant to be some forty-two feet long before being cut to level after having been driven in, and fifteen to eighteen inches in diameter (detailed estimate in 14 II 020, doc. 4). 14 II 020, letters between Morand, Soufflot, and Flachon, 23, 30 April, 7 May 1772.

23 For general comments on the relative uses of wood and metal, see Landes, *The Unbound Prometheus*, 94–5. The merits of wood have been used to suggest that arguments other than those strictly related to the

qualities of a material are often advanced to end a period of technical indeterminacy during which several materials compete for a particular duty. See Guillerme, "Wood versus Iron"; Schatzberg, "Ideology and Technical Choice"; and several essays in Hindle, ed., *Material Culture.*

24 14 II 020, letters between Morand, Soufflot, and Flachon, 9, 14, 19, and 22 May 1772.

25 14 II 020, Flachon to Morand, 14 May 1772; 14 II 022, report from M. Ecuyer countersigned by Le Gendrier, 29 July 1772, and Morand's comments. 14 II 021, 10 December 1772, "Note générale."

26 14 II 020 and 021, congratulations from de la Barbérie, Bertin, Flesselles, Bellecise, and Le Gendrier, January and February 1773 (mentioning use of Morand's "new machine" to drive the posts into the riverbed).

27 Over the years 1773–74, opponents revived the matter of compensation for the Hôtel-Dieu, arguing for instance for a special levy on the bridge's revenues; several navigation accidents also added to the pressures bearing on the builders. Perhaps most troubling for Morand were demands from Flachon and several other associates to raise the bridge to ease the concerns of mariners. Morand resisted their entreaties to avoid reopening what we know to have been a contentious issue. AML, DD 308, 31 December 1773 and 10 January 1774. 14 II 021, letters between Morand and Gendrier, 28 February and 2 March 1773; Morand to la Barbérie, 26 June 1773; Dupuy to Morand, 17 July 1773; exchange between Morand, Flachon, and Soufflot, 2, 5 June, 20, 21, 28 October, 1 November 1774, and 27 February 1775; note by Morand 28 October 1774. 14 II 022, Morand to ?, 23 February 1775; Machério to Morand, 5 December 1775.

28 In the end, Morand used a new cement invented by Loriot that proved less than satisfactory. He had also considered a proposal from Namur (Low Countries), using a mix of tar, crushed shells, and iron clippings (14 II 021, 7 July 1774).

29 14 II 021, Agenda of the assembly of 15 January 1775. The city's fourth alderman was entrusted with this new gate's official key.

30 14 II 024, folder "Pont – recettes: récapitulations." C. Mermet makes the reasonable assumption that most sightseers paid the toll twice, rather than walking all the way to the old bridge (in Dureau et al., *Hommage à Morand*, 98). Engraving commission, 14 II 021, 26 May 1775.

31 Cosperec, *Blois.*

32 Many documents covering the initial stages of Perrache's project in AML, 49 II 21. On 8 December 1777, Perrache was asking for an annual subsidy of 15,000 lt for twenty years and a ninety-nine-year lease on the bridge's toll.

33 AmL, DD 276, exchanges between de Lallié and the intendant, 1776–82.

34 Comments on Perrache's incompetence, his sister's limitations (*impérities* was the word used), the respective faults of architects, technicians, and investors, as well as assessments by de Lallié, Bouchet (first royal engineer of dikes), and Perronet, are found in a series of letters exchanged between these three officials and Laurencin, head of the Perrache company by then, as well as a few printed statements (likely intended for publication; all in AmL, DD 276, dated from 17 January 1783 to 19 April 1783). The architect Chabert was part of this project; he had also done some innovative work on a small bridge across a canal that was also part of Perrache's project (it had collapsed twice by 1778).

35 Detailed information on this project in AmL, DD 276, de Lallié's correspondence, 14 February 1788 to 17 December 1789. We know that on at least one holiday, All Saint's Day 1774, Morand gathered volunteers to keep the work going (14 II 021, 1 November 1774; for mention of inventories, 14 II 020, 2 November 1772).

36 AD 69, 1 C 152, Canal de Givors (see also 1 L 1044); 1 C 162, "Digues du Rhône"; Roux, "Les embellissements du port." For another illustration of the difficulties plaguing even modest projects, see Delvit, "Construire en rivière."

37 AmL, DD 308, distribution of an income of 3,000 lt on 15 November 1775. Morand sold a share to Antoine Terrasse on 25 August 1773 (14 II 022). For a similar list see 14 II 023, 10 February 1776.

38 14 II 022, March 1775, consultation by Guillin de Pougelon to change the company's statutes; letter from Morand, 19 July 1775. Daffaux remained one of Morand's most steadfast bankers, regularly renewing a loan of 50,000 lt given to Morand, as late as 1792 (14 II 007).

39 14 II 022, two letters, Morand to Flachon, 12 August 1775; Morand to Guyot, 25 November and 9 December 1775 (Soufflot had apparently balked at this proposal, supporting Morand at least in part). When, in 1782, the administration considered opening the roads to the east that would enhance traffic on the new bridge, it assumed an original investment of some 600,000 lt (AD 69, Memorandum to M. de la Millière, 1 C 115, 8 January 1782). It is also possible that part of the new agreed-upon figure included rewards for pre-eminent supporters of the bridge, such as Bertin himself, for whom no trace of a payment has surfaced.

40 14 II 022: Morand to Guyot, late August 1775, contesting a debt to Flachon; several receipts from Guyot acknowledging payments by Morand, from 1771 to 1775; and details of all the sums spent by Morand to pay labour associated with the bridge (as of 8 September 1775).

41 14 II 022, request for a loan from Montribloud, 12 June 1773; Morand's acknowledgment of debt to his partners, 1 January 1776 (on 10 February 1776, this sum had risen to 28,363 lt).

42 14 II 022, Morand to de Flesselles, October 1775; Morand to la Barbérie, 28 October 1775.

43 A compromise was reached to move this last boat further south, but the service was soon discontinued in winter and eventually farmed out for only 2,000 lt per year (14 II 023, Deliberations, 1786, 1788, 1789).

44 14 II 022, exchange between Morand and Machério, 5, 8, 13, 19, 25, 26 October, 3 November, 5, 9 December 1775. 14 II 023, 13 February 1776.

45 Morand considered seeking an injunction from the royal council but in the end relied on the strength of well-positioned recommendations. His trip was made more difficult by the fact that Antoinette Levet was sick (Levet to her son Antoine, who was studying in Paris, 14 II 008).

46 14 II 022, note, 12 January 1780.

47 14 II 22, Machério to Morand, 5 October 1775, announcing the policy and a "distribution" of 3,000 lt (another followed on 14 October 1775; see DD 308). For an outline of the management of toll receipts and disbursements, see "Projet d'administration," 14 II 024.

48 Antoine Morand to Antoinette Levet, 22 May 1787, 14 II 035.

49 Antoine Morand received his share in 1785 but may have sold it soon after; he does not appear on lists of owners after that until he replaced his father. His sister (whose married name was Besson) kept her share for a few years. Machério's share may have reverted back to the family (the sale to Machério was registered on 29 June 1780 for the price of 15,000 lt, AD 69, 10 C 1295).

50 The city-side entrance was illuminated from the beginning, and the bridge fully lit by 1785; a protocol was devised to close the doors, ring alarm bells, and summon city guards in case of incident (the guards received twelve sols for each timely intervention, and only half when late; 14 II 023, 1775, 1777, 1785).

51 14 II 024, Memorandum "Pour être dispensé des vingtièmes," undated, but late 1770s; 14 II 022, Flachon to Morand, 30 January 1780. See also undated note on the matter in 14 II 020, suggesting the names of two potential interveners in Paris.

52 AmL, 10 II 004, Levet to Morand, 17 June 1777; in 1779, Morand's own *vingtième* reached 600 lt (24 June 1779).

53 14 II 004, undated note.

54 14 II 020, undated note.

55 14 II 024, "Projet d'administration," late 1775 or 1776. A receiver was
    hired in October 1775 at the rate of 500 lt per year (14 II 022, Machério
    to Morand, 5 October 1775). 14 II 004, Levet to Morand, 28 April and
    2 May 1777.

56 In 1780 Martin felt entitled to free passage for his services in Paris (14 II
    024, 14 September 1780). See also 14 II 022, 15 April 1775, 19 July 1775.

57 14 II 024, 1 January and 26 November 1783, 10, 13, and 17 February
    1784. Morand seems to have preferred to act on a case-by-case basis,
    encouraging individuals to build in the Brotteaux by giving them a few
    thousand free tickets (there are many examples recorded in the book of
    deliberations, 14 II 023).

58 14 II 018, 12 May 1786. Morand also clashed with his partners when it
    was proposed to streamline the bridge's operating budget by checking
    toll tickets only on the city side. He feared the measure would force peo-
    ple entering the city to line up twice, and even entice sightseers to crowd
    the bridge without entering the city and thus not pay (DD 308, date
    unknown).

59 14 II 022, Machério to Morand, 5 December 1775; AD 69, S 2023, 30
    September 1830, and discussions throughout 1867 in S 1376 (Morand's
    arch was just over thirteen metres wide, but in fact reduced to ten metres
    by the footings of the piles).

60 AmL, DD 308, see 17 January 1777, 25 May 1779, 11 July 1782, 3 and
    20 February 1789. There is a small file on the matter in 14 II 022. See
    also Levet to Morand, 14 II 004, 17 June and 4 July 1777, 14 May 1778.

61 14 II 022, Proposition for modification of statutes, by Morand, and
    deliberation, same date, 14 II 023, 27 May 1783 (compromise dated 23
    October 1783).

62 Petition from Morand, 1 June 1789, and letter from his son, 16 June
    1789. Morand's partners argued that ice break-ups were infrequent
    enough that reinforcements to the structure would themselves require
    repair before they were needed for the bridge. A compromise was eventu-
    ally worked out, and repairs completed before the end of the year, to the
    cost of 8,500 lt (see deliberations, 1789, 14 II 023).

63 The directors of this institution argued that the monopoly of 1771 did
    not apply to other bridges (Archives des Hospices Civils de Lyon, Delib-
    erations, A 20, 6 July 1836). A few years before, Antoine Morand had
    thanked the director (likely of the Ponts et chaussées) for making it possi-
    ble to merge the company founded by his father with that created by a
    rival group that had built a third bridge over the Rhône, the pont Charles

x (14 II 035, draft of a letter, Antoine to unnamed director, 3 March 1829).

64 The idea that the city ought to buy the bridge from the company and remove the toll had long been in the air. As early as 1805, Morand's son argued that he was not against the idea, provided that the company received a good price – the lands he owned across the river would likely appreciate more rapidly. Not surprisingly, those implicated in the Perrache project opposed the initiative (14 II 035, Antoine Morand to Antoinette Levet, 18 Ventôse, year 13).

CHAPTER SIX

1 "Figurez-vous une suite de fort belles maisons de cinq ou six étages, bâties aux dépens du ciel, un quay superbe bordé par le Rhône, et orné de trottoirs fort commodes, une vue magnifique en face et des deux côtés, voilà le quay Saint-Clair ... Deux beaux ponts ... communiquent avec une promenade agréable située de l'autre côté du Rhône, appelée les Broteaux. Elle ressemble aux Champs-Elisées." Galle, "Lettres sur un voyage," 350–1.

2 "Maison neuve, située aux Broteaux, vis-à-vis de la rue du Puits-Gaillot, à louer à présent, en toute ou en partie ..." *Affiches de Lyon*, no. 19, 13 May 1767.

3 See Dureau et al., *Hommage à Morand*, 24 (purchase dated 17 April 1778; the property was located in the parish of Chasselay); 14 II 004, Levet to Morand, 3, 9, and 14 April 1779. Payment for this property was apparently completed on 20 June 1792, for a total of 170,000 lt (Dureau, *Inventaire provisoire*).

4 14 II 008, Levet to Antoine Morand, 30 June 1776; 14 II 004, Antoine Morand to Eléonore Morand, his sister, 2 July 1776, 15 May, 8 June, 8 August 1778.

5 14 II 008, Levet to Antoine Morand, 11 November 1776.

6 14 II 013, accounts for the years 1777 and following; these positions were awarded on 5 November 1777 and 1 September 1780 (he had been architect to the archbishop since 1768). Soufflot had also found a faithful supporter in the previous archbishop, Pierre-Guérin de Tencin (who died in 1758).

7 14 II 004, exchange between Levet and Morand, 14, 19, 23, 26, 30 April, 2, 7, 10, 13, 15, 18, 23, 31 May, 3, 13 June 1777. List of rectors of the Hôtel-Dieu in AML, SM 86; Poizieux served from 1776 to 1784.

8 14 II 004, Levet to Morand, 26 April 1777. Morand had tried to diffuse
these rumours several months earlier, arguing that he chose to live in the
Brotteaux for financial reasons (Morand to Soufflot, 11 September
1776). The name de Nervo appears several times in Morand's correspondence.

9 14 II 004, Morand to Levet, 30 April 1777; Guyonnet, *Jacques de
Flesselles*, 62, 115.

10 14 II 004, exchange between Levet and Morand, 28, 30 April, 10 May
1777.

11 14 II 004, Levet to Morand, 31 May 1777.

12 AD 69, 1 C 115, 7 and 17 July 1779; 14 II 018, file "Route de
Villeurbanne," 12 June 1779, 7 March 1781, and several documents
dated 1782 concerning land transactions related to the projected road.
Plans in AmL, 3 SMO 63, 223, 225, and 288. 14 II 004, exchange between
Levet and Morand, 4, 20 March, 3 April 1779. These discussions again
raised tensions within the company: Flachon de la Jomarière wished to
argue that a proper roadway would reduce the damages done by people
opening uncontrolled pathways; Antoine Morand feared that such an
argument would only remind the rectors of the risks associated with
crowds (14 II 035, Antoine Morand to Morand, 24 February 1779).

13 AD 69, 1 C 115, 20 and 29 May 1781, 8 January 1782; 14 II 004, Levet
to Morand, 20 March 1779; 14 II 18, 14 September 1780.

14 AD 69, 1 C 115, folios 150 and following, 1776; 14 II 018, 19 June and
19 November 1787, 17 April, 25 May and 7 June 1789. For a perspective on the problems associated with the *corvées*, see Coste et al., *Un
ingénieur des Lumières*, 69–88.

15 M. Guillin du Montet, an ally and friend of Morand's, felt confident that
land sales would proceed but that the area would not be incorporated in
the city (14 II 035, Antoine Morand to Morand, 20 August 1779). One
of the last indications that Morand had perhaps not abandoned all hopes
for a wall and a canal came in 1782 and 1783, when he tried to prevent
the construction of the Bienfaisance Freemason lodge on a lot just outside
the official plan, objecting that it would stand in the path of what he still
believed to be necessary features (14 II 019, letters to and from Morand,
20 December 1782, 24 February and 6 March 1783).

16 Agreement between the comtes de Lyon and the Hôtel-Dieu, 28 August
1780, in 14 II 018. Morand's plans for the new quarter had first been
aired in his 1764 "Plan circulaire" (see chapter 3), and, to the mind of
some analysts, bore the mark of Soufflot (*Soufflot et son temps*, 78).
Long ago, Morand had seen (and purchased a map of) the newer parts of

Turin, a well-known model of a modern city. The centième denier was a one percent tax levied when a real estate sale was registered with the royal administration, ensuring that a public record of such transactions existed.

17 14 II 004, Levet to Morand, 20 August 1779. Chevalier, "L'urbanisation de la rive gauche"; Barre, "La formation des quartiers lyonnais," 172–6. The plans produced in 1780 and 1781 are found in AmL, 3 SMO 58, 213, 214, 215, and 447 (copies in 14 II 018 and 022). Morand and Décrénice had already clashed, when, between 1767 and 1772, the latter had proposed an ambitious transformation of the right bank of the Saône in front of the Saint-Jean cathedral. Morand, architect to the archbishop, had blocked the project (AD 69, 10 G 613).

18 AD 69, 1 C 297. The January 1780 edict called for hospital properties to be auctioned to ensure best returns. This practice, however, was ill-suited to a long-term plan to sell land on a vast scale. Consequently, each sale required a special dispensation (see for instance AD 69, 1 C 297, 19 July 1785, 9 June 1786, and 1 C 299, 8, 15, and 17 May 1785).

19 14 II 018, agreements, 24 May and 14 September 1780. Plan of the lands exchanged in AmL, 3 SMO 253. This exchange was registered for the nominal price of fifty livres tournois, suggesting that it did not affect the size of Morand's holdings (AD 69, 10 C 1295, 24 May 1780); however, five years later, Morand paid 1,500 lt for an unspecified lot (AD 69, 1 C 299, sale dated 7 September 1785, in list appended to a letter from the rectors to the intendant, 9 April 1787).

20 See appendix 3 for details of sales, and memorandum by Morand, 11 August 1765 (14 II 018) estimating land set aside for public use (146,502 square feet); calculations also in appendix 3.

21 A record of sales by the Hôtel-Dieu between 1781 and 1793 is found in 14 II 018 (with map, surface area, and price). A third of this total, 2.3 hectares, was purchased by Antoine Spréafico, who was rapidly becoming the king of entertainment in the Brotteaux (Vachon, "Antonio Spréafico"). A separate document, attached to a letter dated 9 April 1787 in AD 69, 1 C 299, mentions three other small sales for a total of 11,500 lt, including 1,500 lt for a small transaction with Morand himself.

22 AD 69, 1 C 299, Rectors to Terray, 15 May 1785 (7,000 lt per bichérée, or 0.63 lt per square foot); intendant to la Millière (director of the Ponts et chaussées), 6 December 1786. Between 1782 and 1788, the hospital also sold six lots outside the boundaries of the official plan (covering 278,354 square feet, or some 3.26 hectares, for a total of 69,981 lt). These sales fetched 1.45 sols per square foot initially and 11 sols per

square foot by the end of this short period (the hospital tried to secure a lowering of the first *lods* from the owners of the seigneurial rights over the area, although not all agreed; AD 69, 1 C 298, 4 March 1784).

23 Should funds be used to meet pressing daily needs, reassure worried lenders, or even compensate the administrators whose turn on the board came with hefty financial commitments? See for instance AD 69, 1 C 297, intendant to Calonne and Vergennes, 21 February 1786. Inspections announced 20 July 1785, and carried out from June 1786 to July 1787 (AD 69, 1 C 297).

24 AD 69, not. Dalier, 3 E 3868, 26 July 1760, sale by Soufflot et al. to Genève et al., lot, 281 feet by 105 feet, for 80,000 lt: 29,505 square feet (this lot was to be bisected by a public street); 20 September 1760, sale by Soufflot et al. to L. Roux, lot, 105 feet by 59 feet, for 33,000 lt: 6,195 square feet. 14 II 015, 24 March 1757, sale by Soufflot et al. to Morand.

25 Pérez, "Le lotissement du couvent des Célestins"; 14 II 011, "Prospectus – Société pour l'établissement d'un jardin public" (this sale included buildings that were to be demolished for the most part). Other figures were quoted, not surprisingly, concerning the size of this estate (108,443 square feet or 114,229 square feet in royal units, in 14 II 011, no date, no name, Morand seeking payment for his survey) and the sale (1,260,000 lt, and 1,370,952 lt; see report by Claude Gros, architect and surveyor-inspector of Lyon and Jean-Baptiste Laverrière, architect; 14 II 011, file "Célestins," 20 March 1789).

26 AD 69, BP 2561, purchase of field from Etienne Conte, with *commodo-incommodo* inquest, 4,471 lt, June 1760; copy of Morand's purchase, 3 July 1765, 14 II 018. The 4.5 hectare Abondance estate was purchased for 18,564 lt (plus 16,722 lt for the buildings).

27 This cryptic expression ("machine à faire fortune") was used at the end of a note titled "State of affairs on 1 January 1780," but it is not possible to know with any certitude to what operation it referred (14 II 007). When sales resumed, after the Revolution, Morand's son sold 3,750 square feet for 1,500 francs (the franc being explicitly equated to the pre-1789 livres tournois – again, amounting to eight sols per square foot). Later, but at an unknown date, he drafted a preliminary sale agreement (leaving the name of the buyer blank) to sell 22,750 square feet at the very different price of three francs per square foot, i.e., the equivalent of sixty sols per square foot. It is not clear whether this price reflects the inflation of the mid-1790s or whether this document dates from much later, when prices had risen substantially (for both, see appendix 3).

28 AD 69, 1 C 299, 24 November 1781.

29 For the state of the Brotteaux between 1800 and 1810, see Bertin et al., "Formes architecturales," 12–15. Napoléon's visit is described in Metzger and Vaesen, *Lyon de 1778 au Directoire*, vol. 11.

30 14 II 004, Levet to Morand, 8 June 1779. The warning came with an offer of a rental apartment from two canons of the cathedral chapter.

31 Cottin, "L'abbé Duret."

32 AD 69, 1 C 299, Rectors to Terray, 15 May 1785.

33 Mascoli, "Sur la route de Rome."

34 Even such a modest monopoly could raise the ire of Morand's detractors. They protested, for instance, that he had officially, and with some fanfare, donated street space to the public and yet turned around to sell seating rights. It was also noted that he tended to consider the plantations on and along these pathways as his private property (undated memorandum, signed abbé Guignet, 14 II 018); in the spring of 1779, this public seating business brought two hundred livres tournois to the company (14 II 004, Levet to Morand, 4 May 1779). See his exchanges with the Sr Cardinaly, a Corsican puppeteer (14 II 019, 29 April, 7 May 1776 and 3, 23 March 1777), and the work done on a café and inn in 1778 and 1780. Even before he had built his house, in fact almost immediately after buying the land, Morand had leased some kind of building to a restaurateur who went bankrupt in 1766; a successor failed again in 1792 (14 II 019).

35 Spréafico also owned a celebrated café on the Terreaux, thus being prepared for all seasons (Vachon, "Antonio Spréafico").

36 14 II 019, letters dated 15 December 1783, 20 January 1784, and related accounts. For a detailed account of these early flights, and notably the kind of enthusiasm they raised, see de Cazenove, *Les premiers voyages aériens* (which includes a list of those whose donations financed this first flight); for a broader perspective, see Gillespie, "Ballooning in France and Britain." For her part, Marie Thébaud-Sorger probes an interesting gap between early-modern and modern expectations: early accounts focused exclusively on the wonders of the mechanics of flying and almost entirely ignored the new perspective offered from the sky upon the landscape ("Les premiers ballons"). However, a 1788 visitor to Lyon clearly saw the possibilities offered by flight in this domain: "Quelle exacte topographie eut levé un géographe, à qui son ballon eut servit à la fois de carrosse et d'observatoire!" (What precise topography could a geographer sketch, for whom a balloon could be both a carriage and an observatory! In Galle, "Lettres sur un voyage," 417).

37 14 II 019; Barre and Feuga, *Morand et les Brotteaux*, 65–8, 73–9, 92–4, 99–102.

38 Puitspelu, "Distractions de jadis aux Brotteaux." Morand had rented a small building to a master pyrotechnist in 1786 (at 150 lt per year; 14 II 019).

39 Barre, "La formation des quartiers lyonnais"; Dutacq, *L'extension du cadre administratif.*

40 Chevalier, "L'urbanisation de la rive gauche."

41 Josette, "La formation des quartiers lyonnais"; Clémençon, "La fabrication de la ville ordinaire." For a short perspective on the evolution of attitudes, see Bethemont and Pelletier, "Lyon et ses fleuves."

42 Roche, *La France des Lumières*, chapter 6, notably 183–7. For a focused perspective on the interest of the age in urban matters, see Pujalte, "Le Projet pour le commerce."

43 DD 308, "Memorandum on the Extended Opening of the Porte Saint-Clair," 1789; AD 69, I C 115, 8 January 1782; AD 69, I C 299, 9 April 1787; 14 II 004, Levet to Morand, 31 May 1777; 14 May 1778. The closing of gates was mandated to take place half an hour after sunset in border cities, although Lyon had been granted an extra half-hour to accommodate its business needs.

44 Ruling from the "Maîtrise des Eaux et Forêts, Lyon," AmL, 0001 C 706 760, dated 19 March 1783. The problem was made worse by the fact that the silk industry at the heart of the city's trade entrusted workers with expensive materials, multiplying the risks of theft whenever these valuable supplies could be smuggled out of the city. A substantial industry revolved around the practice: see Hafter, "Women in the Underground Business."

45 AD 69, I C 298, intendant to Vergennes, 4 March 1784. Messance, *Nouvelles recherches*, 68. Recent research supports the idea that the population of Lyon could fluctuate rather rapidly and substantially, perhaps because such a large segment of the population retained links to rural areas (Bayard and Cayez, *Histoire de Lyon*, 48).

46 DD 308, "Memorandum on the Extended Opening of the Porte Saint-Clair," 1789 (p. 36).

47 Jean-Claude Perrot suggests that the eighteenth century turned increasingly to medical metaphors when observers of urban phenomena reached beyond the descriptive level to analyses of functions and then to the very core question of the birth, development, and decline of cities. The seventeenth century had gravitated toward such scientific parallels but limited itself to questions of function (in Bernard Lepetit et al., "Les miroirs de la ville," cx and cxi).

48 The archbishop of Lyon argued that the city was "too narrow" and "too long." Morand had made the same observation in his proposal, illustrated with a comparison to London (14 II 020, Enquête *commodo-incommodo*, December 1771; "Observations ...," 14 August 1769). For the range of arguments presented in favour of expansion, refer to chapter 3 above.

49 In Nîmes, the integration of rapidly growing suburbs into the city apparently raised no objection (Teisseyre-Sallmann, "Urbanisme et société").

50 All bourgeois de Lyon reported for guard duties. The vision of the city as a closed space is the starting point of countless reflections on the transformations of the eighteenth century. See for instance: Lepetit, "L'évolution de la notion de ville" (followed by a discussion edited in Lepetit et al., "Les miroirs de la ville"); *La ville au XVIIIe siècle*; Friedrichs, *The Early Modern City*; Chartier, "La ville chantier"; Ozouf, "Architecture et urbanisme"; Paquot, "Paris et ses limites."

51 Poussou, "De la difficulté." While the word *faubourg* referred to buildings outside the walls of a city, *banlieue* evoked a much larger rural area over which the city retained some jurisdiction.

52 Chartier, "La ville chantier," 121–2, 145–6, 440–50, 452. *La ville au XVIIIe siècle*. Ledoux's plans for the new city of Arc-en-Senans included only two gates through its walls and moats (Ozouf, "Architecture et urbanisme"). The will to enclose cities was still very evident among the engineers of the First Empire (Picon, "De la composition urbaine"). Roncayolo, *Lectures de villes*, chapter 3, "Les murs après les murs."

53 Davis, "The Sacred and the Body Social," notably p. 44.

54 Morineau, "Lyon l'italienne"; Henry, "La Saône, artère vitale."

55 Zeller, "Enjeux d'urbanisme." For the belief in a lower Saône, see for instance the report by G.-M. Delorme to the Lyon Academy (AmL, 49 II 21, 23 December 1771).

56 Lepetit, "Pouvoir municipal et urbanisme" (also "L'évolution de la notion de ville").

57 See the intervention by Marcel Roncayolo in Lepetit et al., "Les miroirs de la ville," cx.

58 Davis, "The Sacred and the Body Social," 54–5. A symbol of Lyon's alienation from the Rhône was to be found in the gardens of city hall, separated from the river by a row of sordid houses. To remedy this truncated perspective, a *trompe-l'oeil* had been painted on the walls of these ill-placed houses (Clapasson, *Description de la ville de Lyon*, 118).

Fernand Braudel insisted on the importance of the Rhône-Saône axis in French history (*L'identité de la France*, 239–71).

59 Paris offers an example of progressive (if not conflict-free) growth, astride a large river (Poussou, "De la difficulté").

60 Roncayolo, *Les grammaires d'une ville*, 332–4; the same author also recalls Jean Ehrard's comment on the two sides of Enlightened references to nature that could support arguments in favour of as well as against change ("L'aménagement du territoire," 511). See also Dockès, *L'espace dans la pensée économique*, introduction and chapter 1; and several comments in Garden and Lequin, eds., *Construire la ville*.

CHAPTER SEVEN

1 ["Le pont Saint-Clair] est infiniment agréable pour les habitants de Lyon qui sans cela n'auraient pu jouir des promenades qui sont sur la rive gauche du fleuve et les plus rapprochées de la ville ; [il] a donné une valeur réelle à des terrains vastes appartenant aux hôpitaux ; ... la construction de ce pont, placé en première ligne sur un fleuve large et rapide et qui a résisté plusieurs fois contre toute attente à l'effort des glaces entraînant avec elles des usines et des moulins, a eu lieu sur des principes nouveaux et a été regardé comme précieuse pour les arts, que jamais ils n'ont été à charge ni au gouvernement ni à la ville ..." "Malgré tous les frais qu'occasionna cette entreprise, elle fut extrêmement avantageuse aux concessionnaires ... Il est notoire que les principaux actionnaires y ont fait une fortune considérable." Plea for the prorogation of the doubling of the toll on the Pont Saint-Clair and counterplea from residents of the left bank (AD 69, 1807, S 2023 and L 1048).

2 "Je prends toujours la moyenne entre notre amour et la nécessité du travail." Morand to Levet, 29 October 1760, 14 II 004.

3 This land reverted back to Morand, who sold it to Spréafico (14 II 018, 29 November 1772; Barre and Feuga, *Morand et les Brotteaux*, 60).

4 14 II 012, letters, plans, accounts dated 31 October, 30, 31 December 1780, 10 May, 7 October 1781, 25 September 1783. Morand had to justify in detail his claim for 5,066 lt, arguing that it amounted to less than the ten percent of the total cost of the project customarily allocated to architects. Michel Gallet suggests that Parisian architects claimed five percent of the project cost, although they could receive more in more complicated cases (*Les demeures parisiennes*, 31).

5 Morand seems, for instance, to have completed the renovation of the Custoderie in 1791 (Hours and Nicolas, *Jean-Antoine Morand*, 24).

6 See 14 II 004, Morand to Levet, 17, 20 June 1777, and many notes exchanged between Morand and the mother superior of the Ursulines in 14 II 013. Guillin du Montet, seigneur of Poleymieux, was one of the first victims of popular violence in the region (26 June 1791), and his brother, Guillin de Pougelon, who had been an early financial backer of Morand, was arrested in the first antirevolutionary conspiracy (December 1790).

7 Drawings and notes in 14 II 013 and 014; many plans have been separated from the original papers and filed in the SMO fonds of the Archives municipales of Lyon.

8 See a range of accounts for hired help in 14 II 010.

9 Undated note to Buisson, 14 II 010. An earlier note (same file), from the 1770s, lists ten on-going affairs, starting with the bridge and transformation to the theatre.

10 In May 1777, locked in a battle over Morand's pension, the manager of the theatre, Lobreau, reclaimed the small space he used to retail ice; Antoinette Levet found an appropriate locale in a few weeks, only to lose it in a sharp confrontation with the owner of the building in 1789 (14 II 004, Levet to Morand, 12–23 May 1777, and 14 II 007, Jordan to Morand, 13, 20 June 1789). For rental disputes, see 14 II 006 and 007.

11 For rental accounts, see 14 II 006 and 007. They collected rent from their building at Saint-Clair (8,000–9,000 lt per year); the house inherited from A. Levet's father (3,000–4,000 lt per year); ten shops in the Terreaux (1,428 lt in 1787); la Paisible (partly rented, mid-1780s, 550 lt per year); and outbuildings, including a building rented to a baker, 300 lt per year, 1784–93, another to a fireworks shop, 150 lt per year, 1786–92, and an enclosed space for animal fights, 200 lt for six months (14 II 004, Levet to Morand, 4 May 1779). Pitiot's house yielded 10,000–11,000 lt, of which they retained an unknown fraction. Revenues drawn from the cultivation of the Brotteaux lands in 1770 included a far from negligible output of 3,230 lt (milk, hay, oats, fruits, poplar trees, and ice; 14 II 019). In 1777 Antoinette Levet calculated that it would be more profitable to farm out the land rather than manage it directly, because of the high cost of labour; a year later, they still hired a new gardener, but in the Year 6, the land was rented for 340 lt per year (14 II 004, Levet to Morand, 19 August 1777; 14 II 019, 22 February 1778, salary of the gardener: 278 lt per year; 14 II 007, inventory, 9 Prairial, Year 6, or 28 May 1797). An estimate of revenues from Machy reached 490 lt for the first seven months of 1793.

12 Between 1764 and 1793, we know of the following sales besides those in the Brotteaux listed in appendix 3: two houses at Saint-Clair, sold in

1764 and 1767 (207,000 lt and 250,000 lt); a house in Briançon, 1776 (3,500 lt). Etienne Levet's testament mentions half a dozen such annuities, but it is not known what became of them (14 II 009, 30 January and 4 May 1754).

13   14 II 004, A. Levet–Morand, 14 April, 12 May, and 5, 12 June 1777. For the central role played by notaries in economic matters of all levels, one may turn to the works of Jean-Paul Poisson, *Notaires et société*, and the critical reminder by Laurence Fontaine, "L'activité notariale."

14   14 II 004, Levet to Morand, 2 May, 12, 13, 20, 27 June 1777.

15   For all these discussions and manoeuvres, see letters between Morand and Levet, dated from 4 March 1779 to 20 August 1779, in 14 II 004.

16   This double statement, dated 1 January 1780, is in 14 II 007. The inventory of Morand's papers, some four years after his death, listed nine such life annuities contracted from 1767 to 1784 (for unspecified amounts; inventory, 9 Prairial, Year 6, or 28 May 1797, 14 II 007). Morand's general record of revenues and expenses from 1767 to 1793 is found in 14 II 006.

17   They were owed, respectively, 17,300, 15,300, 21,056, 12,000, and 50,000 lt (14 II 007, list of obligations, bearing dates ranging from 1760 to 1792). De Glatta's 50,000 loan went back to 3 January 1770, having been renewed in 1784, 1787, 1789, and 1792. Two loans, totalling 40,000 lt, had appeared under the name of Barroud in the 1775 accounts.

18   For recent reflections on these matters, see Fontaine et al., eds., *Des personnes aux institutions*, and Muldew, *The Economy of Obligation*.

19   Morand's first plans reached an estimated cost of 220,000–230,000 lt, and a second draft, meant to spare the city any traffic interruption, 280,000 lt (14 II 012, 16 August 1775; memorandum to the Consulat, no date). 14 II 004, Morand to Soufflot, 11 September 1776; 14 II 012, Morand to Soufflot, 8 January 1778; Morand's plan for a new square, dated 25 August 1778, in AmL, 3 S 270. Morand reported knowing of at least two other proposals, an expensive yet underpriced one for a stone bridge (540,000 lt, proposed by Chabert), and a more modest one, to his mind still overpriced, for a wooden structure (450,000 lt, by de Lallié; see also AD 69, 1 C 115, 21 April 1777).

20   14 II 012, Archbishop to Morand, 30 December 1777.

21   14 II 012, Archbishop to Morand, 16 October 1778. 14 II 004, Levet to Morand, 23 March, 3, 26 April 1779.

22   14 II 004, Levet to Morand, 6, 8, 16 May, 8, 22, 24 June, 1, 9, 12 July 1779. This reform was part of a reign-long attempt at finding new forms

of consultative bodies just short of full representation, one of the key debates of the prerevolutionary decades (Jones, *Reform and Revolution*).

23 Zeller, *Une famille consulaire*, vol. 3, 333–40. 14 II 012, 22 February 1782 (proposal from Pierre Barbier, who also asked for a full tax exemption and the use of a building). It was reported that a royal *lettre de cachet* (a much-abused arbitrary warrant for arrest or imprisonment without trial) was issued against at least one engineer to try and restore some form of serenity to the scene (Cottin, "L'abbé Duret").

24 Metzger and Vaesen, *Lyon de 1778 au Directoire*, vol. 4, at the date of 31 May 1791: Délibération du Conseil général de la Commune de Lyon, Tableau des revenus et des charges, des créances, dettes et besoins ... Construction du pont et des prisons.

25 Hours, *Histoire du pont de Saône*.

26 14 II 004, Morand to Levet, 29 May and 5 July 1777.

27 MacLeod, *Inventing the Industrial Revolution*; Hilaire-Pérez, *L'invention technique*.

28 14 II 004, Morand–Levet correspondence, 22, 29 July, 2, 7, 8, 18, 23, 27 August 1777, 13 March 1779. See also AmL, 704.372 (January–April 1778).

29 AD 69, BP 2561, "*Rapport d'expert*" (June 1759 to May 1761) and an undated note by Morand estimating his claim (14 II 015). Morand's immobilized capital was assessed at 36,000 lt, and his yearly loss valued at three percent. Loss of rental income reached 18,500 lt. Some of the parties objected to the cost of this report. Morand had accused Soufflot and his partners of having compounded his problems by falling behind in their building of the necessary defences against the river.

30 Letters dated 21, 26 April, 19 May, 19 June, 2, 8 August 1777, 26 June and 7 July 1778; and most exchanges between Levet and Morand from March to August 1779 contain references to this battle and the people asked to intervene (14 II 004; see also a proposal to Tolozan in 14 II 015). Morand's grandson suggested that it took another eight years before all was cleared and recorded the settlement at 14,000 lt (1854, Dureau et al., *Hommage à Morand*, 49). Munet, Soufflot, and Tolozan were to be reimbursed by the city – which had had the last word with regard to the final amount of the settlement.

31 14 II 004, Morand-Levet, 21, 26 April, 2, 5, 7, 12, 13, 15, 18, 23, 29, 31 May, 3, 5, 12, 13, 14, 20 June, 4, 25, 27 July, 7, 13, 19 August 1777. Antoinette Levet pressed Bloud particularly hard but also sought help from Bellecise, Grange-blanche, Marte, Muguet; she suspected, among others, Grand, the city's surveyor. The city's actions were partly justified

by the 1764 municipal reforms that prevented it from spending any money on the theatre, and the 1775 clash between the Assembly of Notables and Villeroy over the theatre monopoly (see chapter 1).

32 14 II 004, Morand–Levet, 8 May, 28 June, 3 August 1779; on 12 September 1797, Antoinette Levet gave the revenues from the ten shops to her son, for the remaining two years (see 14 II 007).

33 14 II 011, file sent to de Souligné, directeur général de la Douane de Lyon, and de Morelond, conseiller du roy, Fermier général (payment for this work was delayed; Morand–Archbishop, 14 March and 26 May 1783). Much earlier, Morand had drawn plans for this estate, perhaps for a short-lived project to install the new Conseil Supérieur (payment from Morand to M. Drivon for survey, 31 December 1771; Metzger, *Contribution à l'étude*, 208, and note 1). An ancestor of Victor-Amedeo of Sardinia had given the land to the Celestins in 1407.

34 14 II 004, Levet to Morand, 4, 14, 25 July 1777. Morand's drawings in AML, 3 SMO 84 and 85. Desvouges was notably backed by a Lyon agent de change, M. Madinier, and Gabriel Jars, brother of the noted scientist, who was running a copper mine not far from Lyon.

35 File on the Celestins venture in 14 II 011. The associates were seeking 1.5 million livres tournois, in 150 shares promising a nine percent return. They notably argued of the unique freedom from seigneurial dues attached to this property (*allodialité*), a strong point indeed (see above). Moinecour, "L'urbanisation du quartier des Célestins"; Pérez, "Le lotissement du couvent des Célestins."

36 The detail of Morand's proposals and work is found in 14 II 011. Mention of drawings for a public passageway at the Celestins dated September 1791 (Hours and Nicolas, *Jean-Antoine Morand*, 28). The ground floors and entresols of these houses would also be devoted to commercial pursuits, opening on a series of arcades. Morand estimated construction costs at 47,511 lt for the small houses (42 x 38 feet on the ground), and 86,406 lt for the large (72 x 45 feet).

37 14 II 010, 28 August and 24 September 1792, letters from M. Reux, architect at Bourg-en-Bresse.

38 In 1776 he had asked the secretary of Briançon's city hall to assemble evidence of the participation of his ancestors to that city's council (14 II 002). The Saint-Michel order was a medieval distinction that had been revived by Louis XIV and focused on artistic merit. Parts of the file assembled by Morand in 14 II 003 and 005.

39 On Morand's insistance, Bertin agreed that summer to present his request in Council, but it was apparently ignored. Perhaps because he sensed the

jealousies that his demand could arouse in Lyon, Morand hid his references to this matter behind the curious expression *"marbres verts,"* a reference to his gift to Bertin of green alpine marble vases; 14 II 004, Morand–Levet, 19, 31 May, 5, 19 June, 11, 27 July, 2, 13 August 1777.

40 14 II 004, Levet to Morand, 6 July 1778, 23 March 1779; 14 II 005, 14 April 1781, Vergennes to Tonnerre. When Morand's son, Antoine, reopened the matter, his petitions claimed that the comte de Provence (by then Louis XVIII) had managed to convince his brother, Louis XVI, to grant Morand the ennobling Ordre de Saint-Michel, sometimes in 1788. However, the Revolution broke out before the matter was officially settled (see file, 1819–1822, 14 II 027). Antoine had been eager to help his father's promotion before the Revolution (see letters from Antoine to his father, 3 June 1787 and 19 June 1788 for instance, 14 II 035).

41 1755 accounts book listing purchases totalling 1,457 lt, but the list was likely drawn at a later date (14 II 010), and 1758 accounts recording 1,069 lt (14 II 007). Italian notes in 14 II 005. In 1763, 249 lt were spent on maps, drawings, engravings (14 II 007). Some four hundred engravings and one hundred drawings have reached us among his papers (Dureau et al., *Hommage à Morand*, 81–91).

42 Inventory, 9 Prairial, Year 6, or 28 May 1797, 14 II 007 (or *Hommage à Morand*, annexe 5). The *Encyclopédie ou Dictionnaire Raisonné des Sciences, des Arts et des Métiers* (1751–80) was compiled and edited by Diderot, d'Alembert, and others.

43 He also received all of his father's architectural papers and artifacts (plans, drawings, maps, copper engraving plates, some tools as well as accounts), and some twenty paintings. His mother kept almost as many paintings. 14 II 008; Levet to son, 19 December 1771.

44 Among papers assembled by Antoine Morand, all dating from the last years of the Old Regime, 14 II 001.

45 A survey of Antoinette Levet's correspondence records contacts with some four hundred families in Lyon worthy of a written mention (Karine Charret, "Madame Morand," 11).

46 A helpful guide to the stylistic currents of the age may be found in Wend von Kalmein, *Architecture in France*.

47 Drawings and plans for the Brotteaux buildings are found in the SMO fonds of the AML.

48 14 II 005, two-year lease, starting on Saint Jean-Baptiste day, 1793. The building belonged to the d'Audiffret family, long-time friends of the Morands. For far-reaching reflections on the importance of furniture to elite circles, see Hellman, "Furniture, Sociability."

49 Etienne Levet, Antoinette's father, had leased an apartment for 650 lt while renting five others for close to 1,000 lt (14 ii 009, testament, 30 January and 4 May 1754). See a special issue of the *Cahiers d'histoire*, 44, no. 4 (1999), *Habiter la ville (XVIIe–XXe siècles)*, and Pardailhé-Gallabrun, *The Birth of Intimacy*, 40. Laws facilitating multiple owner-ships within a building only developed in the twentieth century (although it became more common to divide a building among heirs a century earlier, often on a floor-by-floor basis; at least one observer noted before the Revolution that it was not infrequent, in Lyon, for a house to belong to "many people"; Daumard, *Maisons de Paris*, 34, 254; Marchand, *Voyage en France*, vol. 1, 161).

50 *Affiches de Lyon*, no. 36, 7 September 1763 and no. 33, 13 August 1766. 14 ii 008, Levet to Antoine Morand, 19 December 1771. Dominique Julia notes that a growing number of private boarding schools catered to parents seeking something other than the most traditional form of educa-tion offered in older institutions ("L'éducation des négociants"). Antoine had been inoculated against smallpox at the age of five; this was still a hotly debated procedure; see *Affiches de Lyon* (no. 31, 3 August 1763 and no. 9, 39 February 1764).

51 Several letters from Antoinette Levet to her son (14 ii 008), from Antoine to his sister (14 ii 004), and many from Antoine to his mother (14 ii 035).

52 14 ii 004, Levet–Morand, 14, 21, 26, 28, 30 April, 19 May, 29 July, 2, 19 August 1777.

53 14 ii 004, Antoine Morand to his sister, 2 July 1776, 15 May, 8 June, 8 August 1778; Morand–Levet, 6 July 1778.

54 14 ii 004, Levet–Morand, 2 May 1777, 9, 15, 23 March, 3, 17 April, 4 May 1779.

55 Perhaps not surprisingly, events forced the family to reconsider this last provision (report dated 27 Messidor, Year 4, Grenoble, in 14 ii 027).

56 AD 69, Not. H.-F. Brenot, 3 E 3123, marriage Morand–Guilloud, 26 April 1785. A week earlier, Antoine had given his bride 9,000 lt worth of gifts, to which his mother added a set of diamond bracelets valued at 6,000–7,000 lt (note, 14 ii 009).

57 The same day, Catalan signed an official "Résignation d'office" (both documents in AD 69, Not. Guyot, 3 E 5710, 12 April 1785).

58 AD 69, not. Guyot, 3 E 5710, marriage Catalan–Verpillière, 20 December 1784.

59 14 ii 009, folder "Eléonore's marriage," contract 15 July 1786, and addendum to testament, Antoinette Levet, February 1789, 14 ii 008. The revenues of M. de Besson represent a capital of some 200,000 lt.

60 Morand spent perhaps half a year in Paris between 1744 and 1748 and
from December 1753 to late March 1754. He was there again from January to May 1759. We know little of his 1763 trip, but Antoinette Levet
accompanied him for the next trip, from May to August 1768. There
followed visits from November to December 1769, December 1770 to at
least February 1771, and August or September to December 1775. A new
series of trips started in April 1777 (to August), followed by an April-to-
May sojourn the following year (likely in two trips; Antoinette Levet
accompanied him at least on the first of these two visits), and a long visit
from March to August 1779. They both returned to Paris for a month in
the spring of 1788. The details presented in the next paragraph come
from 14 II 005.

61 "I am tired of begging ... let's free ourselves from all this ..." 14 II 004,
Levet to Morand, 28 April 1777, 17 June 1777.

EPILOGUE

1 "La nouvelle de la réunion des trois Ordres ayant été confirmée, le Peuple
s'assembla, et contraignit les propriétaires de maison à manifester la joie
publique par des illuminations ... mais l'excès de cette joie s'étant porté à
un trop haut degré ... le Peuple ... voulant terrasser les derniers efforts de
l'aristocratie, s'est transporté [devant] l'hôtel de M. Tolozan de
Montfort, [a] renversé le corps de garde, forcé les sentinelles, et a taillé en
mille morceaux le Mai ... De là, le Peuple s'est transporté du côté de la
porte St-Clair ... a attaqué le Bureau des portes, pris les registres et autres
papiers, qu'il a brûlés, et les effets, il les a jetés également dans le Rhône.
[Puis] la multitude est venue fondre sur le Bureau des Fermes, situé à
l'extrémité du pont de la Guillotière; elle n'a rien épargné ... et s'est
emparé ensuite d'un entrepôt de vins étrangers ... Alors les esprits, un peu
trop échauffés, se sont livrés tout entiers à leur emportement; le Peuple a
arraché le fusil et autres armes aux soldats ...; il en a blessé, tué et jeté
dans le Rhône plusieurs qui faisaient résistance." BMPD, 350 497, "Récit
sanglant de ce qui s'est passé à Lyon le 3 juillet ...," pamphlet published
on 8 July 1789, six pages in octavo. (BMPD, 350 497).

2 AD 69, 42 L 27 and 28.

3 Maurice Wahl suggests that he may even have been chosen as a deputy to
the Provincial Assembly, which was convened for the first time in 1788
(*Les premières années de la Révolution*, 172).

4 14 II 023, Deliberations of the bridge company, 1790–93.

5 Thirty two sections had been created in January 1790 as electoral districts, neighbourhood assemblies, and administrative units. For recent

accounts of revolutionary years in Lyon see Benoît: *L'identité politique de Lyon*, and "Analyse des violences urbaines"; and Benoît and Saussac, *Guide historique*.

6 The matter of responsibilities for the bloody repression visited upon Lyon has been reconsidered by Paul Mansfield, "The repression of Lyon."

7 Documentation of Morand's role in the siege is in 14 II 022; Arrêt, 16 Frimaire, Year 2 (6 December 1793), AD 69, 42 L 94; transcript of interrogation, on 23 December 1793, published in Hours and Nicolas, *Jean-Antoine Morand*, 50–1; Ruling of the revolutionary tribunal in AD 69, 42 L 27, 5 Pluviose, Year 2 (24 January 1794). Late in November, Morand had obtained a section certificate testifying that he had played no military role in the defence of the city, and a statement from the municipal authorities that he was needed in the reconstruction of the bridge (AD 69, 42 L 130). For the nature of the repression, see Mansfield, "The Management of Terror."

8 Morand to Levet, 27 December 1793, 16, 18 January 1794, published in Hours and Nicolas, *Jean-Antoine Morand*, 48–9 (and mention of letter to mayor, p. 50). Originals in 14 II 005; several more letters (or rather, short notes) in AmL, II 255. On 29 December 1794, Antoine Morand wrote to his mother that he had to "avoid Lyon" (14 II 035, Antoine Morand to Antoinette Levet, 29 Frimaire, Year 3; he was then in Machy). Mansfield, "The Management of Terror," 471.

9 Service to the crown of Savoie, on the Jouffrey side of the family, figured among the arguments advanced by the Morands in their claim to nobility (see above). Antoine's contribution to the 1789 *souscription patriotique* reached 3,200 lt. Documents charting Antoine Morand's career are in 14 II 027.

10 See the list of administrators and representatives for the year 1791, published by Metzger and Vaesen, *Lyon de 1778 au Directoire*, vol. 4. AD 69, 42 L 39, Morand Jouffrey to the Citoyen Général, comité de surveillance, 14 April 1793 (the report itself is not included in file).

11 File in 14 II 027, including a draft of a letter intended to dissociate him from his Lyon connections. Antoine had spent several years in that city, most likely working for his father's cousin, a lawyer (see several letters to his mother, 1782 and following, 14 II 035).

12 Antoine Morand wrote his mother that the Directory's Council of Elders had officially given back the bridge to the company on the third supplementary day of Year 4 (or 19 September 1796; see letter from Antoine Morand to his mother, 14 II 035), but it appears that the company had

recovered its property and the right to collect a toll a year earlier (see decision by commissaries dispatched to the region dated 6 Fructidor, Year 3, or 23 August 1795, AD 69, 1 L 1048). By the spring of 1797, Antoine could report that "Lyon was now very quiet, the elections most orderly ... and it was possible to hope for great improvements in their lot" (14 II 035, Antoine Morand to Antoinette Levet, 10 April 1797). The cost of indispensable repairs to the bridge was estimated at more than 4.6 million livres, a sum that was, however, the equivalent of only 130,000 lt in 1790 terms.

13 AD 69, 1 L 1048. Morand's bridge had also been known by its colour, as the *Pont Rouge*; it became the Pont des Victoires or Pont de la Victoire late in 1794 to honour the successes of revolutionary armies. Two statues by Chinard were placed at its cityside entrance; his early career had been supported by Morand, but he fared well through the revolutionary period. A few years earlier, Antoinette Levet had sought to extricate her personal properties from her husband's confiscated estate; she valued her own share at close to 100,000 lt (14 II 030, petition, undated).

14 On 4 Thermidor, Year 4 (22 August 1796), Antoine Morand Jouffrey bought a 4,022-square-foot lot (adjacent to the house inherited by his wife), confiscated from the Dominican order, for 9,000 lt (AD 69, 1 Q 409, Ventes en exécution de la loi du 28 ventose an 4, no. 203). Much earlier, he purchased a large house confiscated from the Carmelites but on behalf of a third party (19 March 1791, 191,500 lt; AD 69, 1 Q 325, District de Lyon, vente de biens nationaux, no. 150). See an impressive list of his lands in and near Machy in 14 II 030 (drafted for fiscal purposes, no date).

15 Bruyère, "Des monuments aux victimes du siège."

16 Benoît, *L'identité politique de Lyon*. For a short exposition of this thesis, see Benoît, "De l'identité politique lyonnaise." For a comparative approach to the later transformations of cities, see Sutcliffe, *Towards the Planned City*.

17 Dujardin and Saunier, eds., *Lyon, l'âme d'une ville*.

18 Mansfield, "The Management of Terror," 483, 486. Hardouin-Fugier, "Architectes et entrepreneurs."

19 Saunier, *L'Esprit lyonnais*, passim, and p. 188.

20 Hanson, *The Jacobin Republic*.

21 See chapter 1, note 33. Antoinette Levet's maternal aunt was married to an entrepreneur, J. Dufrêne, whose *"fenderie de fer"* (slitting mill) at Saint-Genis-de-Terrenoire went bankrupt; following his wife's advice,

Morand acted as "*syndic*," administrator and representative, to the creditors, among whom he figured for a modest sum (File in 14 11 009, and 14 11 004, Levet to Morand, 2 May 1777).

22 For instance, see the extended family networks behind the insertion in Lyon of the Valesque family (Zeller, "Les Valesque"), or the success of a brother of the Brac who so regularly opposed Morand (Zeller, "Une biographie"). More broadly, see Bamford, *Privilege and Profit*; Forster, *Merchants, Landlords, Magistrates*; Adams, *A Taste for Comfort and Status*.

23 14 11 004, Levet to Morand, 20 March 1760. Some years later, her son felt the need to explain why they never had a third child (14 11 028, notes for an autobiography by Antoine Morand de Jouffrey, started 1 May 1788). For reflections on these questions, see the forum "Demographic Thought and Reproductive Realities, From Montesquieu to Malthus," in *Eighteenth-Century Studies*, 32, no. 4 (1999).

24 Roughly, "Damn business." 14 11 004, Levet to Morand, 7 August 1760.

25 Lespagnol, "Femmes négociants." It is suggested that the late medieval period proved more favourable to women's economic activities (Howell, *Women, Production*).

26 Besides the evidence supplied by Garden's *Lyon et les Lyonnais*, see Davis, "Women in the Crafts," or Hafter, "Women who Wove," and "Women in the Underground Business."

27 Michel Gallet suggests that Parisian architects were much better considered than writers, for instance, and that their duties remained very broad indeed; the profession still remained rather open (*Les demeures parisiennes*, notably chapter 2). Cottin, "L'architecte à Lyon."

28 Malverti, "Ville et régularité."

29 Malverti, *L'idée constructive*, notably Bruno Queysanne, "Architectes et/ou ingénieurs," 9–13, and Loach, "François Cuenot (1610–1686)," 41–63. The Napoleonic regime furthered the role of engineers: André Guillerme, "La formation des nouveaux édiles."

30 For an introduction to a well-worn topic, see Crouzet, *Britain Ascendant*; more precise references in Chapman and Chassagne, *European Textile Printers*, 202, as well as chapters 4 and 10).

31 14 11 035, Antoine Morand to Morand, 19 June 1788.

32 Hirsch, *Les deux rêves du commerce*; see also Bossenga, *The Politics of Privilege*. Bamford, *Privilege and Profit*.

33 See note 54, chapter 3 (with reference to the Archives des Hospices Civils de Lyon, A 19, 1743).

34 Gérard Bruyère goes on to suggest that the next vocation of the Brotteaux – the commemoration of the city's resistance to tyranny, marked a crucial step toward the appropriation of what had been a "*non-lieu*": monuments were needed to pull this nondescript flood plain out of its anonymity ("Des monuments aux victimes du siège," notably 89).

35 On the dearth of heros in Lyon, see Saunier, *L'Esprit lyonnais*, 22.

Bibliography

PRIMARY SOURCES

MAPS OF THE CITY OF LYON

Maps and plans illustrating the transformations of Lyon are available on the Web site of the Lyon municipal archives (see "fonds figurés" at: http://www.archives-lyon.fr). Vital information can also be found in the online version of a publication titled *Forma Urbis. Les plans généraux de Lyon du XVIe au XXe siècle* (Lyon: Archives municipales de Lyon 1997): http://www.archives-lyon.fr/sommaires/forma_urbis.html. Among other important publications:

Debombourg, Georges. *Atlas historique du département actuel du Rhône.* Lyon: Imprimerie Louis Perrin, 1862.
Pelletier, Jean, and Charles Delfante. *Atlas historique du grand Lyon: formes urbaines et paysages au fil du temps.* Seyssinet 38170: Editions Xavier Lejeune – Libris, 2004.
Pelletier, Jean. *Lyon pas à pas. Son histoire à travers ses rues. La Presqu'île, la rive gauche du Rhône, les quais et ponts du Rhône.* Roanne: Horvath, 1986.
Pinol, Jean-Luc, ed. *Atlas historique des villes de France.* Paris: Hachette, 1996.

ARCHIVES MUNICIPALES DE LYON (AMB)

Private Fonds:
Fonds Morand: 14 II 001, 002, 003, 004, 005, 006, 007, 008, 009
    14 II 010, 011, 012, 013, 014, 015, 016, 017, 018, 019
    14 II 020, 021, 022, 023, 024, 027, 028

14 II 030, 035

II 255

II 325; ii 317

Fonds Fleurieu (Perrache):   49 II 3, 10, 21

Series AA Titres (Deeds and Titles):   AA 19, 132

Series BB Actes consulaires, Délibérations consulaires (Council
Decisions/By-Laws, Council Debates):

BB 249; BB 252, 255; BB 260, 265; BB 270, 272; BB 282; BB 293, 294,
296; BB 301–5, 308; BB 310, 311, 312, 313, 315, 316, 317; BB 320,
321, 322, 324, 325, 327, 329; BB 330, 331, 332, 335, 336, 338, 339;
BB 341, 342, 343, 348; BB 360, 361, 363 365, 366; BB 443–7; BB
452–456

Series DD Bien communaux, travaux publics, voirie ... (City properties,
public works, and street matters):

DD 55; DD 256; DD 274, 275, 276, 278; DD 308; DD 330

SM 86 List of rectors; SM 490; SM 491

3 SMO 58, 63, 84, 85, 213, 214, 215, 223, 225, 228, 253, 447

3 S 270

0001 C 704 336 *Mémoire* (Memoranda), 1779

0001 C 706 760 (Ruling, Maîtrise des Eaux et Forêts, 1783)

704.439

704.372

706.344

ARCHIVES DEPARTEMENTALES DU RHONE (AD 69)

Sénéchaussée de Lyon: BP 2561; BP 3603

Series C (Intendance):   I C 114, 115; I C 131–63; I C 142;
I C 152, 156; I C 202; I C 225–6; I C 297, 298, 299

8 C 429–30

10 C 1295

Notaries: 3 E 3123 (Brenot); 3 E 3868 (Dalier); 3 E 4505 (Dubost); 3 E
4733 (Dussurgey); 3 E 5707, 5708, 5710 (Guyot); 3 E 5110 (Berthon
de Fromental); 3 D 5265 (Girard); 3 E 6150–65 (Levet); 3 E 7019
(Perrin); 3 E 9184 (Caillot); 3 E 9709 (Fromental); 3 E 11132 (Durand)

Religious Institutions: 27 H 256; 27 H 428; 10 G613; 10 G 717, 721; 10
G 3814, 3815

2 PL Plan de Lyon, 1786

Revolutionary Archives: I L 1044, 1048; 42 L 27, 28, 39, 94, 130; I Q
325, 409

Ponts et chaussées: S 1338, S 1376, S 2023

BIBLIOTHEQUE MUNICIPALE DE LYON – PART-DIEU
(BMPD)
Fonds Coste: MS 1129; MS 1133 n. 44
117 749 (pamphlet)
115 629 (factum)
350 497 (pamphlet)
Affiches de Lyon
Almanach astronomique et historique de la ville de Lyon
Almanach de la ville de Lyon
*Indicateur alphabétique des curiosités, établissements réguliers et
    séculiers; des personnes de qualité; officiers de judicature, police
    et finances; Notables, bourgeois, négociants, gens d'affaires et
    principaux artistes de la ville de Lyon, avec les noms des rues et
    des maisons de leurs demeures. Pour l'année 1788* (Faucheux,
    Lyon).

ARCHIVES DES HOSPICES CIVILS DE LYON
Archives de l'Hôtel-Dieu
    Fondations, Privilèges (Deeds and Titles, Privileges):   A 19, a 20
    Propriétés, Procédures (Properties, Legal Matters):   B 482–3
    Administration: E 15, E 17; E 1597
Archives de la Charité
    Propriétés, Procédures: B 124, 126; B 325, 343

ARCHIVES DEPARTEMENTALES DE L'HERAULT
C 4271; C 6820 and 6822

SECONDARY SOURCES

Adams, Christine. *A Taste for Comfort and Status: A Bourgeois Family
    in Eighteenth-Century France.* University Park: Pennsylvania State
    University Press, 2000.
Antoine, Michel. *Louis XV.* Paris: Fayard, 1989.
Arbellot, Guy, and Bernard Lepetit. *Atlas de la Révolution Française.*
    Vol. I, *Routes et communications.* Paris: Editions de l'EHESS, 1987.
Aynard, Théodore. *Histoire des deux Antoine et du vieux pont Morand
    sur le Rhône à Lyon.* Lyon: Mougin-Russand, 1886.
Bamford, Paul W. *Privilege and Profit. A Business Family in
    Eighteenth-Century France.* Philadelphia: University of Pennsylvania
    Press, 1988.

Barre, Josette. "La formation des quartiers lyonnais *intra-muros* de rive gauche." *Bulletin de la Société historique, archéologique et littéraire de Lyon* (1998): 157–90.

– *La colline de la Croix-Rousse: histoire et geographie urbaines.* Lyon: Editions lyonnaises d'art et d'histoire, 1993.

Barre, Josette, and Paul Feuga. *Morand et les Brotteaux.* Lyon: Editions lyonnaises d'art et d'histoire, 1998.

Bayard, Françoise. *Vivre à Lyon sous l'ancien régime.* Paris: Perrin, 1997.

Bayard, Françoise, and Pierre Cayez, eds., *Histoire de Lyon des origines à nos jours.* Vol. 2, *Du XVIe siècle à nos jours.* Le Côteau 42120: Horvath, 1980.

Bédarida, Henri. *Parme et la France de 1748 à 1789.* Paris, 1928. Reprint. Geneva: Slatkine Reprints, 1977.

Beik, William. "Louis XIV and the Cities." In *Edo and Paris. Urban Life and the State in the Early Modern Era*, edited by James L. McClain, John M. Merriman, and Ugawa Kaory, 68–85. Ithaca, NY: Cornell University Press, 1994.

Bély, Lucien, ed. *Dictionnaire de l'Ancien Régime.* Paris: PUF, 1996.

Bénedict, Philip. *Cities and Social Change in Early Modern France.* London: Routledge, 1989.

Benhamou, Reed. "Women and the Verdigris Industry in Montpellier." In *European Women and Preindustrial Craft*, edited by Daryl M. Hafter, 3–15. Bloomington: Indiana University Press, 1995.

Benoît, Bruno. *L'identité politique de Lyon. Entre violences collectives et mémoire des élites (1786–1905).* Paris: L'Harmattan: Paris, 1999.

– "De l'identité politique lyonnaise (1793–1905)." *Revue d'histoire moderne et contemporaine* 44, no. 3 (1997): 504–13.

– "Analyse des violences urbaines à l'époque révolutionnaire: l'exemple lyonnais." In *Ville et Révolution française*, edited by Bruno Benoit, 147–62. Lyon: PUL, 1994.

Benoît, Bruno, and Roland Saussac. *Guide historique de la Révolution à Lyon (1789–1799).* Lyon: Editions de Trévoux, 1988.

Bernard, Frédéric. *De Lyon à la Méditerranée.* Paris: Hachette, 1855.

Bertin, Dominique, A. S. Clémençon, B. Dumétier, and M.F. Ligoure. "Formes architecturales et formation urbaine. Le cas de Lyon." *Travaux de l'institut d'histoire de l'art de Lyon*, no. 11 (1988): 7–32.

Bethement, Jacques, and Jean Pelletier. "Lyon et ses fleuves: des berges perdues aux quais retrouvés." *Revue de géographie de Lyon* 65, no. 4 (1990): 300–7.

Bordes, Maurice. *La réforme municipale du contrôleur général Laverdy et son application (1764–1771)*. Toulouse: Faculté des lettres et sciences humaines de Toulouse, 1968.

Bosher, John F. *The Single Duty Project. A Study of the Movement for a French Customs Union in the Eighteenth Century*. London: University of London, Athlone Press, 1964.

Bossenga, Gail. *The Politics of Privilege. Old Regime and Revolution in Lille*. Cambridge: Cambridge University Press, 1991.

– "City and State: An Urban Perspective on the Origins of the French Revolution." In *The Political Culture of the Old Regime*, edited by Keith M. Baker, 115–40. Oxford: Pergamon Press, 1987.

Braham, Allan. *The Architecture of the French Enlightenment*. Berkeley: University of California Press, 1980.

Braudel, Fernand. *L'identité de la France*. Paris: Arthaud–Flammarion, 1986.

Brayshay, Mark, Philip Harrison, and Brian Chalkley. "Knowledge, Nationhood and Governance: The Speed of the Royal Post in Early-Modern England." *Journal of Historical Geography* 24, no. 3 (1998): 265–88.

Brun de la Valette, R. "Louis Tolozan de Montfort. Dernier prévôt des marchands lyonnais." *Rive Gauche*, no. 143 (1997): 19–20.

Bruyère, Gérard. "Des monuments aux victimes du siège de Lyon et de quelques autres pyramides." In *Amplepuis et sa région*, 87–117. Lyon: Archives départementales du Rhône et Union des sociétés historiques du Rhône, 1994.

Burdy, Jean. "Guillaume-Marie Delorme (1700–1782), académicien lyonnais." In *Bulletin de la Société historique, archéologique et littéraire de Lyon* 34 (2004–05): 171–92.

Burnouf, Joëlle, J.-O. Guilhot, M.-O. Mandy, and C. Orcel. *Le pont de la Guillotière. Franchir le Rhône à Lyon*. Lyon: DARA, 1991.

Cahiers d'histoire 44, no. 4 (1999), special issue "Habiter la ville (XVIIe–XXe siècles)."

Cahier de l'Institut d'histoire de l'art de l'université Lyon, no. 1, "Le rôle de Lyon dans les échanges artistiques" (1974), and no. 2, "Le rôle de Lyon dans les échanges artistiques" (1974).

Carvais, Robert. "La force du droit. Contribution à la définition de l'entrepreneur parisien du bâtiment au XVIIIe siècle." *Histoire, économie et société* 14, no. 2 (1995): 163–89.

Cazenove, Raoul de. *Les premiers voyages aériens à Lyon en 1784*. Lyon: Pitrat ainé 1887.

Chapman, Stanley D., and Serge Chassagne. *European Textile Printers in the Eighteenth Century*. London: Heineman, 1981.

Charre, Alain. "Soufflot et l'urbanisme lyonnais." In *Soufflot et l'architecture des Lumières*, 115–23. Paris: CNRS, 1980.

Charre, Alain, and Catherine Servillat. "L'entreprise du quartier Saint-Clair." In *L'oeuvre de Soufflot à Lyon. Etudes et documents*, 21–6. Lyon: PUL, 1982.

Charret, Karine. "Madame Morand, une femme du XVIIIe siècle." MA thesis, University of Lyon 3, 2001.

Chartier, Roger. "La ville chantier." In *Histoire de la France urbaine*, vol. 3, edited by Georges Duby, 109–56. Paris: Seuil, 1981.

Chassagne, Serge, ed. *Une femme d'affaire au XVIIIe siècle. La correspondance de Mme Maraise*. Toulouse: Privat, 1981.

Châtelain, Abel. "Les ponts du Rhône. Etude de géographie humaine." *Les Etudes Rhodaniennes. Revue de géographie régionale. Bulletin de la Société de géographie de Lyon et de la région lyonnaise* 19, nos. 3–4 (1944): 109–39.

Chevalier, Martine. "L'urbanisation de la rive gauche du Rhône à Lyon dans la deuxième moitié du XIXe siècle : quelles politiques pour quels résultats ?" *Bulletin du centre d'histoire économique et sociale de la région lyonnaise*, no. 4 (1988): 5–38.

Chouliaraki, Lilie, and Norman Fairclough. *Discourse in Late Modernity. Rethinking Critical Discourse Analysis*. Edinburgh: Edinburgh University Press, 1999.

Christin, Olivier. "*Ancien Régime* Ballots: A Double Historicization of Electoral Practices." *Constellations* 11, no. 1 (2004): 44–60.

Chuzeville, Sylvain. "Publication et publicité autour du Projet d'un plan général de la ville de Lyon de Jean-Antoine Morand (1766)." In *Claude Nicolas Ledoux et le livre d'architecture en français. Les écrits sur la ville, les programmes et la nature de l'architecture*, edited by Daniel Rabreau and Dominique Massounie, 156–64. Paris: Centre des monuments nationaux – Editions du Patrimoine, 2006.

Clapasson, André. *Description de la ville de Lyon*. 1741. Edited by Gilles Chomer and Marie-Félicie Pérez. Seyssel, 01420: Champvallon, 1982.

Cleary, Richard L. *The Place Royale and Urban Design in the Ancien Régime*. Cambridge: Cambridge University Press, 1999.

Clémençon, Anne-Sophie. "La fabrication de la ville ordinaire. Pour comprendre les processus d'élaboration des formes urbaines, l'exemple du domaine des Hospices civils de Lyon. Lyon-Guillotière, rive gauche du Rhône, 1781–1914." Doctoral thesis, University of Lyon 2, 1999.

Cobb, Richard. *Reactions to the French Revolution*. London: Oxford University Press, 1972.

Collins, James B. "*Translation de domicile*: Rethinking Sedentarity and Mobility in the Early Modern French Countryside." *French History* 20, no. 4 (2006): 387–404.

Cosperec, Annie. *Blois. La forme d'une ville*. Paris: Editions de l'Imprimerie nationale 1994.

Coste, Anne, Antoine Picon, and Francis Sidot, eds. *Un ingénieur des Lumières. Emile-Marie Gauthey*. Paris: Presses de l'Ecole nationale des Ponts et chaussées, 1993.

Cottin, François-Régis. "L'abbé Duret témoin des grands travaux à Lyon." *Bulletin de la Société historique, archéologique et littéraire de Lyon* 24 (1994): 63–81.

– "Le carrefour de Lyon à la fin de l'Ancien Régime." In *Le Rhône. Naissance d'un département*, 51–8. Lyon: Archives départementales du Rhône, 1990.

– "Le chantier du nouvel Hôtel-Dieu de Lyon au XVIIIe siècle." *Bulletin de la Société historique, archéologique et littéraire de Lyon* 31 (2001): 237–52.

– "Trois propositions pour le confluent au XVIIIe siècle." *Bulletin de la Société académique d'architecture de Lyon*, no. 5 (2003): 12–7.

– "L'architecte à Lyon au XVIIIe siècle." In *Soufflot et l'architecture des Lumières*, 103–07. Paris: CNRS, 1980.

Crouzet, François. *Britain Ascendant: Comparative Studies in Franco-British Economic History*. Cambridge: Cambridge University Press, 1990.

Croze, Auguste, Marius Carle, Jean Lacassagne, and E. Mehoz. *Histoire du Grand Hôtel-Dieu des origines à l'année 1900*. Lyon: Audin, 1924.

Cuer, Georges, "Léonard Michon, chroniqueur lyonnais du XVIIIe siècle." In *Amplepuis et sa région*, 71–86. Lyon: Archives départementales du Rhône et Union des sociétés historiques du Rhône, 1994.

Daumard, Louise. *Maisons de Paris et propriétaires parisiens au XIX siècle*. Paris: Cujas, 1965.

Davis, Natalie Zemon. "Women in the Crafts in Sixteenth-Century Lyon." In *Women and Work in Preindustrial Europe*, edited by Barbara A. Hanawalt, 167–97. Bloomington: Indiana University Press, 1986.

- "The Sacred and the Body Social in Sixteenth Century Lyon." *Past and Present*, no. 90 (1981): 40–70.

Debombourg, Georges. *Atlas historique du département actuel du Rhône.* Lyon: Imprimerie Louis Perrin, 1862.

Delfante, Charles, and Agnès Dally-Martin. *Cent ans d'urbanisme à Lyon.* Lyon: Editions LUGD, 1994.

Delphine-Balleyguier, O., trans., *Journal de Mme Cradock. Voyage en France (1783–1786).* Paris: Perrin et cie., 1911.

Delvit, Philippe. "Construire en rivière au XVIIIe siècle : les continuateurs de Colbert sur le Lot." *Annales du Midi* 95, no. 164 (1983): 429–47.

De neiges en glaces ..., 1994. Supplement no. 5 to *Cahier de l'ASER*.

Dockès, Pierre. *L'espace dans la pensée économique du XVIe au XVIIIe siècle.* Paris: Flammarion 1969.

Duby, Georges, ed. *Histoire de la France urbaine.* Vol. 3, *La ville classique.* Paris: Seuil, 1991.

Dujardin, Philippe, and Pierre-Yves Saunier, eds. *Lyon, l'âme d'une ville (1850–1914).* Lyon: Editions lyonnaises d'art et d'histoire, n.d.

Dulaure, Jacques-Antoine. *Description des principaux lieux de France.* 6 vols. Paris: 1788–89.

Durand, Georges. *Le patrimoine foncier de l'Hôtel-Dieu de Lyon, 1482–1791 : contribution à l'étude de la grande propriété rhodanienne.* Lyon: Centre d'histoire économique et sociale de la région lyonnaise, 1974.

Duranton, Henri, and Christiane Lauvergnat-Gagnière, eds. *Journal d'un voyage aux environs de la Loire et de la Saône jusqu'à la mer Méditerranée et sur les côtes du Languedoc et de la Provence* (anonymous). Saint-Etienne: Publications de l'Université de Saint-Etienne, 1993.

Dureau, Jeanne-Marie. *Inventaire provisoire du fonds Morand.* Lyon: Archives municipales de Lyon, 1994.

Dureau, Jeanne-Marie, Claude Mermet, and Marie-Félicie Pérez, *Hommage à Morand. A l'occasion du prêt à usage des papiers Morand de Jouffrey.* Lyon: Archives municipales de Lyon, 1994.

Dutacq, F. *L'extension du cadre administratif et territorial de la cité lyonnaise de 1789 à 1852.* Lyon: Audin, 1923.

Eighteenth-Century Studies 32, no. 2 (1999): Forum "Demographic Thought and Reproductive Realities, from Montesquieu to Malthus."

Ellis, Monica. *Ice and Icehouses through the Ages.* Winchester, Hampshire, United Kingdom: Hampshire Industrial Archaeology Society, 1982.

Expilly, abbé Jean-Joseph d'. *Dictionnaire géographique, historique et politique ..., Vol. 4.* Paris, 1766.

Faron, Olivier, and Etienne Hubert, eds. *Le sol et l'immeuble : les formes dissociées de propriété immobilière dans les villes de France et d'Italie (XIIe–XIXe siècle).* Lyon: Centre inter-universitaire d'histoire et d'archéologie médiévales / PUL, 1995.

Favier, René. *Les villes du Dauphiné aux XVIIe et XVIIIe siècles.* Grenoble: Presses Universitaires de Grenoble, 1993.

Félix, Joël. "Les finances urbaines au lendemain de la guerre de Sept Ans." In *Les finances en province sous l'Ancien Régime,* edited by Françoise Bayard, 179–228. Paris: Comité pour l'histoire économique et financière de la France, 2000.

Feyel, Gilles. *L'annonce et la nouvelle. La presse d'information en France sous l'Ancien régime (1630–1788).* Oxford: Voltaire Foundation, 2000.

– "Négoce et presse provinciale en France au 18e siècle : méthodes et perspectives de recherche." In *Cultures et formations négociantes dans l'Europe moderne,* edited by Franco Angiolini and Daniel Roche, 439–511. Paris: Editions de l'EHESS, 1995.

Flandrin, Jean-Louis. *Histoire de l'alimentation.* Paris: Fayard, 1996.

Fontaine, Laurence. *Pouvoir, identités et migrations dans les hautes vallées des Alpes occidentales (XVIIe–XVIIIe siècle).* Grenoble: Presses Universitaires de Grenoble, 2003.

– "L'activité notariale." *Annales ESC* 48, no. 2 (1993): 475–83.

Fontaine, Laurence, Gilles Postel-Vinay, Jean-Laurent Rosenthal, and Paul Servais, eds. *Des personnes aux institutions : réseaux et culture du crédit du XVIe au XXe siècle en Europe.* Louvain-la-Neuve: Academia-Bruyland, 1997.

Fontanon, Claudine. "L'échec du projet industriel sur les terrains de Perrache, 1826–1832." *History and Technology* 6, no. 2 (1988): 63–94.

Forma Urbis. Les plans généraux de Lyon du XVIe au XXe siècle. Lyon: Archives municipales de Lyon, 1997. A version is currently available on the Web site of the municipal archives of Lyon at http://www.archives-lyon.fr/sommaires/forma_urbis.html.

La formation architecturale au XVIIIe siècle en France. Paris: Comité de la Recherche et du Développement en Architecture, 1980.

Forster, Robert. *Merchants, Landlords, Magistrates: The Depont Family in Eighteenth-Century France.* Baltimore: Johns Hopkins University Press, 1980.

French Historical Studies 19, no. 14 (1996). Special issue on biographies.

Friedrichs, Christopher. *The Early-Modern City 1450–1750*. London: Longman, 1995.

Galle, Léon. "Lettres sur un voyage en France en 1788." *Revue du Lyonnais* 18, 5th series, nos. 5 and 6 (1894): 349–57 and 409–32 (Letters from Mr. C*** de T***, Secrétaire du roi, to Mr. de Br***).

Gallet, Michel. *Les demeures parisiennes à l'époque de Louis XVI*. Paris: Editions du temps, 1964.

Garden, Maurice. *Lyon et les Lyonnais au XVIIIe siècle*. Paris: Les Belles-Lettres, 1970.

Garden, Maurice, and Yves Lequin, eds. *Construire la ville aux XVIIIe–XXe siècles*. Lyon: PUL, 1983.

Gardes, Gilbert. *Le voyage de Lyon*. Lyon: Editions Horvath, 1993.

– *Lyon, l'art et la ville*. 2 vols. Paris: CNRS, 1988.

– "Le monument public français. L'exemple de Lyon." Doctoral thesis, Sorbonne University, 1986.

Garrioch, David. *The Making of Revolutionary Paris*. Berkeley: University of California Press, 2002.

Gascon, Richard. *Grand commerce et ville urbaine au XVIe siècle. Lyon et ses marchands*. 2 vols. Paris: SEVPEN, 1971.

Gillespie, Richard. "Ballooning in France and Britain, 1783–1786: Aerostation and Adventurism." *Isis* 75, no. 2 (1984): 248–68.

Glacière et caves à neige du Rhône. Lyon: Préinventaire des monuments et richesses artistiques, Département du Rhône, 2000.

Goulemot, Jean M., Paul Lidsky, and Didier Masseau, *Le voyage en France. Anthologie des voyageurs européens en France du Moyen-Âge à la fin de l'Empire*. Paris: Robert Laffont, 1995.

Grenier, Jean-Yves. *Séries économiques françaises, XVIe–XVIIIe siècles*. Paris: Editions de l'EHESS, 1985.

Gresset, Philippe. "Un projet d'extension de Bath par R. Adam. Crise et fantaisie dans la ville anglaise." In *La ville régulière. Modèles et tracés*, edited by Xavier Malverti and Pierre Pinon, 65–77. Paris: Picard, 1997.

Gruber, Alain-Charles. *Les grandes fêtes et leurs décors à l'époque de Louis XVI*. Geneva: Dròz, 1972.

Gruyer, Jacques. "La population active à Lyon en 1789." In *Actes du 112e Congrès national des Sociétés savantes, Histoire moderne et contemporaine*, 57–72. Paris: CTHS, 1988.

Guillerme, André. *Bâtir la ville. Révolutions industrielles dans les matériaux de construction. France–Grande Bretagne (1760–1840)*. Seyssel 01420: Champvallon, 1995.

– "Wood versus Iron: The Strength of Materials in Early Nineteenth Century France." *History and Technology* 6 (1988): 239–52.

– "La formation des nouveaux édiles : ingénieur des Ponts et chaussées et architectes (1804–1815)." In *Villes et territoires pendant la période napoléonienne*, 35–57. Rome: Ecole française, 1987.

Gutton, Jean-Pierre, ed. *L'intendance de Lyonnais, Beaujolais, Forez en 1698 et en 1762*. Paris: CTHA, 1992.

Guyonnet, Marie-Claire. *Jacques de Flesselles Intendant de Lyon (1768–1784)*. Lyon: Editions de la Guillotiere, 1956.

Hafter, Daryl M. "Women in the Underground Business of Eighteenth-Century Lyon." *Enterprise and Society* 2 (2001): 11–40.

– "Women Who Wove in the Eighteenth-Century Silk Industry of Lyon." In *European Women and Preindustrial Craft*, edited by Daryl M. Hafter, 42–64. Bloomington: Indiana University Press, 1995.

– "Philippe de Lasalle. From *Mise-en-carte* to Industrial Design." *Winterthur Portfolio* 12 (1977): 139–63.

Hanson, Paul R. *The Jacobin Republic Under Fire. The Federalist Revolt in the French Revolution*. University Park, PA: Pennsylvania State University Press, 2003.

Hardouin-Fugier, Elisabeth. "Architectes et entrepreneurs victimes du siège de Lyon (1793–1794). Hasard ou conséquence professionnelle ?" In *Actes du 112e Congrès national des Sociétés savantes, Histoire moderne et contemporaine*, 99–112. Paris: CTHS, 1988.

Harouel, Jean-Louis. *L'embellissement des villes. L'urbanisme français au XVIIIe siècle*. Paris: Picard, 1993.

Hellman, Mimi. "Furniture, Sociability, and the Work of Leisure in Eighteenth Century France." *Eighteenth-Century Studies* 32, no. 4 (1999): 415–55.

Henry, Paul. "La Saône, artère vitale de Lyon au début du 18ᵉ siècle, d'après la Vue Scénographique de Cleric en 1720." *Centre Presqu'île*, no. 23 (1998): 15–7.

Hilaire-Pérez, Liliane. *L'invention technique au siècle des Lumières*. Paris: Albin Michel, 2000.

Hindle, Brooke, ed. *Material Culture of the Wooden Age*. Tarrytown, NY: n.p., 1981.

Hirsch, Jean-Pierre. *Les deux rêves du commerce. Entreprise et institution dans la région lilloise (1780–1860)*. Paris: Editions de l'EHESS, 1991.

Horn, Jeff. "The Limits of Centralization: Municipal Politics in Troyes during the L'Averdy Reforms." *French History* 9, no. 2 (1995): 153–79.

Hours, Henri. *Histoire du pont de Saône.* Lyon: Jean Andre, 1996.

Hours, Henri, and Michel Nicolas. *Jean-Antoine Morand. Architecte lyonnais 1727–1794.* Lyon: Archives municipales de Lyon, 1985.

Howell, Martha C. *Women, Production, and Patriarchy in Late Medieval Cities.* Chicago: University of Chicago Press, 1986.

Instruction sur les nouvelles mesures à l'usage du Département du Rhône. Lyon: Ballanche et Barret, 1801–02.

Jones, Colin. "The Great Chain of Buying: Medical Advertisement, the Bourgeois Public Sphere, and the Origins of the French Revolution." *The American Historical Review* 101, no. 1 (1996): 13–41.

Jones, P.M. *Reform and Revolution in France. The Politics of Transition, 1774–1791.* Cambridge: Cambridge University Press, 1995.

Julia, Dominique. "L'éducation des négociants français au 18e siècle." In *Cultures et formations négociantes dans l'Europe moderne*, edited by Franco Angiolini and Daniel Roche, 215–56. Paris: Editions de l'EHESS, 1995.

Kalmein, Wend von. *Architecture in France in the Eighteenth Century.* New Haven: Yale University Press, 1995.

Kettering, Sharon. "State Control and Municipal Authority in France." In *Edo and Paris. Urban Life and the State in the Early Modern Era*, edited by James L. McClain, John M. Merriman, and Ugawa Kaory, 86–101. Ithaca, NY: Cornell University Press, 1994.

Kleinclaucz, A. *Histoire de Lyon.* Lyon: Pierre Masson, 1948.

Labasse, Jean. "Réflexions d'un géographe sur le couple ville-fleuve." In *La ville et le fleuve* (proceedings of the Congrès nationale des sociétés savantes 112, 1987), 9–22. Paris: CTHS (Comité des Travaux Historiques et Scientifiques), 1989.

Lamarre, Christine. "La physionomie des villes françaises au XVIIIème siècle: bilan et perspectives de recherches." *Eighteenth-Century Life* 19, no. 3 (1995): 103–11.

– *Petites villes et fait urbain en France au XVIIIe siècle. Le cas bourguignon.* Dijon: Editions de l'université de Dijon, 1993.

Landes, David S. *The Unbound Prometheus. Technological Change and Industrial Development in Western Europe from 1750 to the Present.* Cambridge: Cambridge University Press, 1969.

Le Moël, Michel, and Sophie Descat, eds. *L'urbanisme parisien au siècle des Lumières.* Paris: Action artistique de la ville de Paris, 1997.

Lepetit, Bernard. "Pouvoir municipal et urbanisme (1650–1750). Sources et problématiques." In *Pouvoir, villes et société en Europe,*

1650–1750, edited by Georges Livet and Bernard Vogler, 35–49. Paris: Ophrys, 1983.

- "L'évolution de la notion de ville d'après les tableaux et descriptions de la France 1650–1850." *Urbi*, no. 2 (1979): xcix–cvii.

Lepetit, Bernard, et al. "Les miroirs de la ville: un débat sur le discours des anciens géographes." *Urbi*, no. 2 (1979): cviii–cxviii.

Leroy Ladurie, Emmanuel. "La démographie des Lumières" and "Un urbanisme frôleur." In *Histoire de la France urbaine*, edited by Georges Duby, vol. 3, *La ville classique de la Renaissance aux Révolutions*, 295–310 and 439–81. Paris: Seuil, 1981.

Lespagnol, André. "Femmes négociants sous Louis XIV: les conditions complexes d'une promotion provisoire." In N.a. *Populations et cultures. Etudes réunies en l'honneur de François Lebrun*, 463–70. Rennes: University of Rennes 2, 1989.

Lewis, Gwynne. *The Advent of Modern Capitalism in France, 1770–1840. The Contribution of Pierre-François Tubeuf.* Oxford: Clarendon Press, 1993.

Loach, Judi. "François Cuenot (1610–1686)." In *L'idée constructive en architecture*, edited by Xavier Malverti, 41–63. Paris: Picard, 1987.

Loche, Michel. *Journaux imprimés à Lyon (1633–1794)*. Reprint of no. 229, *Le vieux papier* (1968): 259–84.

Lough, John. *France on the Eve of Revolution. British Travellers' Observations 1763–1788.* London: Croom Helm, 1987.

- *France Observed in the Seventeenth Century by British Travellers.* Stocksfield, England: Oriol Press, 1984.

Lozancic, Nicolas. "Le logement à Lyon aux XVIIe et XVIIe sièces, une approche: le bail à loyer." *Cahiers d'histoire* 44, no. 4 (1999): 537–58.

MacLeod, Christine. *Inventing the Industrial Revolution. The English Patent System, 1660–1800.* Cambridge: Cambridge University Press, 1988.

Maistre, André. *Le canal des Deux mers. Canal royal du Languedoc, 1666–1680.* Toulouse: Privat, 1968.

Malverti, Xavier. "Ville et régularité. Le corps du Génie." In *La ville régulière. Modèles et tracés*, edited by Xavier Malverti and Pierre Pinon, 167–181. Paris: Picard, 1997.

Malverti, Xavier, ed. *L'idée constructive en architecture.* Paris: Picard, 1987.

Mansfield, Paul. "The Management of Terror in Montagnard Lyon, Year II." *European History Quarterly* 20 (1990): 465–96.

– "The Repression of Lyon, 1793–4: Origins, Responsibility and Significance." *French History* 2, no. 1 (1988): 74–101.

Marchand, Jean, ed. *Voyage en France de François de La Rochefoucauld (1781–1785)*. 2 vols. Paris: Honoré Champion, 1933.

Mascoli, Laura. "Sur la route de Rome: l'arrêt à Lyon d'un pensionnaire de l'Académie de France, François-Jacques Delannoy (mars 1780)." In *Lyon et l'Italie: six études d'histoire de l'art*, edited by Marie-Félicie Pérez, Gilles Chomer, and Daniel Ternois, 101–14. Paris: CNRS, 1984.

Messance. *Nouvelles recherches sur la population de la France*. Lyon: Périsse libraires, 1788.

– *Recherches sur la population des généralités d'Auvergne, de Lyon, de Rouen ...* Paris: Durand libraire, 1766.

Mesqui, Jean. *Le pont en France avant le temps des ingénieurs*. Paris: Picard, 1986.

Metzger, Albert, and Joseph Vaesen. *Lyon de 1778 au Directoire. Notes et documents*, 11 vols. Lyon: Librairie générale Henri Georg, 1888.

Metzger, Paul. *Contribution à l'étude de deux réformes judiciaires au XVIIIe siècle. Le Conseil supérieur et le grand baillage de Lyon (1771–1774 et 1788)*. Lyon: A. Rey, 1913.

Meyer, Jean. *Etudes sur les villes en Europe occidentale: milieu du XVIIe siècle à la veille de la Révolution française*. 3 vols. Paris: Société d'édition d'enseignement supérieur, 1983.

Michel. *L'indicateur fidèle, ou, Guide des voyageurs ...* Paris: Rue St. Jacques à l'enseigne du globe, 1775.

Moinecour, Nicole. "L'urbanisation du quartier des Célestins à Lyon (1407–1950)." *Travaux de l'Institut d'histoire de l'art de Lyon*, no. 15 (1992): 38–42.

Morineau, Michel. "Lyon l'italienne, Lyon la magnifique." *Annales ESC* 29, no. 6 (1974): 1,537–50.

Muldew, Craig. *The Economy of Obligation: The Culture of Credit and Social Relations in Early Modern England*. London: MacMillan, 1998.

Nagle, Jean. "Un aspect de la propriété seigneuriale à Paris aux XVIIe et XVIIIe siècles: les lods et ventes." *Revue d'histoire moderne et contemporaine* 24, no. 4 (1977): 570–81.

Nivet, Stéphane. "Prost de Royer: 1729–1784." MA thesis, University of Lyon 3, 2002.

Noël, Jean-François. "Seigneurie et propriété urbaine sous l'Ancien Régime: Autour de la maison de Bertrand d'Argentré à Vitré." *Revue d'Histoire Moderne et Contemporaine* 38, no. 2 (1991): 177–204.

L'oeuvre de Soufflot à Lyon. Etudes et documents. Lyon: PUL, 1982.

Ozouf, Mona. "Architecture et urbanisme : l'image de la ville chez Claude-Nicolas Ledoux." *Annales ESC* 21 (1966): 1,273–1,303.

Paquot, Thierry. "Paris et ses limites." *Proceedings of the Western Society for French History* 24 (1997): 1–8.

Pardailhé-Gallabrun, Annick. *The Birth of Intimacy: Privacy and Domestic Life in Early Modern Paris.* Oxford: Polity Press, 1991.

Papyanis, Nicholas. *Planning Paris before Haussmann.* Baltimore: Johns Hopkins University, 2004.

Pariset, François-Georges, ed. *Histoire de Bordeaux.* Bordeaux: N.p., 1968.

Pelletier, Jean. *Lyon pas à pas. Son histoire à travers ses rues. La Presqu'île, la rive gauche du Rhône, les quais et ponts du Rhône.* Roanne: Horvath, 1986.

Pelletier, Jean, and Charles Delfante. *Atlas historique du Grand Lyon : formes urbaines et paysages au fil du temps.* Seyssinet 38170: Editions Xavier Lejeune-Libris, 2004.

Pérez, Marie-Félicie. "Le lotissement du couvent des Célestins de Lyon à la fin du XVIIIe siècle d'après les papiers de l'architecte Jean-Antoine Morand (1727–1794)." In *Hommage à Marcel Grandjean. Des pierres et des hommes : Matériaux pour une histoire de l'art monumental régional,* edited by Paul Bissegger and Monique Fontannaz, 407–24. Lausanne: Bibliothèque historique Vaudoise, 1995.

– "Soufflot et la société lyonnaise." In Institut d'histoire de l'art. *L'oeuvre de Soufflot à Lyon. Etudes et documents,* 15–20. Lyon: PUL, 1982.

– "Soufflot et la création de l'école de dessin de Lyon, 1751–1780." In *Soufflot et l'architecture des Lumières,* 80–100. Paris: CNRS, 1980.

Perronet, Jean-Rodolphe. *Construire des ponts au XVIIIe siècle. L'oeuvre de J.R. Perronet.* Paris: Presses de l'Ecole nationale des Ponts et chaussées, 1987. Re-edition of Jean-Rodolphe Perronet's *Description des projets et de la construction des ponts de Neuilli, de Mantes, d'Orléans, de Louis XVI, etc.* Paris: Didot fils aîné, Jombert jeune, 1788, and Imprimerie royale, 1782.

Perrot, Jean-Claude. *Genèse d'une ville moderne : Caen au XVIIIe siècle.* Paris: Mouton, 1975.

Pérouse de Montclos, Jean-Marie. *Jacques-Germain Soufflot.* Paris: MONUM, Editions du Patrimoine, 2004.

Picon, Antoine. "De la composition urbaine au 'génie urbain'. Les ingénieurs des Ponts et chaussées et les villes françaises au XIXe siècle." In *Les langages de la ville,* edited by Bernard Lamizet and Pascal Sanson, 169–77. Marseille: Parenthèses, 1997.

– *French Architects and Engineers in the Age of Enlightenment.*
    Cambridge: Cambridge University Press, 1992.

Pinol, Jean-Luc, ed. *Atlas historique des villes de France.* Paris: Hachette,
    1996.

Planhol, Xavier de. *L'eau de neige : le tiède et le frais. Histoire et
    géographie des boissons fraîches.* Paris: Fayard, 1995.

Poidebard, Alexandre. "Etablissement de la place Tolozan et du quai
    Saint-Clair (1749–1764)." *Revue du Lyonnais* 4, series 5 (1887):
    218–22.

Poisson, Jean-Paul. *Notaires et société : travaux d'histoire et de sociologie
    notariales.* 2 vols. Paris: Economica, 1985 and 1990.

Poitrineau, Abel. *Remues d'hommes : essai sur les migrations
    montagnardes en France aux XVIIe et XVIIIe siècles.* Paris:
    Aubier-Montaigne, 1983.

Poni, Carlo. "Mode et innovation : les stratégies des marchands en soie
    de Lyon au XVIIIe siècle." *Revue d'Histoire Moderne et
    Contemporaine* 45, no. 3 (1998): 589–625.

Poussou, Jean-Pierre. "De la difficulté d'application des notions de
    faubourg et de banlieue à l'évolution de l'agglomération parisienne
    entre le milieu du XVIIIe et le milieu du XIXe siècle." *Histoire,
    Economie, Société* 15, no. 3 (1996): 339–51.

Puitspelu, sieur de. "Distractions de jadis aux Brotteaux." *Rive Gauche,*
    no. 154 (2000): 27–9 (excerpt from *Oisivetés du Sieur du Puitspelu* ...,
    by Clair Tisseur, nineteenth-century Lyon architect and erudite who
    wrote under the pseudonym of Nizier du Puitspelu).

Pujalte, Marie-Lucie. "Le Projet pour le commerce et les embellissements
    de Toulouse ou l'idée de progrès des arts par un amateur." In *Claude
    Nicolas Ledoux et le livre d'architecture en français,* edited by Daniel
    Rabreau and Dominique Massounie, 132–42. Paris: Editions du
    Patrimoine, Centre des monuments nationaux, 2006.

Reveyron, Nicolas. "Influence de la charpenterie et rôle des charpentiers
    dans l'architecture de pierre à la fin du moyen-âge à Lyon." *Bulletin
    monumental* 154, no. 2 (1966): 149–56.

Reynard, Pierre Claude. "Public Order and Privilege. Eighteenth-Century
    French Roots of Environmental Regulation." *Technology and Culture*
    43, no. 1 (2002): 1–28.

R.-C. [Ricard-Charbonnet]. *Mémoires d'un Lyonnais de la fin du XVIIIe
    siècle : Précis de la vie de l'auteur.* Lyon: Deleuze, 1838.

Rivet, Félix. *Le quartier Perrache (1766–1946) Etude d'histoire et de
    géographie urbaines.* Lyon: Audin, 1951.

Roche, Daniel. *Humeurs vagabondes: de la circulation des hommes et de l'utilité des voyages*. Paris: Fayard, 2003.

- *La France des Lumières*. Paris: Fayard, 1993.

Roncayolo Marcel, *Lectures de villes. Formes et temps*. Marseille: Parenthèses, 2002.

- *La ville et ses territoires*. Paris: Gallimard, 1997.

- *Les grammaires d'une ville. Essai sur la genèse des structures urbaines à Marseille*. Paris: Editions de l'EHESS, 1996.

- "L'aménagement du territoire (xviiie–xxe siècle)." In *L'espace français. Histoire de la France*, edited by Jacques Revel, 511–643. Paris: Seuil, 1989.

Rossiaud, Jacques. "Les rituels de la fête civique à Lyon." In *Riti e rituali nelle società medievali*, edited by Jacques Chiffoleau, Lauro Martines, and Agostino Paravicini Baglioni, 286–308. Spoleto, 1994.

Roubert, Jacqueline. "L'Hôtel-Dieu de Lyon au xviiie siècle." In *Soufflot et l'architecture des Lumières*, 135–40. Paris: CNRS, 1980.

Rousselle, Aline, ed. *La glace et ses usages*. Perpignan: Presses Universitaires de Perpignan, 1999.

Routier, Jacqueline. *Briançon à travers l'histoire*. Gap: Société d'Etudes des Hautes-Alpes, 1981.

Roux, Isabel. "Les embellissements du port de Bordeaux et l'ordre urbain: 1770–1815." In N.a. *Le Progrès des Arts Réunis, 1763–1815*, 257–64. Bordeaux: CERCAM, 1992.

Sarocchi, Pierre. "Les précurseurs de la construction des ponts métaliques à Lyon au xviiie siècle." *Bulletin de la Société historique, archéologique et littéraire de Lyon* 34 (2004–05): 21–41.

Saunier, Pierre-Yves. *L'esprit lyonnais–xixe–xxe siècle. Genèse d'une représentation sociale*. Paris: CNRS, 1995.

Saupin, Guy. *Les villes en France à l'époque moderne, xvie–xviiie siècles*. Paris: Bélin, 2002.

Schatzberg, Eric, "Ideology and Technical Choice: The Decline of the Wooden Airplane in the United States, 1920–1945." *Technology and Culture* 35, no. 1 (1994): 34–69.

Smollett, Tobias. *Travels through France and Italy*. London, 1766. Reprint. Fontwell, Sussex: Centaur Press, 1969.

Soufflot et l'architecture des Lumières. Paris: CNRS, 1980.

Soufflot et son temps. Paris: Caisse nationale des monuments historiques et des sites, 1980.

Sutcliffe, Anthony. *Towards the Planned City: Germany, Britain, the United States, and France, 1780–1914*. Oxford: Basil Blackwell, 1981.

Tackett, Timothy. *When the King Took Flight*. Cambridge, MA: Harvard University Press, 2003.

Teisseyre-Sallmann, Line. "Urbanisme et société: l'exemple de Nîmes aux XVIIe et XVIIIe siècles." *Annales ESC* 35 (1980): 965–86.

Ternois, Daniel. "L'Hôtel-Dieu de Lyon." In *L'oeuvre de Soufflot à Lyon. Etudes et documents*, 43–75. Lyon: PUL, 1982.

– "Soufflot et Lyon, état des travaux et problématique." In *Soufflot et l'architecture des Lumières*, 81–100. Paris: CNRS, 1980.

Thébaud-Sorger, Marie. "Les premiers ballons et la conquête du ciel. Les dimensions d'une découverte." *Dix-huitième siècle*, no. 31 (1993): 159–77.

Trénard, Louis. *Lyon de l'Encyclopédie au Préromantisme*. Paris: PUF, 1958.

– "Lyon et ses images aux temps modernes." In N.a. *Religion et Politique. Les deux guerres mondiales. Histoire de Lyon et du Sud-Est. Mélanges offerts à M. le Doyen André Latreille*, 473–93. Lyon: Audin, 1973.

Vachon, A. "Antonio Spréafico, glacier-limonadier au siècle des Lumières." *Rive gauche*, no. 143 (1997): 4–10.

Vial, Eugène. "Les anciennes mesures du Lyonnais." *Lyon et sa région*, 1, no. 2 (May–June 1920): no. 6 (December 1920): 179–85.

La ville au XVIIIe siècle. Aix-en-Provence: Edisud, 1975.

Wahl, Maurice. *Les premières années de la Révolution à Lyon (1788–1792)*. Paris, 1894. Geneva: Megariotis Reprints, 1978.

Young, Arthur. *Voyages en France en 1787, 1788 et 1789*. Paris: Armand Colin, 1931.

– *Travels in France during the Years 1787, 1788 and 1789*. Edited by C. Maxwell. Cambridge: Cambridge University Press, 1950.

Zeller, Olivier. "Les Valesque, receveurs des tailles de l'élection de Lyon de 1744 à la Révolution." In *Pourvoir les finances en province sous l'Ancien Régime*, edited by Françoise Bayard, 235–65. Paris: Comité pour l'histoire économique et financière de la France, 2002.

– "L'intensification de la vie théâtrale à Lyon (1761–1788)." *Cahiers d'histoire* 42, no. 2 (1997): 193–216.

– "Géographie sociale, loisir et pratique culturelle: abonnés et abonnements au théâtre de Lyon (1761–1789)." *Revue d'histoire moderne et contemporaine* 44, no. 4 (1997): 580–600.

– "Une biographie de fermier général. Réseaux, apprentissages et stratégies." *Histoire, économie et société* 15, no. 2 (1996): 245–80.

– "Enjeux d'urbanisme à Lyon en 1777. Propriétaires contre promoteurs." *Bulletin du Centre Pierre Léon d'histoire économique et
sociale*, no. 1 (1995): 3–15.
– "Un exemple de gestion immobilière : l'administration du patrimoine
foncier de la famille Petitot (Lyon, 1786–1790)." In *Le sol et
l'immeuble : les formes dissociées de propriété immobilière dans les
villes de France et d'Italie (XIIe–XIXe siècle)*, edited by Olivier Faron
and Etienne Hubert, 253–65. Lyon: PUL, 1995.
– "A l'enseigne du chameau. Manières d'habiter, manières de gérer à
Lyon au XVIIIe siècle." *Cahiers d'histoire* 38, no. 1 (1993): 25–54.
– "En marge du privilège : petits spectacles et théâtre amateur à Lyon
(1785–1787)." In *Théâtre et spectacles hier et aujourd'hui*, Actes du
115ème Congrès national des sociétés savantes, 83–101. Paris: CTHS,
1991.
– *Une famille consulaire lyonnaise de l'ancien régime à la IIIe
République. Les Brac. Racines Alliances Fortune*, vol. 3: *Historique et
documents* 1725–1800. 1990.
– "Politique frumentaire et rapports sociaux à Lyon (1772–1776)."
Histoire, Economie et Société 8, no. 2 (1989): 249–86.
– "Un mode d'habiter à Lyon au XVIIIe siècle : la pratique de la location
principale." *Revue d'histoire moderne et contemporaine* 35, no. 1
(1988): 36–59.

Index